95/

D0200842

DATE DUE

Two Spectacular Seasons

OTHER BOOKS BY WILLIAM B. MEAD

Baseball Goes to War (originally published as *Even the Browns*)
The Official New York Yankees Hater's Handbook
The Explosive Sixties: Baseball's Decade of Expansion

CO-AUTHORED WITH MIKE FEINSILBER

American Averages: Amazing Facts of Everyday Life

CO-AUTHORED WITH PAUL N. STRASSELS

Money Matters: The Hassle-free, Month-by-Month Guide to Money Management

Two Spectacular Seasons

1930: The Year the Hitters Ran Wild
1968: The Year the Pitchers Took Revenge

William B. Mead

Macmillan Publishing Company
New York

Macmillan Publishing Company
866 Third Avenue, New York, NY 10022
Collier Macmillan Canada, Inc.

Library of Congress Cataloging-in-Publication Data
Mead, William B.
    Two spectacular seasons/William B. Mead.
        p.   cm.
    Includes index.
    ISBN 0-02-583731-1
    1. Baseball—United States—History. I. Title.
GV863.A1M44 1990
796.357'0973—dc20   89-12258
                                           CIP

Macmillan books are available at special discounts for bulk purchases for sales promotions, premiums, fund-raising, or educational use. For details, contact:

Special Sales Director
Macmillan Publishing Company
866 Third Avenue
New York, NY 10022

10 9 8 7 6 5 4 3 2 1

PRINTED IN THE UNITED STATES OF AMERICA

To Alden

Contents

Introduction

Baseball resists abrupt change. Twice in history, however, the game has flown out of control, its delicate balance between offense and defense sharply tilted. This is the story of those two seasons, told by the men who experienced them and from the pages of the newspapers and magazines that chronicled their spectacular achievements.

In 1930 the hitters seized the game and splattered it all over the record books. The American League, pitchers included, batted .288, and the National League came in at .303. Hack Wilson of the Chicago Cubs—a rough and boisterous man tailored for Al Capone's Chicago of Prohibition and the oncoming Depression—threatened to become the new Babe Ruth.

In 1968 it was the pitchers' turn. In both leagues, the overall earned run average was under three. Scoring sank to levels below those of the dead-ball era. Denny McLain of the Detroit Tigers became baseball's first thirty-game winner since Dizzy Dean—and yet wound up in bankruptcy, disgrace, and prison. Bob Gibson of the St. Louis Cardinals broke Walter Johnson's record for the lowest ERA in history, and his fierce demeanor epitomized the black anger that was sweeping America in that tumultuous year.

How did it happen? How could baseball change so much? For example, in 1930 Bill Terry of the New York Giants led the National League in batting at .401. In 1968 Carl Yastrzemski led the American League with .301, the lowest championship average in history. Yet Terry's .401 and Yaz's .301 exceeded the league norms by almost exactly the same percentage. Were the hitters of 1930 and the pitchers of 1968 that much better?

Players and managers love to tackle that question, because it lets them spin tales and theories about the mysterious cycles of hitting and pitching. I was fortunate to talk to Bill Terry only a few months before he died in January 1989. You will also hear, in these pages, from Charlie Gehringer, Charlie Grimm, Don Drysdale, Denny McLain, Tim McCarver, and many others. Three men quoted in these pages were active in *both* seasons. In 1930 Al Lopez was a rookie catcher for the Brooklyn Dodgers, Mel Harder was a promising young pitcher with the Cleveland Indians, and Shirley Povich was the precocious sports editor of the Washington *Post*. In 1968 Lopez was managing the Chicago White Sox, Harder was pitching coach for the Cincinnati Reds, and Povich was still editing the *Post*'s sports section. All of them spoke thoughtfully and intelligently about those sharply contrasting seasons, but none claimed to entirely solve the mystery.

The literature of the time shows great alarm among baseball officials during both 1930 and 1968. The guardians of the game feared that the "proper balance" between pitching and hitting was in peril. But baseball adjusted, and in retrospect both 1930 and 1968 stand out. They were extremes, years of excess in a game that prides itself on moderation. They provide a window on their times, and most of all on baseball's enduring battle between hitter and pitcher. They were two spectacular seasons.

PART I

1930: The Year the Hitters Ran Wild

1

"He ain't got no neck."

He did not look like a hero. He stood only five feet six inches
tall. His legs were short and his feet so tiny that he wore size 5½
shoes—the baseball spikes of a child, though boys of that era played
ball in their everyday shoes.

Yet he weighed 190 pounds, most of it concentrated in his muscu-
lar arms and his huge, barrel torso. "He ain't got no neck," said John
McGraw, who scouted him in the bush leagues. Other scouts, watching this oddly topheavy outfielder career around the field, said he
lacked a major league body.

But Hack Wilson could hit, and by this date—October 12, 1929—
he was a slugging star for the Chicago Cubs, champions of the
National League. He had rapped out a triple and a single the day
before as the Cubs, after losing the first two games of the World
Series to Connie Mack's Philadelphia Athletics, stifled the A's 3 to
1, Guy Bush outpitching the great George Earnshaw.

This was the fourth game, Chicago's opportunity to tie the Series,
Philadelphia's chance to take a commanding lead of three games to
one. A capacity crowd of 29,921 jammed Philadelphia's Shibe Park,
cheering their heroes and straining for a glimpse of the Athletics'
legendary owner and manager, Connie Mack. "The Lean Leader," as
sportswriters called him, sat in the dugout attired, like most fans of
the day, in suit and tie, positioning his infielders and outfielders with
subtle waves of his scorecard. Mack was sixty-six and had managed
the Athletics since 1901.

By the seventh inning, the hometown rooters were silent. Mack
had started Jack Quinn, forty-six, one of four major league pitchers

still allowed to throw the spitball. That unsanitary and difficult pitch was banned in 1920, but seventeen spitball pitchers were "grandfathered"—allowed to throw the spitball for the remainder of their careers. Thirteen faded out of the majors during the 1920s. Quinn—who changed his name from John Quinn Picus to John Picus Quinn—was the oldest of the four survivors.

The Cubs got to him for two runs in the fourth and knocked him out with five runs in the sixth, Wilson contributing a key single. Rube Walberg relieved, and the Cubs scored again in the seventh. Chicago's Charlie Root yielded just three hits through six innings. Wilson and his teammates took the field for the last of the seventh with an 8–0 lead. The Series was on the verge of deadlock.

It had opened with a bold gamble by Mack, based on percentages and compassion. The Athletics boasted baseball's best pitcher in Lefty Grove, but the Cubs' lineup was packed with righthanded power. Take a look at the men who batted third through sixth for the 1929 Cubs, all four of them righthanded:

	H	R	HR	RBI	BA
Rogers Hornsby, 2B	229	156	39	149	.380
Hack Wilson, CF	198	135	39	159	.345
Kiki Cuyler, RF	183	111	15	102	.360
Riggs Stephenson, LF	179	91	17	110	.362

The Cubs feasted on lefthanded pitchers. Only one lefty—spitballer Clarence Mitchell of the St. Louis Cardinals—beat them more than once during the season. Two of Mack's best pitchers—Grove and Walberg—were lefties. Grove could throw his fastball past any hitter, but Mack decided to use his lefthanded aces in relief, with Grove as the closer.

He kept it to himself. More than forty years later, Al Horwits, who covered the Athletics for the Philadelphia *Ledger,* recalled for author Jerome Holtzman (*No Cheering in the Press Box,* Holt, Rinehart and Winston, New York, 1973) how Mack hatched his surprise for the Series opener.

In late August, Mack summoned righthander Howard Ehmke to his office and told him he had to let him go. Ehmke, thirty-five, was in his fourteenth major league season and no longer had much on the ball. Mack had used him sparingly.

Tears came to Ehmke's eyes, as they came to the eyes of many athletes in the sports pages of that era. "Gee, Mr. Mack," he said. "I've never been on a pennant winner before, and here this club is winning the pennant. I'd always dreamed that I could pitch in a World Series, and now you're giving me my release."

"Do you think you could pitch in a World Series?"

"There's one good game left in this arm."

Mack told Ehmke he'd get his chance in the first Series game and had him scout the Cubs for the remainder of the season. According to another version of the story, less sentimental but with the same ending, Mack had Ehmke scout the Cubs, heard his report, and asked him to recommend a starting pitcher. Ehmke recommended himself, and Mack went along.

Legend has it that Ehmke burst upon the Cubs like a junkballer from outer space, but in fact *The Sporting News* pictured him on page one of a pre-Series issue, speculating that he might play a major role in the Series. He was a veteran, he was righthanded, and he threw sidearm. "George Earnshaw and Howard Ehmke, little talked of, are apt to prove the stars for Connie Mack," wrote Herman Wecke of the St. Louis *Post-Dispatch,* one of fifty-three writers who picked the A's to win.

The Cubs were picked by forty-two writers, including Bill Cunningham of the Boston *Post.* "I like the way their batters whang the missile, and I think their pitching's good enough," Cunningham wrote. "I don't go in much for Mr. Wrigley's gum, but I think his ball team's pretty sweet."

So were the Athletics, whose number two through seven hitters whanged the missile with these numbers:

	H	R	HR	RBI	BA
Mule Haas, CF	181	115	16	82	.313
Mickey Cochrane, C	170	113	7	95	.331
Al Simmons, LF	212	114	34	157	.365
Jimmie Foxx, 1B	183	123	33	117	.354
Bing Miller, RF	186	84	8	93	.335
Jimmy Dykes, 3B	131	76	13	79	.327

As with the Cubs, these hitters were genuine. Both lineups boasted three future Hall of Famers: for the Cubs, Hornsby, Wilson, and Cuyler; for the A's, Cochrane, Simmons, and Foxx, plus Grove, the pitching ace turned reliever.

Pitching at Wrigley Field in the Series opener, Ehmke stifled the Cubs 3–1. He struck out thirteen, then a Series record. Hornsby, Wilson, and Cuyler fanned twice each. Hornsby said Ehmke's pitches looked easy to hit and must have passed right through his bat. "The Cubs hadn't seen a slow underhand and sidearm pitcher like him all season and naturally were bothered," *The Sporting News* explained.

Simmons and Foxx homered in the second game as the Athletics hammered Pat Malone, the Cubs' twenty-two-game winner, in a 9 to 3 rout. Wilson singled three times, but Mack's pitching strategy clicked again as Earnshaw and Grove, who won forty-four games between them during the season, split the game and matched Ehmke's new record by fanning thirteen Cubs once more.

Earnshaw started the next game, too. Rested from a day off for travel, he worked nine innings and struck out ten. But the Cubs scored three runs in the sixth, and Guy Bush scattered nine Philadelphia hits. Wilson robbed Al Simmons with a catch at the wall: 3–1, Chicago.

As the Philadelphia players came in to bat in the bottom of the seventh inning of the fourth game, Mack told several regulars to go to the clubhouse after the inning. The Athletics were trailing 8–0, and with the game lost Mack thought he'd give his benchwarmers a chance to play in a World Series.

Al Simmons led off the inning with a homer; at least the A's wouldn't be shut out. Jimmie Foxx singled to right. Bing Miller flied to center, and the ball fell for a single when Wilson lost it in the sun. Jimmy Dykes singled to left and Joe Boley singled to right. George Burns, pinch hitting for the pitcher, popped out, but Max Bishop singled to center.

Four runs home, one out, two men on base. Joe McCarthy, the Chicago manager, pulled his pitcher, Charlie Root, and brought in Art Nehf, a veteran who had pitched in four World Series for the New York Giants. Nehf got Mule Haas to hit a routine fly ball to center.

But Wilson lost that one in the sun, too. The ball bounded to deep center field as Boley and Bishop scored. Haas slid home. In the Philadelphia dugout, Jimmy Dykes slapped the man next to him on the back and shouted, "We're back in the game, boys!"

Dykes's rough slap knocked Connie Mack out of the dugout, across the bats lined up in front. Dykes was mortified; he had no idea the dignified Mack had been beside him. "I'm sorry," he said, pulling Mack to his feet.

"That's all right, Jimmy," said Mack. "Everything's all right. Anything you do right now is all right. Wasn't it wonderful?"

The A's had pulled within a run at 8–7. Nehf walked Mickey Cochrane, and McCarthy brought in another pitcher, Sheriff Blake. Simmons grounded to Norm McMillan at third base, but the ball hit a clod of dirt and bounced over McMillan's shoulder for a single. Foxx singled to center, scoring Cochrane to tie the game. Pat Malone relieved Blake and hit Miller with a pitch to load the bases. Dykes drove in the inning's ninth and tenth runs with a double to left that Riggs Stephenson probably should have caught.

The Athletics won, 10 to 8. Never before had there been a World Series inning like it. "The world was stunned," said *The Sporting News.* "It was stupendous, engulfing." For the Cubs, "It was a most mortifying situation."

The most mortified of all was Wilson. Writing in *The Sporting News,* Sam Murphy of the New York *Sun* said that Wilson entered the clubhouse angry and silent. McCarthy told sportswriters that the disaster wasn't Wilson's fault. "The poor kid simply lost the ball in the sun, and he didn't put the sun there," the manager said.

McCarthy tried to console Wilson but the unhappy outfielder pushed his manager aside. "There was fire in his eyes and who knows what was in his heart that minute . . . He seemed dazed as he stepped outside."

There he met his four-year-old son. "Hello, Daddy," the boy said. Murphy continued: "Hack picked up that child, kissed him, hugged him. His sturdy frame shook with emotion. He wept."

That's how they wrote it. Sports pages used to carry poetry as well as tears, and the Chicago *Tribune* produced this, to fit the sad tune of "My Old Kentucky Home."

The sun shone bright in our great Hack
Wilson's eyes—'Tis Sunday, the Mack men are gay—
The third game's won, and Cub pitching's gone astray—
As our Series title fades far away.
Weep no more, dear Cub fan,
Oh weep no more today; for we'll
Sing one song for the game and fighting Cubs,
For the record whiffing Cubs far away.

Things got worse. After an off day Sunday—Pennsylvania law forbade sporting events on the Sabbath—the Cubs led the fifth game 2–0 with two out in the Philadelphia ninth, one man on base, and two strikes on Mule Haas. He homered to tie the score. Simmons doubled, Foxx walked, and Miller singled, driving Simmons home with the run that won the Series.

On the train back to Chicago, Cub players were awakened by a drumming sound. They looked out of their berths and saw Wilson kneeling in the aisle, beating the floor with his fists and cursing. Loyal fans met the Cubs' train in Chicago, and an Associated Press reporter wrote this about Wilson:

"The big fellow forced his way out of a crowd of admirers with tears streaming down his face. 'Let me alone, now, fellows,' he said as he choked and sobbed. 'I haven't anything to say except that I am heartbroken and that we did get some awful breaks.' "

It was quite a comedown. Wilson was fast becoming the Babe Ruth of the National League and would have liked nothing better. Ruth, as sportswriter, attended the Series in civilian clothes, and before the first game Wilson greeted the Babe—one slugger to another. Wilson walked along the Wrigley Field stands, the friendly hero greeting his fans. For the five games, Wilson hit .471 to lead both teams. He made several brilliant catches in the field. But he missed those two fly balls in the Athletics' historic inning. Wilson was the goat, and few Series goats have worn the horns so conspicuously, or for so long. Another Babe Ruth? Ha, said the writers, just look at him. Maybe a sawed-off Babe Ruth.

2

"Sunny Boy Hack"

Despite his humiliation in the World Series, Wilson had reason to look forward to 1930. He was young, strong, and accomplished, a slugger whose home run production had risen each year since he joined the Cubs in 1926. Surely someone would break the Babe's record, and share in the glory and wealth that was uniquely Ruth's.

Baseball's horizons appeared to be unlimited. Sport, like the United States itself, enjoyed an unprecedented burst of enthusiastic prosperity in the 1920s. That decade was "The Roaring Twenties" for the nation, "The Golden Age" for sports. In fact, the two were intertwined. As America became more urban and prosperous, its citizens looked for ways to spend their money and enjoy their leisure time. Many of them turned to spectator sports. As newspapers and the new creation, radio, spread information, they created heroes and heroines. Many of these new giants of American culture were athletes, and they were idolized by children and adults alike. They still are; no other field of accomplishment produces heroes that appeal to so many people of all ages.

Not all the heroes of the 1920s played baseball. Big Bill Tilden aroused interest in tennis, winning Wimbledon in 1920 and 1921, leading the U.S. team to six straight Davis Cup championships, and capturing the U.S. national championship at Forest Hills, New York, six straight times. He won a final Wimbledon in 1930, but by then was beginning to display his homosexuality, which eventually ruined his career and landed him in jail.

Jack Dempsey—like Ruth, a pure slugger—successfully defended his heavyweight boxing championship six times, and then lost it to

Gene Tunney, a 1920s man of a more cerebral stripe; after beating Dempsey in the 1927 "long count" rematch, Tunney retired to study philosophy at the Sorbonne.

The dignified Bobby Jones, widely admired because he remained a "pure" amateur rather than turning professional, won the U.S. Open golf tournament three times in the 1920s. He won the British Open in 1926, the first amateur in twenty-nine years to do so. In 1930 he won what was then regarded as golf's "grand slam"—the U.S. and British Opens and Amateurs. With no more worlds to conquer, he retired. Walter Hagen, a dapper symbol of the twenties himself, won the PGA four straight times, from 1924 through 1927, and captured the British Open four times, in 1922, 1924, 1928, and 1929.

Football fans applauded the heroics of Illinois' Red Grange, "The Galloping Ghost." He won All-American honors three straight years, then turned professional, attracting new followers to a fledgling professional sport. Knute Rockne became a legend of leadership at Notre Dame, where the "Four Horsemen," so named by sportswriter Grantland Rice, led the Irish to an undefeated season in 1924 and a victory over Stanford in the Rose Bowl.

Women won the right to vote in 1920 and began to emancipate sports as well. Helen Wills became a tennis heroine, winning the U.S. singles championship three straight years. Annie Oakley, veteran star of Buffalo Bill's Wild West Show, broke the women's trapshooting record by smashing 98 of 100 targets at sixteen yards. Swimmer Gertrude Ederle set a world record for the 150-yard freestyle in 1925; a year later she became the first woman to swim across the English Channel, and in so doing beat the previous record, set by an Italian man, by nearly two hours.

Johnny Weissmuller gained fame for his swimming championships—and later for his acting, film after film, in the role of Tarzan. Man o' War retired to stud in 1920 after winning twenty of his twenty-one races, and the decade's racing hero was jockey Earl Sande ("Gimme a handy man like Sande . . ."), who won the Kentucky Derby three times and rode Gallant Fox to the Triple Crown in 1930.

Baseball was America's most popular sport going into the 1920s, and thanks to Ruth it retained and expanded its leadership. The sport almost foundered in scandal when eight members of the Chicago

White Sox—"the Black Sox"—were indicted in 1920 for throwing the 1919 World Series in exchange for bribes from gamblers. Baseball moved to cleanse its reputation by hiring Kenesaw Mountain Landis, a stern federal judge, and naming him commissioner with virtually unlimited powers. Landis expelled the eight Black Sox from baseball for life, and otherwise imposed rectitude.

But no one bought a ticket to see him play. People came to see the heroes of the game, and as the anxieties of World War I gave way to the optimism of the new decade, baseball was blessed with a hero of unprecedented stature. Babe Ruth was crude and unlettered, but he could hit the baseball a mile, and he changed the game, attracting fans who lacked patience for the defensively oriented brand of baseball that was so treasured by insiders.

Off the field, Ruth was a flamboyant and boisterous man about town, the very epitome of the happy-go-lucky 1920s playboy. He had a smile and a presence that captivated everyone who saw him. He drove flashy cars, frequented speakeasies, dressed like a million bucks, and always had a pretty girl on his arm; sometimes she was his wife. He was the sun and moon of sport's Golden Age. No wonder Hack Wilson, and dozens of lesser players, wanted to be just like him.

Before Ruth, teams played for one run—a single, a stolen base or a bunt, a hit-and-run play. Ty Cobb epitomized this slash-and-run style, and its proponents sanctified it as "scientific baseball." Home runs were rare because the ball was dead, and because dirty, scuffed balls were kept in play.

When Ruth hit 29 homers for the Boston Red Sox in 1919, he broke the old major league record by five. The fans loved it, and the rule makers began tilting the game toward the hitter. In 1920 the spitball was banned, and umpires were told to put new, clean balls in play.

Sold to the Yankees, Ruth electrified baseball by pounding 54 home runs in 1920. The power splurge was all Ruth's; Cy Williams of the Philadelphia Phillies led the National League with 15, and Ruth's closest competitor in the American League was George Sisler, who hit 19 homers for the St. Louis Browns.

To promote still more homers, the ball was livened. A few players began ringing up some bigger numbers. Cy Williams, who was proud of the 15 homers he hit in 1920, hit 41 in 1923. Rogers Hornsby, then with the Cardinals, doubled his home-run output two years in a row—9 in 1920, 21 in 1921, 42 in 1922.

But the home run, and especially the glamour surrounding it, was still the property of Babe Ruth. No one hit as many home runs as the Babe, and no one hit them as far. Anchoring the Yankee dynasty of the 1920s, Ruth proceeded to break his own home-run record three times—54 in 1920, 59 in 1921, 60 in 1927. There was nothing cheap about those numbers; no other *team* in the American League hit as many as 60 homers in 1927.

Ruth's home runs were something to see. "High and long," recalled Mel Harder, a star pitcher for the Cleveland Indians. "They looked like golf balls going out." Sad Sam Jones pitched twenty-two years in the American League, covering Ruth's entire career. "Babe Ruth could hit a ball so hard, and so far, that it was sometimes impossible to believe your eyes," Jones told author Lawrence Ritter.

"Ruth was the best who ever walked out there," said Doc Cramer, an outfielder who broke in with the Athletics in 1929 and played twenty years in the American League. "He could pitch, he could play first base, he could play the outfield. He was a very good fielder—a crackerjack. He could *throw*. On a single to right field, you didn't go from first to third on Ruth. If you did he'd throw you out."

The Yankees, whose 1927 and 1928 world champions are often cited as the greatest team in baseball history, fell to a distant second place in 1929. Connie Mack had learned the value of the home run; Jimmie Foxx and Al Simmons combined for seventy-seven. A few older Yankees were slipping—Bob Meusel, Waite Hoyt, Herb Pennock. Miller Huggins, "The Mighty Mite" who had managed the Yankees to six pennants, fell ill late in the 1929 season and died September 25. "The finest little fellow in the world has left us," said Ruth, who served as a pallbearer at Huggins's funeral.

But Lou Gehrig was in his prime, and Ruth, at thirty-four, was as big as ever. In 1929 he batted .345 and hit forty-six home runs to lead the league in round-trippers for the tenth time. Even with the Yankees out of the race, Ruth was far and away baseball's most publicized star.

In public stature—pure celebrity value—Ruth stood above everyone else of his era, athlete or otherwise. No one measured up to the

Babe—not President Hoover or Thomas Edison, not even Charles Lindbergh, not Al Jolson or Charlie Chaplin, not Greta Garbo or Albert Einstein or Al Capone. "He was an amazing man," said Jimmy Reese, a young Yankee infielder who was a close friend of the Babe's. "He saved baseball. After that 1919 scandal he brought it back. He had more charisma than anybody who ever played the game." Reese spoke from long experience; in 1988 he was still in the major leagues, working as a coach for the California Angels.

Since baseball was far and away America's dominant sport, its stars were expected to provide sports-page copy year-round. None filled the role as well as Ruth, whose ebullient personality and hearty living habits enhanced his reputation. He indulged children, signed endless autographs, and posed for any crazy picture a promoter or photographer dreamed up. He dressed and traveled in style; Reese remembers riding in the Babe's sixteen-cylinder Cadillac. He ate, drank, smoked, and whored hugely. His teammates loved him, and so did the public. Yankee Stadium, which opened in 1923 with a crowd of 74,200 on hand, was aptly nicknamed "the house that Ruth built."

By 1930 the public needed Ruthian relief. On October 24, 1929— ten days after the A's wrapped up the World Series—the stock market crashed. Panic spread through the financial world; the dizzying bull market that epitomized the "Roaring Twenties" was mortally wounded. Unemployment was increasing, and though Hoover said that "prosperity is just around the corner," not everyone believed him.

With his usual sense of go-to-hell timing, Ruth picked the Depression winter of 1929–1930 for a contentious holdout. He had finished up a three-year contract at $70,000 a year and asked for $100,000. The Yankees offered $75,000. Ruth said he'd take $85,000 a year for three years. The Yankees froze at $75,000. "Ruth has taken more money from the Yankees than I have," said Colonel Jacob Ruppert, the wealthy brewer who owned the team.

Ruth traveled to Florida, where he was pictured on the beach and the golf course. A newspaper cartoon ridiculed him for demanding a higher salary than Hoover's—the president was paid $75,000. In the best holdout tradition, Ruth indicated that he didn't really need to play baseball anymore. Although a wild spender, he had been squeezed into a savings plan by his manager, Christy Walsh. Ruth released a statement claiming that "I'm good for $25,000 a year for life even if I quit baseball today." He said he'd saved $150,000 in the past three years. "If you think that figure's padded, call the president of the Bank of Manhattan or the Equitable Life Assurance Company," he said.

Dan Daniel, a legendary New York sportswriter, was one of Ruth's many buddies in the press corps. The Yankees were about to play their first spring training exhibition game of 1930, and as Daniel recalled the story for author Jerome Holtzman (*No Cheering in the Press Box*), camp was getting dull with Ruth out of uniform. Daniel decided Ruth should sign and told him so.

"I said, 'What's the matter with you? Did you know that this afternoon in Union Square in New York there was a riot? A lot of people were rioting for bread.'

" 'What did you say?' he said.

" 'A lot of people in New York are rioting for bread. They're broke. There's a depression. And you're holding out for $85,000 a year while they're starving. It's making a very bad impression and hurting baseball.'

"He told me, 'Why don't people tell me these things?' "

Ruth asked Daniel what he should do, and Daniel told him that Ruppert probably would agree to $80,000, and Ruth should take it.

"Babe said, 'Bring him around. I'll sign for $80,000 before noon tomorrow—and if I don't I'll turn my uniform in and go home.' "

It was a rainy day. Daniel passed the word to Ruppert and wrote a long story for page one of the following day's New York *Telegram,* an afternoon newspaper. But the next morning the sun was shining. Ruth no longer was in a hurry to sign, and certainly didn't want to leave Florida. "I've changed my mind," he told Daniel.

Daniel faced the nightmare of every newsman. His story would be on page one that afternoon, and unless Ruth fell into line, the story would be utterly false.

"Babe," he said, "you sign for $80,000 or you turn in your uniform. You're not going to do this to me."

The amiable Ruth agreed, so Daniel went looking for Ruppert—who, to the sportswriter's consternation, was no longer in a hurry to close the deal.

"Colonel," said Daniel, "I'm in a heck of a hurry. I wrote this story and I'm stuck with it if you don't back me up."

He herded Ruppert to the hotel, where Ruth was waiting. They shook on the deal. Dan Daniel, frightened sportswriter, had nailed down his scoop.

Ruth's salary was stunning—forty times the wage of the average American worker. One dollar in 1930 bought about as much as $7.40 in 1989, so in today's terms Ruth's $80,000 salary was worth about $590,000. Today, that's not much more than an average player makes.

But in 1930 no other ballplayer made more than a fraction as much as Ruth. The same winter, Lefty O'Doul of the Phillies held out for $17,000, Babe Herman of the Brooklyn Dodgers for $18,000, Edd Roush of the New York Giants for $20,000, and Burleigh Grimes of the Pittsburgh Pirates for $25,000. Goose Goslin of the Washington Senators was holding out against an offer of $10,000 plus a bonus based on performance, the amount to be determined by Clark Griffith, owner of the club.

These were not journeyman players. Roush, Grimes, and Goslin are in the Baseball Hall of Fame. O'Doul led the National League in batting in 1929 at .398, with 32 homers and 122 runs batted in, and Herman was close behind at .381, 21 homers, 113 RBI. The Giants wouldn't yield to Roush, and he held out all season. The Phils said O'Doul was already the team's highest-paid player at $8,000; he settled for a $500 raise. The Pirates ducked Grimes's contract by trading him to the Boston Braves in April, and the Braves traded him to the Cardinals in June; the man was *expensive.*

A reporter asked Edward G. Barrow, the Yankees' rather stuffy general manager, whether baseball would ever have another $80,000 player. "No!" he replied. "No, you will never hear of another ball player getting that kind of money. Even if another Ruth came along, he wouldn't be able to command it, because he would be just another Ruth, and that means he would not be a novelty."

You sure no one will make that much? the reporter pressed. "I'm sure there will never be another one on *this* ball club," replied the Yankee executive, who of course had no way to foresee the spending habits of George Steinbrenner. Barrow earned a niche in the Hall of Fame for his executive skills, but he was a lousy prophet. Ten years earlier, after Ruth hit twenty-nine homers, Barrow predicted that the Bambino would wisely settle in as a singles hitter, Ty Cobb style, having satisfied his childish urge to hit home runs. Barrow's foolish attitude was shared by many baseball traditionalists, who considered the home run a pollutant.

Ruth seemed pleased with the contract, which covered two years at $80,000 per. "I'm going to put most, if not all, of it right in the old sock," he said. "We've got enough to get along on anyway, and we will stick the old pay checks in that trust fund to keep the family in bread and butter when I'm old and graying."

Thanks to Christy Walsh, Ruth indeed had other sources of income. One venture fell through that winter, Ruth's Home Run Candy running afoul of the thirty-five-year-old copyright on the Baby Ruth bar, which had been named after the baby daughter of President and Mrs. Grover Cleveland. In September 1930, Ruth lent his name to a new haberdashery on Broadway. He was there for the opening, and a newspaper photographer caught him selling Babe Ruth brand hats to his teammate, Lou Gehrig; the new Yankee manager, Bob Shawkey; the famed Notre Dame football coach, Knute Rockne; and a leading radio sportscaster of the day, Graham McNamee.

Babe Ruth underwear is prized by today's memorabilia collectors, but his haberdashery didn't survive the early years of the Depression. However, most of Ruth's investments were uncharacteristically conservative, thanks to Christy Walsh.

Tax rates were negligible by today's standards, but Ruth didn't like paying income tax. "He complained like hell," recalled Jimmy Reese. "He made about $20,000 in endorsements, whatever, so he wound up making $100,000. The next year in spring training he said to me, 'What do you think those damned IRS people did? Know how much they stole from me? Three thousand dollars! What do you think of those bastards?'

"I said, 'Yeah, tough luck, Babe.'"

Other accounts have pegged Ruth's total income at about $200,000. His salary and fame aroused envy in other players, who began to realize that home runs paid off. One player who yearned for Ruthian fame was a grandiose self-promoter named Art (The Great) Shires, who played first base for the Chicago White Sox and fancied himself a boxer as well. Shires gave himself his immodest nickname, and after outhitting Ruth and Gehrig in a series in 1929, he sent this poem to New York editors, protesting their failure to properly publicize his feats:

> You may rave about Babe—you may rave about Lou.
> Why be so snooty—the great Shires is good too.

In a hotel altercation later that season, Shires punched out his manager, Lena Blackburne, and roughed up two hotel detectives. That winter, Shires turned boxer. In Chicago, he knocked out one Mysterious Dan Daly in thirteen seconds of the first round. Daly said he took a dive, and the Michigan Boxing Commission alleged that another fixed fight had been arranged in Detroit between Shires and a fighter known as Battling Criss. Shires was suspended by the boxing commissions of thirty-two states, and *The Sporting News* editorially wrung its hands: "It will never do to have a suspended boxing hired man playing baseball in the big leagues."

Notoriety sells tickets, and a Chicago promoter got the bright idea of booking a fight between Shires, of the White Sox, and Hack Wilson, of the Cubs, who had won a few headlines with his own fisticuffs. Like Ruth, Wilson came from tough roots. He was the illegitimate son of a hard-drinking mill worker and a sixteen-year-old factory girl. Bench jockeys back then were neither delicate nor—to use a current term—"socially aware." They called Ruth "nigger," claiming his facial features looked Negroid, and they called Wilson "bastard," a worse insult then than today. Wilson's odd, stubby appearance gave the bench jockeys more ammunition. Among other things, they called him "Caliban," after Shakespeare's savage and deformed slave.

On July 4, 1929, Wilson was getting an earful from the Cincinnati Reds. He charged into their dugout, and it took a pile of men to restrain him. The Cubs and Reds were booked on the same train that night, and on the platform Wilson knocked down Pete Donohue, a Cincinnati pitcher. Wilson was briefly suspended, but he was a popular man in Chicago and Cub fans leaped to his defense, a Chicago alderman coming up with this analysis: "Mr. Wilson is a fine young man, and I know that Mr. Donohue deserved to be struck in the mouth. Otherwise Mr. Wilson would not have struck him there."

Later that season Wilson charged into the stands to silence an abusive milkman. The milkman sued Wilson for twenty thousand dollars, claiming Hack had opened his lip with a punch, but a judge ruled that Wilson acted in self-defense.

So Wilson was the perfect match for Shires, the two ballplayers filling up winter space on the sports pages with their pugnacious declarations. It was small stuff compared to Ruth's holdout, but it was better than nothing. Wilson spent his winters in Martinsburg, West Virginia, his wife's hometown and the place where he first played minor league ball. The bout would give him a rare chance for winter publicity.

Shires took the first dig. "Hack will lose sight of my gloves just as he lost sight of the ball in the World Series," he said.

Wilson responded in kind. "Right here and now I want to tell Mr. Shires that I am one of those hearty mountaineers from West Virginia, the class of people who do things without bragging about them. Down here we knock poundage off each other, so if Mr. Shires has any superfluous flesh on his body, he won't need any training to get it off after we get together."

Wilson was promised fifteen thousand dollars, not to mention the off-season notoriety. The Cubs were embarrassed to have one of their star players engaged in such an absurd spectacle, so Wilson, in deference to the team, took on the ring name "Battling Stouts"—a strange flight of logic, since without Wilson's fame as a ballplayer there would be no fight.

As things turned out, Stouts did no Battling. Shires had a warmup bout against a center for the Chicago Bears, George (The Brute) Trafton. Trafton beat Shires in a boring five-rounder. The best punch was landed by Bill Flecktenstein, a guard for the Bears, who hit the ring announcer for calling the boxers a couple of bums.

The Shires versus Wilson publicity balloon lost its air, and the fight was canceled. Cub management and Wilson's wife, Virginia, had been trying to talk him out of it, anyway. Wilson explained his position this way: "I had a feeling that I owed it to the quiet, dignified players of the major league to slap down this braggart, but Trafton took care of the matter."

Wilson's tears of the previous October were dried by the time he reported for spring training in 1930 at Catalina Island, California. In fact, Wilson, like Ruth, was an immensely cheerful and likable man, and though he had a temper he could enjoy a joke at his own expense. He was popular among his teammates, and his misplays of the 1929 World Series became the jokes of spring training. They called him "Sunny Boy Hack." When fly balls were hit into the sun, Cub players shouted "Wilson!" In the hotel dining room, Wilson pulled the window shade and asked the maitre'd to dim the light so he wouldn't misjudge his soup.

A boy pestered Joe McCarthy, the Cubs' manager, for a ball one day, and McCarthy pointed out to Wilson, who was shagging fly balls. "Son, do you see that fat fella out there in the outfield?" McCarthy asked. The boy said he did. "Well," McCarthy said, "you just stand behind him and you'll get more baseballs than you know what to do with."

But Wilson craved more fame. It was the custom back then for newspaper syndicates to run ghostwritten accounts of World Series games under the bylines of star players. Wilson got himself a ghostwriter and a syndicate for the 1929 Series, but the syndicate couldn't find any newspapers willing to buy. Newspapers carried Series accounts under the names of four Cubs—manager Joe McCarthy, slugger Rogers Hornsby, pitcher Guy Bush, and colorful first baseman Charlie Grimm. Later, Wilson announced his resolve:

"I'll have a ghost writer in the next World Series, even if it's played at the Polo Grounds. I notice that Babe Ruth sits in the press box in civies with his ghost writer as a body guard. Just watch my home run smoke next year!"

Thanks largely to the lively ball, hitting and home runs had been increasing throughout the 1920s. Ruth's fame and wealth were attracting more and more emulators. As spring training opened in 1930, Joe Vila, the New York *Sun*'s veteran baseball writer, noted a rash of exhibition homers. "The players, keeping in mind Babe Ruth's $80,000 contract, are doing their level best to knock the ball over the fences," Vila wrote.

Baseball traditionalists like Vila were unabashedly against the power trend. "Home run hitting actually dominates the national pastime," he reported. "It serves to discourage youngsters who possess natural pitching skill, but are forced, through apprehension, to donate their time to other positions."

E. S. Barnard, president of the American League, proposed to cut "cheap home runs" by requiring thirty-foot screens atop outfield walls that were within 325 feet of home plate, and twenty-foot screens for walls that ranged between 325 and 350 feet away. A year before, screens had been erected at Sportsman's Park in St. Louis, Baker Bowl in Philadelphia, and Forbes Field in Pittsburgh. Barnard's proposal would have required screens at the home parks of the Yankees, Giants, Dodgers, Athletics, Tigers, Red Sox, Indians, Reds, and Cubs.

Barnard said the screens wouldn't affect Ruth's mighty blasts, but would dampen lesser hitters. In 1929 Chuck Klein of the Phillies hit 43 homers—only three fewer than Ruth. Mel Ott of the Giants hit 42, and Wilson and Hornsby hit 39 apiece. No one quite said so, but the idea was to preserve the God—Ruth—while putting down his pretenders.

But the same day Barnard floated his proposal, Ruppert, the Yankee owner, shot it down. "Not for the next two years, anyway," he said, mindful of his salary obligation to Ruth. Ruppert realized that the screens would stop some of Ruth's drives just like anybody else's. He couldn't afford to kill the goose that laid baseball's golden egg—Ruthian homers. The idea was quietly dropped.

In the baseball dialogue of the time, to act against home runs was to take the high moral ground. Despite overwhelming evidence to the contrary, most baseball observers still considered Cobb, when in his prime, a better hitter and a more valuable player than Ruth. "I think the time has come for a swing toward the Ty Cobb type of baseball," said Waite Hoyt of the Yankees. But he was a pitcher.

Looking back, it is easy to pinpoint 1930 as a hinge year between the prosperity of the twenties and the Depression of the thirties. But it wasn't clear at the time. The stock market had crashed and unemployment was rising, but it was hard to tell whether the economy would consider sliding or turn back up. U.S. automakers made more cars in 1930 than ever before; the reality of the Depression did not set in until the following year.

Anyway, government didn't know what to do about a depression. John Maynard Keynes, the British economist, published his *Treatise on Money* in 1930, but the notion that government should spend the economy back to health was considered too radical for serious consideration. President Hoover and leaders of Congress thought it wiser to float a surplus.

Baseball, however, saw the deepening Depression as a threat to attendance and took precautions of its own. Home runs had boosted attendance before. Maybe more home runs would bring more fans to the ballpark. So in 1930 the owners put a little more juice into the ball—particularly the ball used in the National League, which had a lot of good hitters but did not have Babe Ruth. The lively new ball was thrown into play just as the major leagues were cresting with a breathtaking number of truly superior hitters—the kind of talent edge that offense occasionally achieves over defense, and vice versa. The hitters of 1930 didn't need a hotter ball, but they got it.

3

"Baseball tonight!"

The rules haven't changed much, but a baseball game was quite a different spectacle in 1930 than it is today, and fans got their baseball news in a different way.

Loudspeaker systems were installed in 1929 at the Polo Grounds, home of the New York Giants, and in 1930 at Shibe Park, where the Philadelphia Athletics played. At other major league stadiums, a man with a megaphone—the kind used by high school cheerleaders—announced the batteries before the game, bellowing his announcement three or four times, at different parts of the grandstand and bleachers.

That was it. No lineups, no national anthem, no player introductions, no announcement of who was stepping in to bat. Scoreboards were operated by hand and gave the score, inning by inning, plus batteries and scores of games in other cities; nothing more. You could not tell the players without a scorecard, because the players did not have their names on their uniforms.

Most of them did not even have numbers. As manager of the Cardinals in the early 1920s, Branch Rickey had gone too far by putting numbers on the backs of his players. Both fans and players saw the numbers as demeaning, like something worn by convicts. "I did not mind the public criticism," Rickey said later. "That sort of thing has not often changed any program I thought was good. But the effect upon the team was bad and busted up team morale completely. The players were embarrassed all of the time. They really didn't want to show themselves on the field. Because of the continuing embarrassment to the players, the numbers were removed."

The Yankees broke tradition by using uniform numbers in 1929.

Ruth wore number 3 because he batted third in the lineup, Gehrig was number 4 because he batted cleanup, and so on. The Washington Senators and Cleveland Indians adopted uniform numbers in 1930, and the rest of the American League leaped to numbers in 1931. The National League followed in 1932. You can't rush these things.

Radio was treated with similar skepticism. In April 1921 a radio station carried a boxing match, the first sporting event ever broadcast. That summer, station KDKA of Pittsburgh broadcast a baseball game. At the time, it was considered a novelty, not a breakthrough. In 1922 the World Series between the Yankees and Giants was broadcast in a few Eastern cities, with sportswriters Grantland Rice and Bill McGeehan announcing. Madison Avenue paid little heed; the last two games weren't aired for lack of a sponsor.

In 1924 station WMAQ of Chicago began broadcasting home games of the Cubs and White Sox. Other teams gave radio a try, but not without misgivings. It hadn't occurred to anyone that a radio station could be offered exclusive play-by-play rights and charged for the privilege. In ballparks where they were allowed, radio announcers were treated like sportswriters. A team like the Cubs, who thought additional fans would be attracted to Wrigley Field after hearing games on the radio, got plenty of it; by the late 1920s five stations were carrying Cub games.

The NBC and CBS radio networks were born in 1926 and 1927, respectively, and baseball broadcasting became more skillful and professional. Newspapermen had done most of the local work, but NBC hired Graham McNamee and CBS took on Ted Husing. McNamee tended to mispronounce names and err on facts, but he was entertaining and colorful. Husing elevated the profession; he did his homework, and went on the air armed with factual and interesting information.

A single announcer seemed plenty, and the private broadcasting booths of today were unheard of. Broadcasters sat alongside writers in the press box. During the 1929 World Series, NBC listeners heard an irritated sportswriter complain, "McNamee, will you please pipe down?"

As with television years later, club owners argued whether radio broadcasts boosted attendance by attracting new fans or hurt attendance by making it easy to enjoy the game without buying a ticket.

Several baseball teams continued to bar radio broadcasts. The three New York teams did not permit them until 1939. Writing in the New York *Sun* in April 1930, Grantland Rice said there was much talk in baseball circles of cutting out World Series broadcasts.

Trying to split the difference, the St. Louis Cardinals and Browns decided to allow broadcasting in 1930, but only if the announcers gave straight play-by-play, with no commentary—this from teams whose games were later aired by Dizzy Dean and Harry Caray. At the time, however, the keep-it-dull ruling struck baseball purists as sensible. "This should be mutually satisfactory to both the fans and the magnates, for there are some announcers prone to wander far from the actual occurrences on the field," reported *The Sporting News,* which little knew how prophetically it spoke.

Television was already being developed—Bell Labs demonstrated an experimental color TV in 1929—and Grantland Rice anticipated difficulties between the commercial orientation of this future medium and the academic character of college sports. "In case of a war between the broadcasting companies and the colleges," he wrote, "it might be necessary for the former to start a new line of universities, grab off most of the famous coaches and build up a football schedule of their own." Rice's tongue may have been in his cheek, but some critics might say that his suggestion was not all that far from the eventual marriage of television, money, and college football.

Although radio was immensely popular, stations did not, as they do today, carry frequent reviews of sports scores—or, for that matter, of news or weather. Few cars were equipped with radios. Most fans got their baseball news from the newspapers, which devoted more space to sports than they do today and delivered sports results much more quickly.

Baseball games were shorter. Hitters and pitchers didn't fidget around as much as they do today, pitching changes were fewer, and the time between innings was not extended for the sake of broadcast commercials. Most games started at 3:00 P.M. or thereabouts and were over by 4:30 or 5:00. Workers en route home could buy an afternoon newspaper with the game results, including a box score and a play-by-play. Presto!

"Within a half-hour after the game, newsboys would be yelling 'Cards win!,'" recalls Bob Broeg, who was an eager fan in 1930 and grew up to become sports editor of the St. Louis *Post-Dispatch.* "You could stick your two cents through the street-car window and get the paper."

These final editions put the baseball news on page one or used a wraparound sports section on top of the rest of the paper. "Newspapers were head cheese back then," says Broeg, and indeed they were. Most big cities had at least one morning newspaper and several afternoon papers, so the homeward-bound commuter could choose his favorite paper, or even his favorite sportswriter.

The competition was fierce. Sam Muchnik recalls covering the Cardinals for the St. Louis *Times.* He was twenty-five years old in 1930. Muchnik became a wrestling promoter in 1932 and promoted wrestling matches in St. Louis until his retirement in 1982:

"St. Louis had four papers. The *Post-Dispatch,* the *Star,* and the *Times* in the afternoon, and the *Globe-Democrat,* a morning paper. I was the youngest of the four writers traveling with the Cardinals. The *Post* had Roy Stockton, who was a veteran. Martin Haley covered for the *Globe.* Red Smith, with the *Star,* was just a little bit older than me.

"They played the games in the afternoon about three o'clock. There were no night games at that time. The *Times* had what they called a pink sheet, the *Star* had a green sheet, and the *Post-Dispatch* had an orange sheet. On top of the paper, wrapped around.

"A Western Union operator would sit next to each writer for an afternoon newspaper. We'd dictate the play-by-play. We tried to get the game in for the final, and usually we got it in. We had a set lead—'Cardinals won' or 'Cardinals lost.' Then they'd pick up the play-by-play. We didn't have much time to get a story in.

"That was true everywhere. When the Giants played here, twelve or fifteen writers would come in. New York had about fifteen newspapers back then, most of them afternoon newspapers.

"I remember real well the first time they ever gave out sandwiches in the press box. It was at Wrigley Field in Chicago. About the middle of the game they gave us sandwiches and Coca-Cola or coffee. Then the other teams started doing it. Now you go in the press box and you can have a full meal.

"It was quite a thing to make the trips. Were the trains air-conditioned? No. You had to open the windows up. Though we didn't have the niceties that they have now, it was real nice being on the train and talking to the ballplayers. You got to sit down and talk to the guys, go in the dining car and have dinner with them. We wrote a lot of feature stories on the ballplayers. I managed to get my stories by being friendly with a lot of the players. I bought my first car in 1929. A Ford roadster. Dizzy Dean rode with me in that car, and Jack Dempsey rode with me.

"There was a friendliness that I don't think exists today. In those days they'd sit in the hotel lobbies and talk baseball, where today they're reading the *Wall Street Journal.*"

Shirley Povich, for many years the sports editor of the Washington *Post,* agrees with Muchnik. "It was more romantic in those days," Povich says. No newspaperman had a more romantic introduction to the trade than Povich, who grew up in small-town Maine with no thought of becoming a writer. In 1988 Povich, an octogenerian, participated in the *Post*'s World Series coverage, writing in the witty and gracious style that has endeared him to Washington readers over seven decades. In an interview, he recalled his unusual professional training:

"I grew up in Bar Harbor. My summer job was to go to the golf course and caddy for those aristocrats who played golf and sailed all summer. Every caddy had a number. You took turns. My number was 23—as they say, '23 skiddoo!'

"This capitalist came to play, and it was my turn to caddy for him. I had no idea who he was. On the second hole he hit a ball with a big spade mashie. He hit it over the green into the woods. And he said, 'Nobody will ever find *that* ball.' And I said, 'Perhaps.' I went over there and picked it up. He said, 'That's a great piece of caddying!'

"It turned out to be Edward B. McLean, owner of the Washington *Post.* I became his private caddy. Three years later, he said I should go to his college, Georgetown University, and work on his newspaper."

* * *

So Povich, just out of high school and with nothing better to do, traveled to Washington.

"I was sixteen years old, or just seventeen. The first day I was in town I went out to see him. The butler, who was an old friend of mine from Maine, took me around to the first tee of his private golf course—McLean Gardens. Mr. McLean was *so* happy to see me. He introduced me to the three people with him. He said, 'Mr. President, this is Shirley Povich. He's the greatest caddy in America, and he's going to caddy for you today.'

"I caddied that day for President Harding, and that's the beginning of the story. It was 1922. I enrolled at Georgetown, and Mr. McLean sent me to see the general manager of the *Post*. I knew nothing about newspapers. In a quick effort to get rid of me, the general manager sent me to the city room. He didn't want me lousing up the composing room or the press room. The city room was a dump, a repository for all the incompetents. I worked there, and late in 1924 I got into sports."

Povich fondly recalled the Western Union operators who transmitted play-by-play to the *Post* during a game, and later transmitted the story, often looking over the writer's shoulder and sending code just a sentence or two behind the typewriter:

"One day I'm in Boston with a Western Union operator. The Senators are tied for the league lead with Cleveland. We're playing one game in Boston, and Cleveland is playing a doubleheader. Cleveland has already lost the first game. They're playing the second game.

"We lose to Boston, 11 to 3. Made twelve errors. Played lousy ball. I'm waiting on the second Cleveland game. It looks like the Indians are going to lose it. I'm writing for my own amusement.

By Shirley Povich
Washington *Post*

Boston, May 18—The Nats fell into the shithouse today and came up with the league lead.

"I suddenly realized that the operator is looking over my shoulder and sending. I said, 'Halt! Halt!' "

Only two umpires worked major league games in 1930—one behind the plate, one on the bases. Players did not wear helmets, even though knockdown pitches were perfectly legal and were much more common than they are today. Outfield walls were not padded, and there were no warning tracks. In left field at Boston's Fenway Park and throughout the outfield at Cincinnati's Crosley Field, the field sloped upward as it approached the fence.

Fields were not well groomed, and bad bounces were common. Gloves were tiny by today's standards; a fielder really did need two hands to be sure of a catch. After retiring the side, infielders and outfielders tossed their gloves in the grass behind them. This foolishly hazardous practice persisted until 1954.

Prohibition was in effect; plenty of beer in speakeasies, but none at the ballpark. There were no ballgirls or bat days, no trivia quizzes or DiamondVision, no waves or trumpet charges. The Chicken and the Phillie Phanatic were decades ahead, but the ground was broken for today's costumed clowns by Al Schacht and Nick Altrock, two former pitchers who coached for the Washington Senators. The Senators needed all the help they could get at the box office, so Schacht and Altrock developed pantomime comedy routines that entertained fans for years. They became a fixture at Senator games and were hired year after year to entertain before World Series games. Schacht was the star and was dubbed "The Clown Prince of Baseball."

Promotion may have been primitive by today's standards, but baseball executives did try to attract new fans. Most baseball patrons were male, yet many more women than men were free in the afternoons. The St. Louis Browns had inaugurated "Ladies Day" early in the century, and in 1930 the Chicago Cubs raised the weekly event to a stampede. With sluggers like Wilson, Hornsby, and Cuyler, the Cubs were fun to watch, and Wrigley Field was a pleasant enough place to spend the afternoon. When the 1930 season started, a woman—or a lady—could get two free tickets to a Ladies Day game.

The promotion was a runaway success. On one Ladies Day 21,000 women came in free; a week later, 31,000. William Veeck, Sr., the

Cubs' general manager, cut the ladies back to one ticket apiece. They had to be ordered by mail, and orders were cut off after 17,500 tickets were mailed out—one for every seat in the upper deck, yielding a weekly mass of femininity unique in athletic annals. The ladies kept ordering. With the Giants coming to Chicago for a Ladies Day game in August 1930, Veeck had to climb over ten bags of mail to get to his office. Other teams, including the Giants, started their own Ladies Days.

All games were played in daylight, and in retrospect it is hard to understand why. According to baseball researcher Oscar Eddleton, a night exhibition game was played in 1880, just one year after Edison invented the light bulb. In 1909 a Massachusetts inventor, George F. Cahill, developed a portable lighting system for ballparks and traveled the country trying to sell it. Cahill's lighting system was demonstrated at several exhibition games, including one at the home park of the Cincinnati Reds and another at the White Sox home grounds in Chicago. The lights worked, the fans were enthusiastic—and professional baseball continued to spurn the innovation.

In 1930, with the Depression threatening attendance, this devotion to baseball tradition became too much for the minor leagues to bear. Des Moines, Iowa, of the Class A Western League, announced that it would play its first home game of 1930 under the lights. Des Moines opened on the road, and Independence, Kansas, of the Class C Western Association, won the honor of staging the first night game in organized baseball. M. L. Truby, president of the team and a wealthy oil man and jeweler, put up the money in a cooperative venture with the Giant Manufacturing Company of Council Bluffs, Iowa, which manufactured the lighting system.

On the night of April 28, 1930, the Independence Producers beat Muskogee, 12 to 2, in organized baseball's first night game. The same night, the Kansas City Monarchs played the first night game of the Negro leagues, using a portable lighting system. Four nights later, Des Moines played under what a local sportswriter called "33,000 candle power of mellow light" and scored eleven runs in the first inning en route to a 13 to 6 drubbing of Wichita. The electric bill, according to *The Sporting News,* came to $25. The game was attended by C. C. Slapnicka, a Cleveland scout, who reported that he "did not see a man flinch from a ball, either batted or thrown."

The fans certainly did not flinch; more than ten thousand attended. The minor leagues, which had resisted night baseball for so long, now rushed to embrace it. By the end of May, twenty teams had lights or were installing them. Attendance doubled and tripled, giving the minors a badly needed financial boost. William Wrigley, Jr., decided to install lights at Wrigley Field—in Los Angeles, home of the Cubs' top minor league affiliate.

Giant Manufacturing and other makers of lighting systems began hard-sell advertising in *The Sporting News,* like this message from the Outdoor Sports Illuminating Company of Des Moines: "Smashing triumph! Night baseball. 300% increase in attendance at Des Moines, where we installed General Electric equipment."

Minor league cities that continued to hold out were scorned. Four of the six teams in the Piedmont League had lights by mid-July of 1930. The two that did not, Henderson and Raleigh, North Carolina, were not drawing as well at home and asked for a visitors' cut of the night gate receipts while on the road. The other four teams not only refused, but told Henderson and Raleigh to install lights or get out of the league.

But the major leagues would not budge. Reporting on a meeting of major league owners in July 1930, the New York *Sun* had this to say:

Players are not agreed that moonlight baseball is anything more than a novelty. The grounds can be lighted, it is true, but the game is not the same as the sun-kist sport. In fact it is almost impossible to see a curve ball. It is a guess about low-thrown balls. Up in the air the ball can be easily spotted if new balls are kept in circulation.

In view of all the reports received the magnates, off the record, decided to go slow on shifting to the night game. Whether there will be a test is not known. Most of the powerful club owners don't want to shift, for they feel that they have made millions in the game as it stands and it is feared that the quality of players will deteriorate.

The attitude of most owners was reflected by Clark Griffith, owner of the Washington Senators. With the Senators in New York to play the Yankees in early September of 1930, Griffith attended a minor league night game in Newark, New Jersey, and spoke of it with sarcasm. "Nothing to it for anyone who wants baseball instead of a mere show," Griffith reported. Newspaper accounts of the controversy rarely mentioned the compelling fact that most people work during the day, and thus might be more likely to attend a game at night.

Only one major league owner, Sam Breadon of the Cardinals, openly campaigned for night baseball. Breadon was a native of New York's Greenwich Village who moved to St. Louis and became wealthy as an automobile dealer. He gave a summer picnic in 1930 for writers from New York and St. Louis, and told them night baseball was sure to come to the majors. "It makes every day a Sunday," he said.

Breadon needed a boost; the Cardinals were not drawing, even though they were a contending team. According to writer Frederick G. Lieb, the National League gave Breadon permission to play night games in 1932, and he offered to pay for installation of lights at Sportsman's Park, which was owned by the St. Louis Browns, with the Cardinals as tenants. Philip de Catesby Ball, owner of the Browns, refused—and the Browns paid the price, drawing all of 112,558 fans to their home games in 1932.

In 1935 Larry MacPhail broke tradition by installing lights at Crosley Field, Cincinnati. Very gradually, other major league teams followed, although for a decade the number of night games was strictly limited. In 1988 lights were installed at Chicago's Wrigley Field—the last holdout. It was fifty-eight years after night baseball first came to organized baseball, and traditionalists still were not ready for the change; Wrigley was bathed in light, but shrouded in journalistic mourning.

In fact, the Cubs didn't hold out as steadfastly as many people think. They bought a lighting system after the 1941 season, intending to install it in time for night play in 1942. Then the Japanese bombed Pearl Harbor, and Philip Wrigley, William's son and heir, patriotically donated his lighting equipment to the war effort.

In minor league towns of 1930, night baseball was hardly welcomed by other purveyors of evening entertainment—notably the movies and Putt-Putt golf, which was wildly popular in 1930. Borrowing the meter of Longfellow's "Excelsior," one Jack Jones penned this poem for an August 1930 edition of *The Sporting News:*

The shades of night were falling fast,
When down the town's main street there passed
A bloke who packed a bunting sign,
Emblazoned with a strange design:
    "Baseball tonight!"

His brow was low, the jaws beneath
Were opened wide to show his teeth,
And with a fog-horn voice, he roared
The message of his painted board:
    "Baseball tonight!"

"What's this," the theater owner cried.
"How come no customers outside?"
But still the bloke of forehead low,
Broadcast his message, to and fro:
    "Baseball tonight!"

"Hey, cut that out! I'm gonna fight,"
The boxer moaned, "This here ain't right!"
But, drowning out the street car bell
The low-brow bloke went on to yell:
    "Baseball tonight!"

"For heaven's sake, give us a rest!"
Cried Putt-Putt folk in loud protest.
His voice was hoarse, but raucous still,
And so he roared with lusty will:
    "Baseball tonight!"

At dawn the copper on his beat
Espied the victim 'cross the street.
Bruised, injured, beaten, damnified—
He whispered once, before he died:
    "Baseball tonight!"

4

"Unless the home run burlesque is curbed in some way . . ."

At Griffith Stadium in Washington on April 17, President Hoover threw out the first ball of the 1930 season. Umpire Roy Van Graflin caught it, and the visiting Boston Red Sox edged the Senators, 4 to 3. It was a rare moment of hope for the Red Sox, who were on the way to their sixth straight last-place finish, the legacy of Harry Frazee's sale of Babe Ruth and other Red Sox stars to the Yankees a decade before.

The Athletics opened at home on a note of worry. Al Simmons, their great slugger, was holding out. The night before, Connie Mack had announced that Spence Harris, a weak journeyman picked up from the Senators, would play left field in Simmons's place.

But Simmons wanted to play. As his teammates began warming up on the field, he signed his contract. The Philadelphia fans roared when he walked onto the field, and applauded when he came to bat in the first inning, with a man on base. George Pipgras was pitching for the Yankees in an opening-day meeting of the two teams expected to compete for the American League pennant.

Simmons homered. Lefty Grove stifled the Yankees, and the A's won, 6 to 2.

The Cubs were favored to repeat in the National League. Their lineup looked even more powerful, with Gabby Hartnett, their star catcher, back after missing most of 1929 with injuries. But the Cubs suffered two early-season misfortunes. On May 27 pitcher Hal Carlson died in his sleep from the effects of poison gas inflicted upon him in World War I. Death, said *The Sporting News,* "took him where umpires never miss a perfect strike and nobody ever bellows, 'Take him out!' "

Two days later, Rogers Hornsby broke his left ankle. The injury stripped the Cubs of a devastating hitter, the National League's Most Valuable Player in 1929.

"To this day, I've never seen a right-handed hitter hit that good, and that includes Joe DiMaggio," said Charlie Grimm, Hornsby's teammate with the Cubs and a major league manager for nineteen years. Clyde Sukeforth, a catcher with the Cincinnati Reds in 1930, recalled the awe with which other p'ayers regarded Hornsby: "When he would hit in batting practice, everybody would stop and watch. Every player, on both teams."

Hornsby was an outstanding second baseman, too, but he had an aversion to pop flies and always asked his shortstop and first baseman to take them all. Woody English was the Cub shortstop. "Hornsby would say, 'Oh, look up at that sky! It's high today. You take all the pop flies you can get, Wood. Come on, Wood!'"

Most baseball historians have relegated Hornsby to a spot behind Ruth and Cobb, and perhaps behind a few other hitters, but take a look at what Hornsby *averaged* for the five seasons from 1921 through 1925:

H	R	HR	RBI	BA
216	123	29	140	.402

No one else—not even Cobb—ever *averaged* .400 for five years. Cobb never hit more than twelve homers in a season, and indeed scorned the home run as if a single were somehow superior, but Hornsby twice led the league in homers. And he wasn't swinging wildly from the heels; he hit over .400 both of those seasons.

Hornsby's hitting declined sharply in 1926, but his stature increased. As the Cardinals' playing manager—he succeeded Branch Rickey, who was fired and kicked upstairs to the front office—Hornsby led the Cardinals to their first pennant. In the seventh inning of the seventh game of the World Series, he waved in Grover Cleveland Alexander from the bullpen to face Tony Lazzeri of the Yankees. The bases were loaded. Alexander punched out Lazzeri in one of the most famous strikeouts in baseball history and the Cardinals beat the Yankees, Hornsby tagging Babe Ruth for the final out as the Bambino tried to steal second base.

But Hornsby was a dour man, difficult to get along with. He held out for fifty thousand dollars a year for three years. Sam Breadon, the Cardinal owner, got mad, and on December 20, 1926, he traded Hornsby to the New York Giants for Frankie Frisch, a star second baseman, and Jimmy Ring, a pitcher. St. Louis was shocked. The Chamber of Commerce passed a resolution of protest, and the mayor tried to get the deal reversed. Hornsby was a St. Louis institution; he had even bought Branch Rickey's stock in the team, when he succeeded Rickey as manager. To avoid a conflict of interest between Hornsby the player and Hornsby the investor, the league ruled that the slugger would have to sell his Cardinal stock before reporting to the Giants. He held out for a fat profit and got it.

New York was only the first stop for Hornsby, who became a baseball nomad. In 1927 he hit .361 for the Giants, scored 133 runs, drove in 125, and filled in as manager when John McGraw was out sick or missing for other reasons—a habit McGraw acquired in his later years. McGraw and Hornsby were alike in their managing approach. That is to say, they rarely said anything nice to their players, and never hesitated to chew a player up and down for the slightest mistake.

Perhaps feeling that Hornsby was stealing McGraw's show, the Giants traded Hornsby to the Boston Braves that winter for a couple of nobodies. The Braves were a lousy team, but Hornsby managed them in 1928 and led the league in batting at .387. Hornsby knew the Braves needed money, so he encouraged them to sell him. They did, to the Cubs, for five players and $200,000. It was a record, almost double the $110,000 the Yankees paid for Babe Ruth in December 1919.

Hornsby came dear, but the Cubs had stolen Hack Wilson from the Giants in 1926 when the New York front office slipped up and forget to protect Wilson from the annual player draft of minor leaguers; the Giants had farmed Wilson to the minors for some final seasoning. The Cubs also got a bargain in Hazen (Kiki) Cuyler, a hitting and base-stealing star acquired from the Pittsburgh Pirates in November 1927 for two journeymen. With Hornsby out in 1930, the Cubs leaned harder on their other stars, particularly Wilson.

"The Boy With the Mountainous Chin," as the sportswriters sometimes called Wilson, came out of the gate slowly in 1930. He drove in only one run in the season's first six games and didn't hit his first homer until the next day. He went on a tear in May. On June 1 "The Hardest Hitting Hydrant of All Time"—another disparaging Wilson nickname—drove in six runs with two homers, a double, and a single as the Cubs routed the Pirates, 16 to 4, behind Guy Bush. Wilson was leading the National League with sixteen homers and was mentioned as a threat to Ruth's record of sixty.

Everyone was hitting. *The Sporting News* expressed concern: "Unless the home run burlesque is curbed in some way the sluggers will knock out 1,500 four masters this year." They had hit a record 1,350 the year before.

Rallies were immense, and pitchers absorbed terrible punishment; relievers were not called upon as readily as they are today. On May 12, in Chicago, the Giants scored six runs in the second inning and seven in the third, helped by a home run by Mel Ott and two doubles by Fred Lindstrom. Larry Benton, the New York pitcher, carried a 14 to 0 lead into the fifth inning, and little seemed amiss when Cliff Heathcote homered for the Cubs; 14 to 1.

In the Cub sixth, Wilson and Hartnett walked, and Clyde Beck homered; 14 to 4. In the seventh, Heathcote led off with his second homer, and, after one out, Wilson homered to right. So did Charlie Grimm. Les Bell flied out and Hartnett fanned for what would have been the third out, but Shanty Hogan, the Giant catcher, dropped the ball and then threw it wildly, Hartnett reaching second. Beck homered again; 14 to 9. Benton had yielded four homers in the inning, and McGraw decided he was weakening. He brought in Joe Heving, who gave up six hits and three runs, but no homers. The Giants won, 14 to 12, the Cubs having run out of outs.

Also threatening Ruth's record was Ruth himself. The Yankees and Athletics were stacked with sluggers, and when they collided the home runs fell like rain. In late May, the Yanks and A's played three doubleheaders in four days, and the hitters gorged. On a Wednesday afternoon, thirty thousand fans crowded Shibe Park. Ruth hit three straight homers in the first game, and Ben Chapman hit another for the Yankees, but the A's countered with a barrage of hits, including a homer by Foxx, and won 15 to 7. Simmons and Jimmy Dykes homered in the nightcap as Philadelphia made it a sweep, 4–1.

In Thursday's opener, Ruth hit two homers. Chapman and George Pipgras, the Yankee pitcher, hit one each, and Pipgras stopped the Athletics; 10 to 1, New York. The nightcap was a firestorm. Gehrig hit three homers and drove in eight runs; Foxx hit two and drove in six; Lazzeri hit two doubles and drove in four. Ruth homered; so did Simmons and Dykes. The Yanks scored nine runs in the first two innings, but after six it was tied, 12 to 12. Earnshaw relieved for Philadelphia, then Grove, but the Yanks kept hitting; 20 to 13, New York.

On to New York for two more Saturday. Ruth drove in seven runs in the twin bill, homering in both games to give him eight in six games, a new record. The Yankees swept, 10 to 6 and 11 to 1. Noting a need for pitching help, the Yankees had pressed an outfielder and $50,000 on their Red Sox cousins for Charley (Red) Ruffing, who had lost forty-seven games for Boston in the last two seasons. Ruffing stopped the A's in the nightcap, starting a distinguished tenure in New York that would land him in the Hall of Fame. "I don't know what heaven looks like," Ruffing said of the trade, "but that's how it seemed."

The ball was carrying, and Ruth predicted that he'd hit about seventy-five home runs. But on July 2 he jumped for a ball, caught a finger on the outfield screen, and lost the nail. The team doctor said the Babe would be out for a while, but he played the next day, his finger bandaged. Two days later he hit his thirty-second homer, putting him more than twenty games ahead of his record pace of 1927. But his slugging tailed off. He finished the season with forty-nine homers—no record, but enough to lead the league.

Although the Athletics and Yankees carried heavier lumber, the Washington Senators, of all people, led the American League by four games going into a Memorial Day doubleheader—morning and afternoon—at Philadelphia. Walter Johnson was managing the Senators in a classic test of managerial adaptability—the best pitcher from the dead-ball era, now trying to win with the rabbit ball.

Johnson put together the best pitching staff in baseball. Four of his starting pitchers won fifteen games each and the fifth, southpaw Lloyd Brown, won sixteen. The staff ERA was 3.96—the only staff in either league that yielded fewer than four earned runs a game. Still, the pitching looked awful to Johnson, and he talked of returning to active duty, though he was forty-two and hadn't pitched for three years. Clark Griffith, the Senators' owner and a great pitcher in his own day, counseled The Big Train to steam down.

The Washington lineup boasted excellent hitters in Heinie Manush, Joe Judge, Ossie Bluege, Sam Rice, and Sammy West. Shortstop Joe Cronin, a former schoolboy tennis champion from California, suddenly blossomed into a star. The running and weightlifting vogue among athletes was still a half-century away, but Cronin was a skinny shortstop without power and decided to do something about it. Over the winter he ran several miles a day and hacked logs with an ax. His six-foot frame gained thirty pounds, to 180, and he suddenly joined the league's elite hitters.

Cronin became a perennial all-star, and managed the Senators to their final pennant, in 1933. In October 1934 he married Mildred Robertson, the niece and adopted daughter of Griffith. Tom Yawkey, the millionaire who by then had purchased the Boston Red Sox, offered Griffith $250,000 for Cronin. Realizing that the family soup was getting a bit thick with son-in-law, shortstop, and manager rolled into one, Griffith—with Cronin's acquiescence—took the deal. It sounded callous, but in fact Griffith knew that his daughter and son-in-law could expect a brighter financial future under the wealthy Yawkey than he could provide them with his bootstrap Senators.

In 1930 Cronin's emergence as a strong hitter impressed everyone. "In the clutch," said Connie Mack, "I'd just as soon have Cronin up there for me as anybody I can think of. I'll go further than that. With a man on third and one out, I'd rather have Cronin hitting for me than anybody I've ever seen, and that includes Cobb, Simmons and the rest of them."

On Memorial Day 1930, however, Mack settled for his own Aloysius Szymanski, or rather Al Simmons; players of that era liked to Americanize their names. In the opener, Washington's Ad Liska, a junkballer, had the A's and Lefty Grove beaten 6 to 3 with two out in the last of the ninth and nobody on base. But the Washington catcher, Muddy Ruel, ignored a pop foul that he could have caught, and the A's got consecutive singles from a couple of guys named Spence Harris and Dib Williams—the Flynn and Blake of the lineup, with Simmons stepping to bat as the mighty Casey.

Liska had retired Simmons four straight times, but this time Casey did not strike out. Simmons homered to tie the score and send the game into extra innings. Simmons doubled in the eleventh inning, singled in the thirteenth, and was stranded both times. He doubled in the fifteenth, and when Foxx beat out a slow roller toward third Simmons overran third base and got caught in a rundown. He scrambled back safely, but felt his right knee pop.

"Standing on the bag I could feel it swelling up under my uniform," Simmons later told writer John P. Carmichael. "By the time Boob McNair singled and I scored the winning run it was becoming stiff."

Between games, Mack summoned the team physician, a strong Athletics fan. The doctor said Simmons should be hospitalized but could wait a few hours—in case he was needed to pinch hit in the nightcap.

He was. Trailing 7 to 3, Philadelphia loaded the bases in the last of the seventh. "Looks like this is the time and the place," Mack said to Simmons. "This is what Dr. Carnett meant and you know what he said. Walk around the bases if you can."

Simmons homered off Bump Hadley and walked around the bases behind three teammates. "My, that was fine, Al!" Mack said as Simmons hobbled back to the bench.

"We won in the ninth," Simmons told Carmichael, "and down came Carnett and lugged me off to the hospital." Simmons was the hero of the sweep, but Foxx played a good supporting role—eight hits, fourteen total bases. The Athletics beat the Senators the next two days and soon were on top again.

In mid-June the Cleveland Indians climbed into first place. The Indians boasted a superb hitter in Earl Averill, who hit .339 and drove in 119 runs, and one of the game's finest pitchers in young Wes Ferrell, who won twenty-five games. They also had their share of rabbit-ball sluggers. Ever hear of Johnny Hodapp? He hit .354 for the Indians in 1930, with 121 RBI. Guys named Dick Porter and Eddie Morgan hit .350 and .349, respectively; Morgan had 26 homers and 136 RBI.

On June 15 a record crowd of thirty-five thousand overflowed Cleveland's League Park to cheer on the first-place Indians against the Yankees. As was the practice back then, fans without seats were allowed to stand in the outfield, behind ropes. Fly balls hit into the outfield crowd were ground-rule doubles. Ruth walked his first four times up, then hit his twenty-first home run. Gehrig drove in seven runs, homering to right and powering a second homer out of the park in left. Herb Pennock went the route for New York, and it was a long route indeed. He pitched a sixteen-hitter and won, 17 to 10.

The Indians wilted. The Yanks scored 1,062 runs to lead the major leagues. (In 1987, a big year for hitters, the Detroit Tigers led the majors with 896 runs. In 1988 the Boston Red Sox led with 813.) But the Yankee pitching was weak, and they never really challenged for the lead. The Senators played with remarkable consistency and pulled into first place once again in July. Manager Johnson credited the *loss* of his best relief pitcher, Garland Braxton, who was traded June 16 for Art (The Great) Shires. "Braxton was always warmed up as a relief man," explained Johnson. "The pitchers used to figure that if they did not halt the enemy in a few rounds they would get help from Braxton. Now they go in the box determined to stay the limit." The Senators won sixteen of twenty-four games, fifteen of them complete games by the starting pitchers.

But the Athletics had good pitching, too, and great hitting. In a devastating road swing in July, they scored ninety-seven runs in eight games, winning all of them while averaging twelve runs and fifteen hits a game. They scored ten runs in one inning at St. Louis, then, the next day, nine runs in the first three innings. In Chicago, Foxx hit a ball clear over the left field stands at Comiskey Park, the first player to do so. Comiskey was properly baptized; three years before, Ruth had cleared the right field roof. Foxx had a gentle nature, but his strength and slugging earned him a brutal nickname: "The Beast."

Mel Harder broke in with the Indians in 1928, at the age of eighteen—just in time to pitch to Ty Cobb and Tris Speaker, who were finishing their careers, and to yield Cobb's final home run. By 1930 Harder was a regular starter. He pitched twenty seasons in the major leagues, all with Cleveland. Harder was considered one of baseball's best curveball pitchers. He won twenty or more games twice and finished with 223 victories, although the Indians never won a pennant during his career. Harder later coached for the Indians. He was pitching coach for the Cincinnati Reds in 1968, making him one of the few men whose careers spanned the thirty-eight years that separated baseball's seasons of extremes—the great hitting year of 1930 and the great pitching year of 1968. In the summer of 1988, Harder reminisced about 1930 in an interview:

"We had a good bunch of hitters in the league. The Athletics were in their second year of having a real tough club. They had Jimmie Foxx and Al Simmons, Bing Miller, Mickey Cochrane. All good hitters. The Yankees still had Gehrig and Ruth, Lazzeri, fellows like that. Even the White Sox had good hitters, and the St. Louis Browns.

"We were very careful with the Babe. His job was to hit home runs. If he wanted to go for singles and doubles he probably would have hit for a higher average. But he was known for the home run, and that's where all his color came from. The fans would rather watch him hit a home run than see him hit a couple of doubles or triples or whatever.

"We tried to make good pitches to him all the time, and if we walked him, we walked him. Trouble with the Yankee lineup was, when you got through with the Babe, why, Gehrig was there. Gehrig was strong. He could hit the ball a long ways like Ruth. Sometimes he'd hit three home runs in one day—nothing to it for him, I guess. Gehrig had his feet farther apart than Ruth. Gehrig could hit straightaway—left field, right field, all around.

"As a combination, Foxx and Simmons were pretty close to Ruth and Gehrig. They were great with handling the bat, you know, and strong. Foxx, by golly, you talk about line drives!

"Weak spots? No, no. The only thing that saved you a lot of times was when they didn't time the ball—hit under it or topped it or something like that."

Charlie Gehringer, the Detroit Tigers' great second baseman, admired Foxx as one hitter to another. "I liked to see him hit," Gehringer said. "He hit the ball as hard as anybody I ever saw, including Ruth. He was probably the only guy who ever hit a ball out of the Tokyo Stadium. You ever see that stadium? It goes on for miles, and he hit one out."

The Athletics also had Grove, the ultimate stopper. Grove, like Red Ruffing, was a coal miner's son, and he was tough. He made an unusual sociological pairing with the Athletics' other ace, George Earnshaw, who came from a wealthy family and had attended an exclusive prep school.

Doc Cramer, a young outfielder with the Athletics in 1930, was Grove's teammate for ten years, first with the A's and then with the Boston Red Sox. Cramer hit .296 over twenty big league seasons and played in two World Series fourteen years apart—with the Athletics in 1931, and with the Detroit Tigers in the wartime year of 1945, when Cramer was forty years old. I asked Cramer about his old teammate in 1988, and he had no trouble remembering the great lefthander:

"Grove was all man. Ornery. Wanted to win. Didn't care how he won. He just stood out there and threw the ball. Threw it hard. He didn't have the curve. That was the funny thing about Grove. Everybody in the league knew what they were going to hit at. He just threw it right on by 'em. Did he throw faster than Bob Feller? Oh yeah. I know he did. I hit off both of 'em."

Charlie Gehringer broke in with the Tigers in 1924, played nineteen seasons with Detroit, and faced Grove for seventeen of those years. Gehringer was called "The Mechanical Man" because he hit so well and so consistently. He led the American League in batting in 1937 with a .371 average, and wound up with a career batting average of .320. He was elected to the Baseball Hall of Fame in 1949. Gehringer was a quick and sure-handed fielder; he is considered one of the greatest second basemen in history. He is a Michigan native, was still living (and playing golf) in the Detroit area in 1988, and is one of the most beloved of all-time Tiger heroes. He found Grove a tough customer:

"Grove was outstanding. I don't think anybody could compare with him. Maybe Walter Johnson. I saw Johnson in the tail end of his career. He could still throw awfully hard, but not as hard as Grove. I wish they'd had a speed clock in those days.

"He hardly ever threw a curve. Mostly fastballs, which made him, you would think, easier to hit. But by the time you made up your mind whether it was going to be a strike or not it was too late."

* * *

In 1961 Jimmy Dykes, the Athletics' third baseman in 1930 and later a major league manager for twenty-one years, told Hal Lebovitz of the Cleveland *Plain Dealer* about Grove's temper. As with Bob Gibson of the Cardinals almost forty years later, Grove's teammates learned to leave him alone on the day he would pitch.

"On the day he was pitching it was suicide for a photographer to try to take his picture," Dykes said. "He'd throw the ball right through the lens. If you don't think he could throw a ball through a camera, go ask the Libby-Owens people. They had made this marvelous new thing. Unbreakable glass. They figured it would be great advertising to have Grove throw his fastball at the glass just to prove how strong it was. Lefty went for the idea. There was money in it, of course.

"He whistled one at the glass and nobody ever heard any more about the experiment. The ball went clean through. Made a perfect circle.

"I was his good friend off the field so I was the only one allowed to go near him when he was on the mound. If I saw his blood pressure going up, I'd get the ball and hold it awhile. I'd go near him, but not too near.

"He'd snarl, 'Gimme the ball.'

"I'd step back and say, 'Now wait a second, Lefty.'

"He'd say, 'Gimme the ball.'

"I'd say, 'This is your old buddy, Jimmy, talking. Just relax.'

"He'd just keep repeating, 'Gimme the ball,' and the instant I'd get close enough, he'd grab it."

In 1930 Grove grabbed it for twenty-eight wins against five losses. Mack used him freely in relief, a common practice back then; Grove had nine saves. His ERA of 2.54 was far and away the league's lowest. It was the third of nine ERA championships for Grove, an unparalleled achievement. In his *Historical Baseball Abstract,* Bill James rates Grove the greatest pitcher of all time.

Earnshaw won twenty-two games for the A's, and Rube Walberg won thirteen. The Yankees actually outscored the Athletics, averaging 6.9 runs a game to Philadelphia's meek 6.18. Even in 1930, the Year of the Hitter, pitching made the difference.

The Athletics took the lead to stay on July 13. They clinched the pennant September 18 in a game started by Earnshaw, finished by Grove, and decided by Simmons, who hit a homer and three singles. For 1930, it was just your average ballgame: Athletics 14, White Sox 10.

5

"The wind caught the ball . . . and it conked me. It could have happened to anybody."

At Pittsburgh's Forbes Field on June 23, the Brooklyn Dodgers, a surprise contender, demonstrated the kind of play that endeared them to their fans—and, in some ways, to their opponents as well.

Two were out in the Brooklyn sixth, with one man on base. Heinie Meine, the pitcher with the rhyming name, was working for the Pirates.

Johnny Frederick singled. Wally Gilbert hit an inside-the-park home run. Babe Herman homered. Del Bissonette singled. So did Rube Bressler. Glenn Wright tripled, bringing home the fifth and sixth runs of the inning. Mickey Finn doubled. Al Lopez singled. Jumbo Jim Elliott, the Dodger pitcher, also singled, Lopez stopping at second. Frederick, up for the second time in the inning, got his second single. Lopez, trying to score, was thrown out at the plate. The Dodgers had *concluded* their inning with ten straight hits.

Jewel Ens, the Pirate manager, decided Meine had suffered enough, having yielded fourteen runs and nineteen hits, the last ten of them in a row. Leon (Moose) Chagnon faced the Dodgers in the seventh. He quickly yielded a double to Gilbert and another homer to Herman. Bissonette grounded out, but the Dodgers had tied a major league record with twelve straight hits. They won, 19 to 6.

These Dodgers were the "Daffiness Boys" of manager Wilbert Robinson, a cheerful and rotund gent who was affectionately known as Uncle Robbie. He had managed the Dodgers since 1914 and was used to playing third fiddle in New York, behind the Yankees and Giants.

In 1930 the Dodgers were good *and* daffy. Robinson had the league's best pitcher in Dazzy Vance, still an overpowering fastballer at age thirty-nine. Someone said that Lefty Grove could throw a lamb chop past a wolf; Vance, said his teammate Johnny Frederick, "could throw a cream puff through a battleship." The Dodgers had two other good pitchers in Ray Phelps and Dolf Luque—"The Pitching Pearl of the Antilles" in the kind of melodic nickname that became popular in the 1930s. Al Lopez, a rookie catcher, played superbly. So did short-stop Glenn Wright, first baseman Del Bissonette, and center fielder Frederick.

Most of all, the Dodgers had Babe Herman, a great hitter who was capable of dazzling defensive plays. Unfortunately, poor Herman is best remembered for his breathtaking goofs. In 1922 Herman, batting .416 for Omaha, was released by his exasperated manager after a fly ball hit him on the head.

Herman, as always, had a logical explanation. "It was a foul ball that started to go into the stands," he told sportswriter John Lardner. "The minute I turned my back, though, the wind caught the ball and blew it out again, and it conked me. It could have happened to anybody."

But it happened to Herman, and it grew into a legend. Herman didn't think it was fair. After all, it was a foul ball, and it happened in the minor leagues. Asked later whether he had *really* been hit on the head by a fly ball, Herman replied, "Absolutely not. On the shoulder, yes, but not on the head."

Herman's baserunning was the stuff of history. On May 30, 1930, Herman, leading off first base, stood and watched as Del Bissonette's towering fly ball cleared the right field screen at Ebbets Field. There was no chance the ball would be caught, but Bissonette thought it might hit the screen and was running hard. Not so Herman; Bissonette passed him between first and second base, and was declared out. His home run was pared to a single.

On September 15, in the heat of the pennant race, Herman did it again. This time the unfortunate slugger was Glenn Wright, and Herman wasn't the only roadblock. Wright, a star National League shortstop for a decade, later recalled the incident for writer Eugene Murdock:

"We were playing the Cubs and it was a close game. We had two men on and I hit a fly ball to left. I wasn't sure it would reach the bleachers, so I put my head down and turned on the gas. I remember stepping on somebody's foot at first base, but didn't think much about it so intent was I on getting around the bases. I noticed a lot of traffic at second, too, as I finally looked up and saw the ball in the bleachers.

"Well, I had passed Babe Herman and somebody else on the base lines and wound up with a single for my home run."

On the subject of another legendary episode, John Lardner wrote, "Floyd Caves Herman never tripled into a triple play, but he once doubled into a double play, which is the next best thing."

Herman explained that one to Jim Murray of the Los Angeles *Times:*

"In the first place, they said I tripled into a triple play, but there was one out so how could I do that? Also, they forget I hit in the winning run in that game. Now, here is what happened.

"DeBerry was on third, Dazzy Vance was on second, and Chick Fewster was on first. We were playing the Braves and George Mogridge hung a curve, and I hit it four feet from the top of the wall in right. DeBerry scores to put us ahead 3 to 2. Vance runs halfway to third, then he runs around third, then he starts to run back. Fewster is on third, so he starts back to second.

"Now, I got the throw beat, and I slide into second. Safe. Right? So, now, somebody hollers to Jimmy Cooney, the shortstop, and he throws home. Al Spohrer chases Vance back to third. Now, I go to third on the rundown and, naturally, I slide into third. Safe. Right.

"Now, I was called out for passing Fewster, but Vance is on third and it's his bag by the rules. Spohrer begins tagging everybody, but I am already out. It's like sentencing a dead man. Now, there are only two out, but Fewster wanders out to right field to get his glove and Doc Gautreau, the Braves' second baseman, chases him and tags him out.

"You see, there never were three men on third exactly. See how everything gets mixed up?"

* * *

The incident led to this apocryphal question and answer, one fan to another:

"The Dodgers have three men on base."

"Which base?"

Robinson, the Dodger manager, took an optimistic view. "That's the first time this season the team has been together," he said.

Herman was a frequent contract holdout, partly because he wanted more money and partly because he wanted an excuse to skip spring training. That, too, seemed to be something the writers got wrong, as Herman explained when, in later years, he was with the Chicago Cubs. "You got the wrong idea entirely," Herman said. "I am not holding out. I just don't want to sign this bleeping contract the Cubs have sent me, because the dough ain't big enough."

In Brooklyn, Herman was so often portrayed as a bumbler that he once asked a New York writer to cut it out. "People will think I am a joke ballplayer and that will hurt my reputation," he said.

"I never thought of it that way," the reporter replied. "From now on I promise I'll stop poking fun at you."

"Thanks," said Herman. He pulled the stub of a cigar out of his coat pocket and stuck it in his mouth. The writer reached for a match, but Herman puffed on the cigar, and smoke curled from it. "Never mind," said Herman. "It's lit."

The writer reacted. "What I just said doesn't go," he said. "It's all off. Nobody who carries lighted cigars around in his pocket can tell me he isn't a clown."

Misplays and all, Herman was a treasure. He hit .393 in 1930, scored 143 runs, hit 35 homers and drove in 130 runs. He was a strong and graceful lefthanded batter. In *Pride of the Yankees,* the movie about Lou Gehrig's tragic life, Herman—not Gary Cooper—played Gehrig in the batting scenes. His zany quotations to the contrary, Herman was intelligent; after leaving baseball, he became a prosperous businessman.

Herman was the muscle and heart of the 1930 Dodgers, who led the league much of the season despite some truly awful episodes. On June 15 the Cardinals presented the Dodgers with three early runs on an outfield misplay. But the Dodgers fought back with five errors of their own, two of them by second baseman Mickey Finn, who fielded as if he had swallowed his name. Andy High, a Brooklyn castoff who haunted his old team all season, came up with two men on base via errors and tripled them home. He came up later with a man on, courtesy of another error, and homered.

Dazzy Vance was pitching for the Dodgers. He hit Taylor Douthit twice with pitches, but pitched to him in the Cardinal ninth after an error by Bissonette put one runner on. Douthit tripled him home and scored on an error by third baseman Wally Gilbert: 9 to 4, St. Louis; losing pitcher, Vance. Pitching for the Dodgers was never easy.

But the team played well, fighting the Cubs for first place. Vance hit a losing streak, but the Dodgers got a pitching lift from Watson Clark, described in *The Sporting News* as a "Mississippi swamp dweller with a sleepy expression and a curious, ambling gait." The Cubs were getting strong pitching from Pat Malone, Guy Bush, and Charlie Root.

Both teams were hitting. On June 23 the Cubs routed the Phillies at Wrigley Field 21 to 8; Hack Wilson had five hits, including his twenty-second homer, and drove in four runs. The Cubs won twenty-four games in June, taking three of four from the Dodgers to slip into first place June 29.

Even as a contender, the Dodgers kept things light. After losing four straight games, Robinson decided that a dose of freedom might help. With the Dodgers clinging to first place by one percentage point, the Brooklyn manager let Herman pick the batting order July 4. Herman indulged his teammates, nearly all of whom wanted to try a new slot. The team won.

In the opener of a doubleheader at Ebbets Field on July 21, the Cardinals led 8 to 6, having scored all eight runs on homers, two of them by pinch hitters Jim Bottomley and George Puccinelli. In the last of the ninth, Brooklyn got two men on base and Robinson sent Harvey Hendrick up to pinch hit. Flint Rhem, the St. Louis pitcher, got two strikes on Hendrick, who then homered—the third pinch-hit homer of the game—to win it 9–8. The Cardinals took the nightcap 17–10, leaving the day's statistical wreckage to be added up—54 hits, 44 runs, 7 homers, 3 triples, 8 doubles, and—oh, yes—11 errors. Brooklyn fans got into the game, too, as two pop bottles narrowly missed umpire Ted McGrew.

The Cubs took advantage of the split to regain first place as Root beat the Giants 6–0 with the help of two homers by Wilson. The Dodgers traveled west and a writer asked a Brooklyn player whether the players were tight. "Why, this team doesn't even hustle all the time, much less tighten up," replied the player, whose identity the writer discreetly protected. "Without doubt," the writer went on, "the Robins have lost more games this summer through loafing than through any over-anxiety to win." He expressed hope that the team would "find a happy medium in the mental attitude." (The Dodgers were often referred to as the Robins, an abbreviation of their manager's name.)

Al Lopez started his distinguished major league career as Brooklyn's catcher in 1930. Lopez caught for nineteen seasons and managed for seventeen more. He caught 1,918 games, a record until Bob Boone caught his 1,919th in 1987. Lopez managed the Indians to a pennant in 1954 and the White Sox to a pennant in 1959. He is a hero among that legion of fans who root against the Yankees, because without those two interruptions the Yankees would have won every American League pennant from 1949 through 1964.

Lopez retired from managing after the 1965 season, but was lured back by the White Sox in 1968. With Mel Harder and Leo Durocher, he is one of three men active in both 1930 and 1968—baseball's seasons of extremes. Lopez was elected to the Baseball Hall of Fame in 1977 and served on the Veterans Committee of the Cooperstown shrine. In 1988 he reminisced about 1930, the first of his thirty-six years in the major leagues, and about the Dodgers' lowly status in New York:

"The Giants and the Yankees were the favorites in New York. They had outstanding teams during those years, so the team everyone picked on was the Dodgers. Any time the Dodgers did anything wrong, they were called all kinds of names. Well, yes, they ended up with three men on third base one time. But a third baseman with the Giants chased the winning run across the plate, and that other guy [Fred Merkle] forgot to touch second base.

"Herman turned out to be a great ballplayer. I think he belongs in the Hall of Fame. I roomed with him. He was a great guy, great family man. The jokes about him? I'll tell you what happened. He was a first baseman, and he had a bad year in 1927 with Brooklyn, which had a bad club. The following year Brooklyn came up with a fellow by the name of Del Bissonette, who had had a tremendous year at Buffalo. They were going to make him the first baseman. I reported to Brooklyn in 1928 in the spring, at Clearwater. I was on the scrubeenie team. Robinson put Herman in right field on our team, and we went out and beat the regular club that day. Herman hit three homers.

"The next day Herman was on the regular club in right field. He went from first base to right field just like that, and he wasn't an outfielder. He had to learn. But by 1929 he was a greatly improved outfielder. He played that right field wall at Ebbets perfect. He had a good arm, good speed, and he became a good outfielder.

"But they gave him the reputation of being kind of a joke. They gave him a bad rap, I think. It's still hurting him, because I tried to get him in the Hall of Fame but he didn't get enough votes.

"Wilbert Robinson was a fine man. I thought he did an outstanding job. He had a lot of patience, and everybody on the club liked him. He didn't use too many trick plays. He just played commonsense baseball. He believed in big pitchers. He wanted guys who could throw hard, guys who could really fire the ball. He had Vance, and he had Watty Clark. Vance came up late. He was thirty-one years old when he came up. He was a great pitcher. Dazzy Vance had a great record against the Cubs, and the Cubs were one of the greatest hitting teams I ever saw. Vance used to strike out thirteen, fourteen, fifteen of them. Mostly with fastballs. Vance never threw a change of pace. He had a good curveball, but he threw mostly fastballs.

"I believe the best pitch in baseball is the fastball. With Dazzy Vance and Dizzy Dean and Lefty Grove and those guys, whenever they threw a changeup they were doing you a favor. The old saying in baseball is, 'Never throw a lousy hitter a change of pace.' You have to overpower them. And you don't throw too many change of paces to guys like Williams and DiMaggio and Musial. You might fool them with one, but don't throw it again.

"Ebbets Field was a great place to play. The players loved to play there because the fans were right on top of you. They were great fans, and you could hear every word anybody said. It looked like everybody was in the ballgame. There was a lot of action. The right field fence was short down the line. You could hit the ball out of the ballpark. Lefthand hitters had a great advantage. In 1930 there was just a bleacher in left field. Sometimes the ball would bounce on one hop into the stands for a home run. Then they changed it [in 1931] to a ground-rule double.

"The Cub ballpark was a real tough ballpark to hit in. It's much easier now than it was back then. In those days they had a wooden bleacher in left field and they had a bleacher in right field. It looked like the wind was blowing all the time from left field in. Most of the Cub hitters were righthand hitters, and they all went to the opposite field—Hartnett and Hornsby, and Woody English. Hack Wilson was a right-center field hitter in the Cubs' ballpark. Grimm was the only lefthander on the club. He hit straightaway. Never pulled.

"We were in first place with about two weeks to go. The Cubs were right up there and the Giants were, too. And the Cardinals."

Brooklyn's continued success prompted this poem by Grantland Rice of the New York *Sun:*

Ballade of Bombast

Back where the memory of any man
To the contrary runneth not,
Even the rabidest Flatbush Fan
Granted the Dodgers were not so hot.
They couldn't share in a Series pot:
Victory shied from the Brooklyn brow.
But what of the 1930 spot?
Where are the Dolorous Dodgers now?

Year upon year just an also ran,
Minus a Jackson, a Frisch, an Ott.
A club eternally on the pan,
Rating a second division slot,
The worst of it was the best they got!
And ne'er a break did the fates allow.
But what of today? Is it all a plot?
Where are the Dolorous Dodgers now?

Once but an oddly assorted clan,
An oila podrida—lousy lot
Now they've a Wright to be in the van
(Pardon the pun, but 'tis true, eh wot?)

They've got what one might call "eclot;"
Vance is an ace and the Babe's a wow!
Infield as tight as a canny Scot—
Where are the Dolorous Dodgers now?

Roscoe McGowan, a Giant advocate, was allowed this stanza in reply:

Prince, tell the experts who voice the rot
That the Royal Robins are sure to bow
Ere this season's end to a Giant swat
Where are the Dolorous Dodgers now?

6

"McGraw could do anything with the Giants he wanted. . . . He was mean."

Few teams leaped on the rabbit ball of 1930 with more zest than the New York Giants, and few baseball men mourned the death of peck-and-run baseball more than the Giants' aging manager, John J. McGraw.

McGraw had managed the Giants to ten pennants, and it was—and is—heresy to criticize his managing. But by 1930 his health was bad, his handling of pitchers was questionable at best, and his yearning for the old days seemed to belie the strength of his own lineup. He cursed his players and treated them like fools—or, at best, like ignorant tools of his own superior baseball mind. At least two of his best players loathed him. Lightning may strike as you read this, but here it is: McGraw, by 1930, was a poor manager.

He had a heckuva team. Check this lineup, slots two through seven:

	H	R	HR	RBI	BA
Freddy Leach, LF	178	90	13	71	.327
Fred Lindstrom, 3B	231	127	22	106	.379
Bill Terry, 1B	254	139	23	129	.401
Mel Ott, RF	182	122	25	119	.349
Shanty Hogan, C	132	60	13	75	.339
Travis Jackson, SS	146	70	13	82	.339

Lindstrom, Terry, Ott, and Jackson are in the Hall of Fame, as is Carl Hubbell, the team's pitching ace. The bench was good, too. Veteran Bob O'Farrell shared the catching duties with Hogan, hit .301 and drove in 54 runs. Doc Marshall, Ethan Allen, Andy Reese, and Pat Crawford combined for another 94 RBI. The Giants hit .319, the highest team batting average of the twentieth century, and their 143 home runs were second in the league in 1930 only to the Cubs. Terry was the last National Leaguer to hit .400.

You can't fault the pitching, either. Here's the Giant rotation:

	W	L	ERA
Fred Fitzsimmons	19	7	4.25
Carl Hubbell	17	12	3.76
Bill Walker	17	15	3.93
Clarence Mitchell	10	3	3.98

Good as it was, the pitching could have been better. "The only man who thought you could win with one pitch was John McGraw," Hubbell told Bob Oates of the Los Angeles *Times* in 1981. "McGraw wanted us to throw a curve on every pitch. Any time you threw a fastball on McGraw's team and it beat you, you got fined." With McGraw calling the pitches, Hubbell once threw seventeen straight curves.

A few years later, Hubbell elaborated in an interview with author Walter M. Langford:

"He called every damn pitch, see, and every damn one was a breaking ball. It would be a curveball or a screwball. He didn't think you had enough sense to throw a fastball . . .

"He had the news media so conned with his Little Napoleon bit that after every home game he'd go into the little room that was his office. Nobody interviewed McGraw. Nobody! So he'd get in his little room, and he'd bring in the old sportswriter Bozeman Bulger, who was about as old as McGraw.

"Nobody would say a word but McGraw would write out everything that happened in the ball game. If they had won the game, it was about something he had done, and if they lost, it was about what some dumb ballplayer had done wrong. Bozeman would take the report out and say, 'Well, fellows, here's McGraw's report.' And they would write their stories accordingly."

* * *

Bill Terry, the Giants' leading hitter, was a forceful personality himself and never did get along with McGraw. "He'd call the pitches until you got in a tough spot," Terry said of McGraw. "Then he would throw the job on the shoulders of the catcher."

Like most men who played for him, Terry admired McGraw's grasp of the game. McGraw disciples have been among baseball's best managers—Terry, Frisch, Hughie Jennings, Billy Southworth, Casey Stengel. But sinus trouble had aged McGraw prematurely by 1930—he was fifty-seven, but looked and acted much older. And though the players of 1930 were docile by today's standards, they were a new breed to McGraw.

Burleigh Grimes, who pitched under McGraw in 1927, told author Donald Honig that if a player tried to explain a misplay by saying, "I thought . . ." McGraw would cut him off this way: "What with? You just do the playing. I'll do the thinking for this club."

That did not sit well. Edd Roush's season-long holdout was partly an aversion to playing for McGraw, and it may have cost the Giants the 1930 pennant. Terry's feelings about McGraw were shared by Fred Lindstrom, an intelligent man who later served as postmaster in Evanston, Illinois, and coached baseball at Northwestern University. Lindstrom described McGraw this way:

"McGraw was one of those fellows who had managed in an era when it was common practice to abuse ballplayers verbally. Later on you had a different breed of ballplayer—Terry, Jackson, myself—who resented being verbally abused. He lost some of his effectiveness doing that. He'd just call you unsavory names if you made an error or played the ball badly.

"He never thought he was mean. He just thought that was one way to get the best out of you—driving you, compelling you on to greater things. I liked him in that he was an impetus. Put you on your toes. He was also a good judge of human nature. He knew exactly what you could do. All human beings have days they don't put out as much as on other days. He had that sixth sense to know when those days came around. He never allowed for the fact that you had a good day yesterday. He wanted to know what you had done today."

* * *

Bill Terry, a testy man himself, played under McGraw for eight seasons and succeeded him as manager in 1932. He managed the team to pennants in 1933, 1936, and 1937. After leaving baseball he became a successful automobile dealer in Jacksonville, Florida. Terry discussed his old manager in 1988:

"We didn't have any good times together. They were all tough. If you played ball for him it had to be tough. He was just that type of manager.

"In the olden days he probably had to use a lot of that toughness. He had tough fellows playing with him. Abuse players? Yes, if he could get by with it. But with me he got the wrong man. We used to have all kinds of arguments. He and I didn't speak for the last two years."

As a young player, Al Lopez observed McGraw and was aware of the Giant manager's strong influence:

"McGraw could do anything with the Giants he wanted. He was like the general manager. He paid the players their salaries. He could make trades.

"He was mean. They tell me, by God, he called Lindstrom all kinds of names one time and Lindstrom chased him all over the clubhouse.

"We beat them in a ballgame in 1930. He had Fred Leach playing left field, and I was the hitter with a man on first base in the ninth inning. I hit a line drive into left field and Leach tried to make a shoestring catch out of it, and it got by him. The guy on first base scored the tying run and I went to third base on the play. The next guy hit a fly ball out to left field and I scored, and we beat them 3 to 2.

"At that time we played ballgames at one o'clock, and the game was over about three o'clock or three-thirty. They tell me he held the players in the clubhouse until eight o'clock that night. He wouldn't let anybody take their uniform off. There were no lights under the stands then, and they had a hell of a time finding their way out.

"On the other hand, I understand that if you did something real good for him he'd put one hundred dollars in your locker.

"All those guys had the utmost respect for him. For years I played for Casey Stengel at Brooklyn and Boston. George Kelly was a coach over there. All they talked about was the old man. The old man did this and the old man did that. By God, everybody tried to copy the way he played ball."

For all their antipathy, Terry and Lindstrom turned in the years of their lives in 1930. So did Travis Jackson, Shanty Hogan, and Fred Leach. Besides Rogers Hornsby, who did it three times, Terry is the only National Leaguer of this century to hit .400. "I put together the greatest season of my life," he later said in a *Saturday Evening Post* story. "Everything I hit seemed to land safe, and there were 254 of them to tie the league record."

McGraw, never the diplomat, was asked during the season to name the best first baseman in baseball. He picked Lou Gehrig. But Terry's achievement was given this flowery accolade in the 1931 *Reach Official Base Ball Guide:* "In the season of 1930 there stepped forward a stalwart hitter who became the second .400 per cent hitter the National League has known since 1899 . . . bay leaves aplenty for William Harold Terry, first baseman of the Giants, who was 32 years old on October 30, 1930. He is a throwback to the mauve decade." (The mauve decade was a nickname for the 1890s, when Ed Delehanty and Jesse Burkett batted over .400 in the National League.)

Today's hitters use light, thin-handled bats and break a lot of them. Not so Terry, as he later told Lyall Smith of the Detroit *Free Press:* "I'll still have one record all to myself as a .400 hitter no matter what happens this year or any one. I started the 1930 season with two favorite bats. Both of them were 42-ouncers. I used one of them every day until I finally broke it late in June. Then I used the other one the rest of the year and wound up with my 254 hits and my .401. On just two bats, mind you."

In reward for his big season, Terry got a $7,000 raise—but not for long. "When I failed to lead the league in batting for 1931 by a matter of .0002 McGraw slashed my salary $5,000," he wrote.

In fact, Terry barely led the league in 1930 at .401. Babe Herman hit .393, Chuck Klein .386, and Lefty O'Doul .383. In 1931, playing with a less lively ball, Terry barely lost the batting championship. He and Chick Hafey of the Cardinals both hit .349 but, as Terry said,

Hafey had an edge of .0002. The ball had a lot to do with it both years, and McGraw had a lot to do with the deadening of the ball in 1931.

The lusty hitting of 1930 caused much comment, and in mid-July McGraw proposed that the distance between the pitching rubber and home plate be reduced from sixty feet six inches to fifty-eight feet. He delivered a veritable sermon, quoted approvingly by Joe Vila of the New York *Sun.*

"I don't care what the manufacturers of the ball used by the major leagues say," McGraw said. "It is lively, and every sensible baseball man knows it. Why, most of the pitchers are scared to death when they are sent to the mound. The home run slugging has taken the heart out of them. Here the season is only half over and more than 800 home runs have been made in the big leagues. Home runs are about as numerous as singles and they have revolutionized the game.

"The lively ball has taken three great features out of baseball. I mean bunting, base-stealing and long-distance throwing. How often do you see a man thrown out at the plate by an outfielder? When a player reaches first base he no longer tries to steal because the fellow behind him is likely to knock out a four-bagger. Slugging dominates baseball. The scientific inside methods when I was a player have gone and it is too bad."

McGraw showed Vila a dirty, scuffed baseball. He said it was the last of three balls—only three—used in a game in 1916. McGraw continued:

"Here is a ball that was in use in 1916, when the Giants won 26 straight games. You can see that the cover is a bit loose and the seams are more prominent than in the present-day ball. It was easier for the pitchers to get winning results with this ball of 1916 than with the one they are compelled to use today. The manufacturers say that the modern ball is made with better material. That may be true but, just the same, it travels farther and with greater speed when hit hard than the old style ball.

"I would suggest, for the improvement of baseball in general, a change in the pitching distance. Fifty-eight feet would be about right instead of sixty feet six inches. In that case pitchers who find it difficult to last through nine innings today because of the greater strain put upon them would be improved.

"The rule providing for throwing out a ball the moment it roughens or soils should be abolished. There never was a bit of sense in it. So long as the ball remains inside of the playing field and isn't ripped or torn it should be kept in use.

"It is getting extremely difficult to find good young pitching prospects. The restrictions put upon them by the rules are discouraging. Of course, there are pitchers who are better than the average and are able to win consistently. But the rough treatment most of them receive is a lesson to the youngsters who are beginning to take up the game as a profession.

". . . It is a puzzle to me why some of the pitchers go to pieces so quickly. That is why I think placing the mound fifty-eight feet from the home plate will do a lot of good."

McGraw's suggestions were not adopted, but Al Lopez believed that McGraw's influence had a great deal to do with the deadening of the ball in 1931. Lopez, then the Brooklyn catcher, described an incident in 1930 that may have brought the controversy to a head:

"We were playing the Giants. The Giants and Brooklyn were great rivals then. They had a boy by the name of Leroy Parmelee, a big strong pitcher who threw hard. Every pitch was like a slider. The ball broke away from you. Glenn Wright was up at the plate and he was fooled on the ball, because the ball kind of sailed away from him like a slider. He swung one-handed and pulled it down the line, up in the upper tier of the Polo Grounds, which was about 265 feet. He hit it up there one-handed.

"McGraw blew his stack. He said, 'How can you play baseball like this?' He wanted to play hit-and-run. He was a great manager for figuring out plays for them—going to right field with a man on second base, trying to hit behind the runner, all that kind of thing. From what I heard, McGraw put up a big beef that he couldn't play baseball this way. And they came in with a dead ball, and the averages went way down."

In Hubbell, the Giants had a pitcher of historic stature. He was twenty-seven years old in 1930 and had his best years after Terry became manager, winning twenty-one games or more for five straight seasons starting in 1933. In the 1934 All-Star Game he recorded one of the enduring achievements of baseball history, striking out Babe Ruth, Lou Gehrig, Jimmie Foxx, Al Simmons, and Joe Cronin in succession.

Hubbell's best pitch was the screwball, a curve that breaks down and in instead of down and out. For a lefthander, as Hubbell was, it provides a down-and-away breaking ball to righthanded batters. "That thing he threw up there, it looked like it stopped," said Lopez. "You swung at it, and then it came again. The damndest screwball I ever saw."

"Most pitchers aren't loose-jointed enough to throw it," Hubbell told writer Bob Oates. "It's an unnatural pitch—just the opposite of a curve. The ball comes out of the back of your hand with a wrist snap. You're going against the grain, in other words—throwing out of the back instead of the front."

Hubbell almost didn't make the major leagues. The Tigers brought him up in 1926. Ty Cobb, the Detroit manager, looked at Hubbell's screwball and told him to stop throwing the peculiar pitch. Two years later he was pitching for Beaumont in the Texas League and happened to start a game in Houston when that city was hosting the Democratic National Convention—the one that nominated Al Smith for president.

Dick Kinsella, an Illinois politician and a delegate to the convention, doubled as a scout for the Giants. As Hubbell related the story to writer Walter Langford, Kinsella decided to take an afternoon off from the convention, went to the ballgame, and saw Hubbell win in extra innings, 2–1. He called McGraw, gave Hubbell a strong recommendation, and the Giants quickly bought Hubbell.

The Giants started fast in 1930, slumped in May, then climbed back into contention and stayed close all season. Terry was no shoo-in for the batting title. On July 17 the league leaders stacked up like this:

Showboat Fisher, St. Louis	.424
Lefty O'Doul, Philadelphia	.407
Chuck Klein, Philadelphia	.403
Babe Herman, Brooklyn	.387
Riggs Stephenson, Chicago	.387
Bill Terry, New York	.386
Paul Waner, Pittsburgh	.375

But Terry was smoking. At the Polo Grounds on July 26, he hit two homers, lined out two other hits and drove in the winning run as the Giants edged the Phils, 5–4. He hit in fifteen straight games, with a batting average of .467. Lindstrom, a savvy place-hitter, picked up his pace in August as the Giants won three of four games in Pittsburgh, then four straight in Cincinnati. Coach Dave (Beauty) Bancroft filled in as manager while McGraw took time off to tie up the business affairs of his late brother.

Even Hubbell had his bad days with the rabbit ball—and rabid hitters—of 1930. In Philadelphia on May 23, Hubbell benefited from a homer by Terry in the eighth and a three-run shot by Ott in the ninth. But the Phils nicked Hubbell for seventeen hits, including a homer by Pinky Whitney, and won 9–8. On June 16 King Carl was protecting a one-run lead in the top of the ninth. The Cubs loaded the bases with none out. Hubbell retired Kiki Cuyler and Hack Wilson on short flies, but Riggs Stephenson's infield single pushed across the tying run. Charlie Grimm then homered for an 8 to 4 Chicago lead. Shanty Hogan opened the Giant ninth with a homer—New York's fifth solo shot of the day—but that was it: 8 to 5, Chicago.

On August 31 the Giants beat the Boston Braves 4 to 3 in the first game of a doubleheader before forty thousand fans at the Polo Grounds. In the nightcap, Mel Ott—twenty-one years old, and already in his fifth season with the Giants—hit three homers and a double, driving in six runs. But veteran George Sisler homered for Boston, and Wally Berger, the Braves' sensational rookie, knocked out three of Boston's eighteen hits: 14 to 10, Boston. Across town at Ebbets Field, the Dodgers rapped the Phils for twenty-three hits including homers by Babe Herman, Glenn Wright, and Rube Bressler: 14 to 3, Brooklyn. The Cardinals beat the Cubs. Chicago, Brooklyn, and New York were neck-and-neck, with St. Louis getting close.

7

"... if the right fielder had eaten onions at lunch the second baseman knew it."

The Philadelphia Phillies opened the 1930 season with high hopes. They had finished fifth the year before, but Lefty O'Doul led the league in batting at .398 and Chuck Klein broke the National League home run record with forty-three. In 1930 Grover Cleveland Alexander was back for a swan song at age forty-three, and Burt Shotton, the Phillie manager, said Alexander might win twenty games and pitch the Phils to a pennant, as he had fifteen years before.

Klein and O'Doul held out in 1930, but both came into the fold for less than ten thousand dollars. Klein stepped up for his first Florida exhibition game and hit two homers. "I am in fine shape this year after a winter of bowling," he said. In the slapdash scouting system of that era, Klein, an Indianapolis steel-mill worker, had been spotted while playing semipro ball by Adolph Stallman, a Prohibition agent, who recommended him to Evansville, Indiana, of the Three-I League.

Les (Sugar) Sweetland, a thirteen-game winner in 1929, pitched a shutout to start the Phils on the right foot. But a shadow hung over the team. It was cast by the right field barrier of their home park, Baker Bowl, a rusting relic of the 1890s.

Whoever designed Baker Bowl should have erected a skyscraper instead. The stadium was ringed with a high wall. Even the clubhouse, in center field, was two stories tall. The Phils dressed on the top floor, with a commanding view of the patchy green surface. "Down on the field it was like a hole," recalled Ray Benge, a Phil pitcher from 1928 through 1932.

The right field wall stood forty feet high, but it was only 280 feet from home plate to the right field corner, 300 feet to the right-center power alley. With Klein—and others—lining repeated homers over this barrier in 1929, the team's president, William F. Baker, struck a noble pose. "The home run is too cheap so we have to do something about it," he said. He erected a twenty-foot screen.

There it stood: sixty feet of barrier, only 280 feet from home plate. Today's most inviting wall, the Green Monster in left field at Boston's Fenway Park, is distant by comparison at 315 feet—and short, too, at thirty-seven feet two inches.

Of Baker Bowl, Red Smith wrote, "It might be exaggerating to say the outfield wall cast a shadow across the infield, but if the right fielder had eaten onions at lunch the second baseman knew it." Pinky Whitney, the Phils' third baseman, gave a hitter's viewpoint: "It was a dime shot to the wall, but not to get over it." Benge said, "Standing on the mound it looked like you could reach back there and thump that wall."

The hitters thumped it plenty. As far back as 1913, sportswriter Sid Mercer wrote scornfully of "the Philadelphia cigar box." The Phils' Gavvy Cravath, a righthanded hitter, learned to push fly balls over the short wall often enough to lead the league in homers six times during the teens.

As the rabbit ball gained more zip, the Baker Bowl cigar box took on the characteristics of a pinball arcade. Bing! Bing! Bing! Twice in 1929 the Phils played host to doubleheaders in which fifty runs were scored (Brooklyn 26, Philadelphia 24; St. Louis 34, Philadelphia 16).

Then came 1930 and the ball that Ring Lardner called "a leather-covered sphere stuffed with dynamite." The stitches on the National League ball were low, almost countersunk, making it difficult for pitchers to throw a breaking pitch. The Phillies, a team never in contention, quickly became the most startling symbol of the season's thunderous hitting.

Ray Benge suffered the 1930 season without much complaint. A stoic sort, he was called "Silent Cal," the nickname of former president Calvin Coolidge. Benge survived 1930 and pitched twelve years in the major leagues. But he remembered Baker Bowl and the rabbit ball of 1930 very well:

"It looked like the infielders had slowed up. But they just didn't have a chance to move. That ball was by 'em. That ball was so lively you'd throw it and look for a mole hole to get in. It was a railway express on the way back. Sakes alive, you'd duck a ball and it would be a two-base hit. There was a lot of fellows who got hurt when that ball was so lively.

"They had that sixty-foot-high right field wall. It was sheet-iron, tin, on a brick wall, and a twenty-foot screen on top of that. I was a pitcher, not a long-ball hitter, and I hit balls off that wall. You just had one way to pitch. That was outside to lefthanders, inside to righthanders. But a lot of the righthanders wouldn't pull it. They'd punch the ball to right and ping it off that wall."

In 1930 the *entire* National League hit .350 at Baker Bowl. The pinging produced a lot of two-base hits. A fair number were ground-rule doubles, as drives punched through the rusty metal wall and rattled to the ground behind, lost forever. Most pings bounced to the right fielder, who didn't need much of an arm to challenge runners. Klein, the Philadelphia right fielder, became a ricochet artist. He rang up forty-four assists in 1930, one of the more secure records of the twentieth century.

As for his own pinging, Klein led the league with fifty-nine doubles. Pinky Whitney hit forty-one and gave the wall a lot of credit. "I hit a bunch of pop flies against it," he said.

Games were long. On June 16 the Phils pulled ahead of the Pirates 16 to 3 after six innings. The Pirates came back with eleven runs, but fell short. The final score was 18 to 14, Philadelphia, with homers by the Phils' Klein, O'Doul, Don Hurst, and Fred Brickell.

In the nightcap of a doubleheader on July 23, the Phils attacked the Pirates with twenty-seven hits, including two homers by Hurst. Not enough; the Pirates won, 16 to 15, on a homer by Pie Traynor in the thirteenth inning. The Cubs came to Philadelphia the next day and the two teams banged out seventeen hits each; Chicago won, 19 to 15. Two days later a pregame band concert put Hack Wilson in high spirits. He marched around the field with a bat on his shoulder, soldier-style. When the game began he hit his thirty-fifth homer, then his thirty-sixth and thirty-seventh. The Cubs won, 16 to 2.

Not all of this resulted from the lively ball or the pinball ballpark. The Phils had powerful hitting and pitiful pitching. Here's the Phillie murderers' row of 1930:

	H	R	HR	RBI	BA
Barney Friberg, CF	113	62	4	42	.341
Lefty O'Doul, LF	202	122	22	97	.383
Chuck Klein, RF	250	158	40	170	.386
Pinky Whitney, 3B	207	87	8	117	.342
Don Hurst, 1B	128	78	17	78	.327

We could throw in the catcher, Spud Davis, who hit .313, but that was *below* the team batting average of .315. A couple of subs named Monk Sherlock and Harry McCurdy batted .324 and .331, respectively. Fresco Thompson, the captain and second baseman, came in at a disgraceful .282.

"I could have hit .300, though," Thompson told writer Jack Orr. "I was going along fine, hitting around .320, but the other guys were so ashamed of my average that they wouldn't let me take batting practice. I wasn't allowed even to speak to O'Doul and Klein. Yeah, I was captain, but it was like being foreman of a WPA gang."

The Phils banged out 1,783 hits, a record unmatched even since the season has been expanded to 162 games. Home and away, they averaged 6.05 runs a game. But they gave up 7.69. Here's the Phil pitching rotation:

	W	L	ERA
Fidgety Phil Collins	16	11	4.78
Ray (Silent Cal) Benge	11	15	5.70
Les (Sugar) Sweetland	7	15	7.71
Claude (Weeping) Willoughby	4	17	7.59

Hal (Ace) Elliott was the top relief pitcher. He went 6–11, 7.67, with no saves. The kind of savior the Phils needed does not wear spiked shoes.

"Those pitchers were really awful," Thompson told Orr. "Once I took the lineup to home plate. I had written in the pitcher's spot, 'Willoughby—and others.' Bill Klem, the umpire, didn't think it was funny and made me cross it out. I was right, though, and in the first inning, when we were changing pitchers, I yelled, 'See, Bill, what'd I tell you?' "

Sweetland and Willoughby held down so much combat duty on the mound that local sportswriters wove their names into a patriotic song:

> My country 'tis of thee
> Sweetland and Will-ough-by
> Of thee I sing.

Playing third base, Pinky Whitney had plenty of time to observe his pitchers. "Willoughby had pretty good stuff, but when he had to pitch he couldn't pitch," Whitney recalled. "The long ball got him." The Phillie starters worked in relief, too, and Willoughby rested while awaiting the call. "You'd have to send someone out to the bullpen to wake him up," said Benge.

In 1978 George T. Wiley, a history professor at Indiana University of Pennsylvania, had his History of Baseball class undertake the macabre task of analyzing the Phils' line scores of 1930. They counted forty-five games in which the Phils yielded ten or more runs. In seventeen of those games, Phillie pitchers coughed up fifteen or more. Whitney, for one, wasn't surprised to hear it. "They were all long games in Baker Bowl," he said. "It was all-day baseball."

Given the dimensions of Baker Bowl, Grover Cleveland Alexander's achievements there are stunning. Pitching for the Phils from 1911 through 1917, he *averaged* twenty-seven wins a year and led the league in shutouts five times. But that was in the dead-ball era and it was before World War I. Serving in France with the U.S. infantry, Alexander came under heavy shelling. He lost his hearing in one ear, developed epilepsy, and became an alcoholic. Yet he continued to pitch well, and in 1930 the Phils hoped he could hang on for another season.

Whitney told writer Walter Langford about Alexander's epileptic symptoms: "Sometimes he'd have one of those spells out on the mound and we'd get around him and pull his tongue out. And then he'd get up and throw the next ball right through the middle of the plate."

But after pitching ineffectively in nine games, Alexander was sent down to the Dallas Steers of the Texas League. In mid-July he twice failed to show up for games. The Steers offered him for the waiver price of fifteen hundred dollars, but there were no takers. Alexander was released. *The Sporting News* was not sympathetic. "Baseball has given Grover Cleveland Alexander a fair chance," the newspaper editorialized. "It appears that he no longer feels that he owes baseball or the public even a partial return for the advantages and opportunities that it has proferred him."

Chuck Klein was posthumously elected to the Hall of Fame in 1980. Like a politician who credits the home folks for his success, Klein might well thank good old Baker Bowl. He played seventeen years in the major leagues, seven of them—and part of another— with the Phillies before they moved to Shibe Park in 1938. Klein led the league in home runs four times, in runs and slugging average three times, in hits, RBI and doubles twice each, and in batting average once—all from 1929 through 1933, when the ball was swift and Baker Bowl was home.

Researcher Dave Hewson of Eugene, Oregon, compared Klein's home-and-away batting averages for the seasons 1929 through 1932. The results:

	Overall BA	At Baker Bowl	Away
1929	.356	.391	.321
1930	.386	.439	.332
1931	.337	.401	.269
1932	.348	.423	.266

When Baker Bowl was dedicated in 1895, it was given this lofty mandate:

". . . Our park rules have never changed and never will change. They prescribe temperance, order and discipline. They proscribe gambling, betting, profanity, obscenity and disorderly conduct, as well as Sunday ball playing at home or abroad. . . .

"While always aiming for the highest place, our players, proud of their past reputation, prefer to sacrifice both championship and place rather than win either by trickery, rudeness, or other conduct unworthy [of] their good name or the approval of the ladies and gentlemen whose refining presence honors their contest for supremacy on the ball field."

* * *

The 1930 Phillies could second that. Before the refining presence of 299,007 fans, they sacrificed both championship and place, batting .315 as a team but finishing dead last, a fitting monument to the Year of the Hitter. As Pinky Whitney said, "In my day, you had to be humble if you played for the Phillies."

8

"I go to Capone's place of business. Why shouldn't he come to mine?"

With the help of the rabbit ball, baseball squeezed one more year out of the Roaring Twenties. Fans like hitting, and attendance in 1930 hit 10.1 million, a record total that was not topped until 1945. As the decade brought deeper economic depression, attendance declined. Salaries were cut drastically. From his peak of $80,000 a year in 1930 and 1931, Ruth was slashed to $52,000 in 1933, to $35,000 in 1934—and still was baseball's highest-paid player.

In 1930, however, America was less occupied with the Depression than with Prohibition. The tenth anniversary of this "great social and economic experiment," as President Herbert Hoover called it, was observed January 16, 1930. In New York, the Women's Christian Temperance Union opened its anniversary celebration with song:

> We praise thee, oh God
> For the victory grand
> That has driven the open saloon
> From our land.

In dissent, Congressman Oliver of New York said that Prohibition had "driven liquor from the bar to the boudoir, from the saloon to the salon, from hops to hips, from keg to kitchen." A huge criminal industry was industriously filling the demand for beer, wine, and liquor; competing mobs settled many of their disagreements with machine guns.

The public favored repeal. The *Literary Digest,* a leading magazine, conducted a nationwide poll in 1930. The results were front-page news: Wets 3,342,366, Drys 1,464,098.

Neither Hoover nor Congress responded. Fans attending the third game of the 1931 World Series in Philadelphia treated Hoover like a bartender who wouldn't turn on the taps. Morning newspapers reported that the president and his wife would be attending the game. Police gathered in front of the Athletics' dugout as the Hoovers arrived. The president waved his hat and smiled, and there was a scattering of applause.

Then someone booed. The boos grew in volume and changed to a chant:

"We want beer! We want beer!"

Thousands of fans were chanting, and sportswriter Joe Williams described the incident in the present tense. "It has the swing and resonance of a college cheer at a football game," he wrote. Hoover ignored it. As the president and his party rose to leave after the eighth inning, the public address announcer asked the crowd to be silent and stay seated. But these were Philadelphia fans, and they were thirsty.

The chant began again: "We want beer!"

Billy Sunday, a National League outfielder turned evangelist, was among those who fanned the moralistic fervor that brought about—and preserved—Prohibition. Sunday didn't hit much in his eight seasons with the Cubs, Pirates, and Phils, but he became a heckuva preacher. "Avoid the hellish booze that makes a man's brain a mud puddle!" Sunday preached. Congressmen feared the wrath of Prohibitionists. Many of them continued to vote "no" on the roll calls, "yes" when a drink was offered.

So did many other Americans, ballplayers included. Although it was against the law, drinking was quite socially acceptable—even chic. In what today would be called the "home section," the New York *Sun* of March 26, 1930, hailed built-in home bars as "a new field in modern interior decoration . . . as light and heady as an aperitif."

"In those days it was Prohibition and unless you really hunted for it you couldn't find it," Joe Cronin told an interviewer. "They didn't have cocktail parties or beer in the clubhouse. A lot of players were not drinking at all. Of course if a guy wanted to find it, he found it."

In Washington, D.C., members of Congress bought liquor from an obliging gent known as "the man in the green hat." Reminiscing in 1988, Shirley Povich of the Washington *Post* recalled Prohibition:

"There were all kinds of speakeasies in Washington. As many as you liked. The code word was, 'Benny sent me.' On the road, if you couldn't find a drink yourself you could always ask the bell captain. He could always find you a drink.

"We were barnstorming up from the South one time and got to Chattanooga. Vinnie Flaherty [another Washington sportswriter] and I were going to give a little party for the baseball writers and a few of our favorite ballplayers. So we asked the bell captain where we could get some whiskey. He said, 'I'll have to take you to the man.'

"He took us to the man down at the river. He took us aboard a scow. The man on the scow said, 'What do you want?' At the end of the scow he had a rope or a chain, and he brings up a big washtub full of whiskey bottles, up from the bottom of the river. He said, 'What do you like, mate? Red or white?' Red was bourbon and white was gin."

Bootleg liquor could be expensive, as Povich illustrated with another anecdote:

"A friend of mine, a notable drinker, was traveling with the team. In Cleveland he said, 'Where can we get some whiskey?' I said, 'Call the bell captain.' He called the bell captain, and the bell captain brought up a bottle of bourbon. A quart. My friend said, 'How much is this?' The bell captain said, 'Fifteen dollars.' That was lots of money in 1930.

"My friend's reply was wonderful. He said, 'This is the first time I've paid what good whiskey is worth.' "

Liquor was as illegal in 1930 as cocaine is today, but neither Commissioner Landis nor anyone else in baseball tried to keep players from drinking or worried about their effect as "role models" to the young. Babe Ruth and Hack Wilson, to name just two, were heavy drinkers and made no secret of it. Wilson was arrested at a drinking party one year and at a speakeasy another year, to the accompaniment of lighthearted newspaper stories. When police entered the speakeasy, Wilson tried to climb out a men's room window, headfirst, and got stuck; he was arrested from the posterior.

Bill Veeck, the beloved baseball man whose father, William Veeck,

Sr., ran the Chicago Cubs during Wilson's playing days, recalled a Wilson hangover in 1930. Young Veeck walked into the clubhouse with a message for the Cubs' trainer, Andy Lotshaw, and found him preparing Wilson for that day's game. Veeck related the incident in his autobiography, *Veeck—As in Wreck* (Holtzman Press, Evanston, Illinois, 1962):

"Andy had Hack in one of those big, high old tubs, sobering him up. In the tub with Hack was a 50-pound cake of ice. Well, what would you do if a 50-pound cake of ice jumped into your bathtub with you? You'd try to jump out, right? That was precisely what Hack was trying to do. Enthusiastically, but not successfully. Every time Hack's head would bob up, Andy would shove it back down under the water and the cake of ice would come bobbing up. It was a fascinating sight, watching them bob up in perfect rhythm, first Hack's head, then the ice, then Hack's head, then the ice . . . That afternoon Hack hit three home runs."

After games, wrote Veeck, Wilson and a couple of dozen friends would hit speakeasies on the North and West sides of Chicago, with Wilson picking up the checks. Few of these establishments were fancy saloons. Most were "beer flats," private homes where a man could get "needle beer"—near-beer, which was legal, with grain alcohol added. Wilson also frequented The Hole in the Wall, a gangster hangout in Cicero, a Chicago suburb that became the mob's virtual property. His drinking buddies included Cub pitcher Pat Malone, other players—and young Bill Veeck.

Wilson was a Chicago hero, but as a local celebrity he could not measure up to Alphonse (Scarface) Capone, who in March 1930 got his picture on the cover of *Time* magazine. The occasion was Capone's release from prison, where he had served a year for carrying a gun without a permit.

Back in Chicago, where he ran the nation's most infamous bootlegging operation, Capone, thirty-six, said he was ready to retire. Capone was a Cubs fan, and so was his rival, Bugs Moran. The Cubs used to put on an entertaining pregame show, with fancy fungo hitting and a razzmatazz infield drill, and the gangsters came early to see it.

"They used to come out and watch us practice," recalled Charlie Grimm, the Cub first baseman. "They'd sit right behind our bench, and there was never a peep out of them."

One day, however, Capone peeped at Gabby Hartnett, the Cubs' catcher, and Hartnett walked over to Capone's box to autograph a ball for Capone's twelve-year-old son. A newspaper photographer happened to catch them, and the picture—the Cubs' star catcher publicly obliging the country's most notorious gangster—appeared in newspapers throughout the United States.

Judge Kenesaw Mountain Landis, the baseball commissioner, was outraged. He summoned Hartnett for a scolding and ordered the league presidents to forbid any conversations between players and spectators. Landis also told the teams to stop announcing the next day's starting pitchers, since that information was useful to gamblers, but sportswriters successfully protested that stricture, pointing out that if the Judge really wanted to keep gamblers in the dark he should keep the schedule a secret, too.

Hartnett's reaction was mild. "I go to his place of business," he said of Capone. "Why shouldn't he come to mine?"

Not that the Cubs catered only to bootleggers. John Dillinger, the bank robber and killer, watched the games, too. "Dillinger used to come in every day and sit all by himself in the right-center field bleachers," Grimm said.

Gangsters were regarded as celebrities.

Woody English, the Cub shortstop, remembers Chicago speakeasies as easy to find and secure from police interference. "In Chicago there were several cops who ran a place right near the ballpark," said English. "In St. Louis right near the ballpark they had an old German beer garden. It was nice and cool in there after a game."

According to Bill Terry, he and other players on the Giants kept Wilson's drinking under control when he was playing with the New York team. In Chicago, Joe McCarthy, the Cubs' manager, used a soft stick with Wilson.

"Joe McCarthy was a great psychologist," recalled Charlie Grimm. "He loved the guy [Wilson]. On the road Joe would frequently have him up to his room and talk things over. He kept him straight."

* * *

Compared to the modern era, the ballplayer's world of 1930 was different in many ways, as Mel Harder, the former Cleveland pitcher, recalled:

"We played all day games, and after your game, why, everyone who wanted to have a few beers would head for a bootlegging place—a speakeasy, some of them called it. We knew all the spots. In those years some of the best places to get a steak was a sort of bootleg place that sold whiskey and beer. We used to do a lot of our eating in those speakeasies. There was no trouble finding them. When a visiting club would come to town, why, they'd ask a local ballplayer, and they'd find out right away where to go. In New York, by golly, they seemed to be wide open. I don't think the beer was as good as what they're brewing today, but it tasted just as good.

"I hate to see people today complain about air travel. They never traveled by train in the summertime, I'll tell you that. Were the trains air-conditioned? No, not until later. Hot trains, hot taxis, hot hotels. They had fans in the clubhouses, but that's the only thing. The showers were just so-so. You couldn't cool off, period.

"We didn't know any different. The fields weren't manicured like they are today but that's the way we expected it. Just like our clothes [uniforms]. By golly, the only way they fitted you was around the waist. You didn't have the knees tailored and all that stuff. Ours looked like we were wearing bloomers a lot of the time. Hot? Yeah, they were. We wore them a long time before they had them cleaned, too. Several games? More than several. They'd just dry them and brush them off and we'd put 'em back on again.

"We didn't make any money, and we didn't know any better. Because of the Depression, your best friends were out pushing a rake somewhere for the WPA. So you didn't squabble about salaries so much. In 1928 I made $350 a month for six months. That wasn't bad money in those years. Back in 1933 we all took a 10 percent cut in Cleveland. The club wasn't making any money."

Al Lopez, the Dodger catcher, recalled the heat:

"The bad part about it was, there was no air-conditioning any place you went. It was hot, that's all. The uniforms were real heavy. We'd go into Cincinnati and St. Louis in July and August and it was miserable. Sometimes the temperature wouldn't go under one hundred day or night. In St. Louis they had fans in the hotel rooms. You had to put a quarter in, and it would last two hours. It blew hot air, so we had to call downstairs to tell the boy to bring up a pitcher of ice and put it in front of the fan, to get a little cool air. That would last about fifteen minutes, because it melted that ice right away. So then we'd tell the boy to bring us a bucket of ice. That would last maybe thirty or forty minutes. Sometimes we ended up sleeping in the bathtub with ice in the water, just to get some sleep. Other times we'd take a sheet and a pillow and go across the street from the Chase Hotel and try to get some sleep in the park. But still it was real hot."

Charles A. Lindbergh glamorized air travel by flying across the Atlantic in 1927, but businessmen, ballplayers, and other ordinary people traveled by train. In late August of 1930 the Athletics bought outfielder James Moore from the Dallas Steers. Connie Mack told him to report as soon as possible. He expected the young outfielder to show up in three or four days.

But Moore took Mack's instructions seriously. The Athletics were playing in Boston. Moore caught an airplane out of Dallas at 8:00 A.M. on a Wednesday. It landed at Columbus, Ohio, at 6:45 P.M. No planes were available to New York, much less Boston, so Moore took a train Thursday and got to New York at 9:30 P.M. Friday morning he caught a flight to Boston, arriving in time to walk into the clubhouse as the game entered the seventh inning. Dallas to Boston in only two days!

The Sporting News described Moore's "wild plane flight" from Texas. Moore said he was dizzy on arrival, the plane having reached 125 miles per hour. As for Mack, "when the Lean Leader heard about it, he nearly fell out of his chair."

Mack told Moore, "I wanted you to lose no time getting here, but I never wanted you to take an airplane." *The Sporting News* said Moore, a "daring young man," was a team hero because of his swift travel.

Other innovations were equally suspect. Dial telephones came into use, but the White House refused to accept them. Without asking, the phone company installed dial phones in Senate offices, and the senators voted them out. "Number please" returned to the World's Greatest Deliberative Body.

In April 1930 Hoover declared the Depression at its end. "We have now passed the worst," he said, "and with continued unity of effort, we shall rapidly recover." Things got worse instead, and in the fall of 1930 the vague statistics about unemployment were dramatized by an imaginative business promotion. The International Apple Shippers Association got the bright idea of selling its surplus to unemployed men, on credit. The sight of numerous men selling apples on street corners quickly became an indelible image of the Depression.

The stock market continued to decline in the early 1930s, and one of its many victims was Connie Mack, owner and manager of the Philadelphia Athletics. Mack reportedly bought stocks on the advice of Ty Cobb, who made a fortune on Coca-Cola stock and who finished his playing career with the Athletics in 1928. Whether or not Cobb played a role, Mack had invested in stocks, and the Depression decimated his entire portfolio. Doc Cramer, an outfielder with the Athletics from 1929 through 1935, says Mack's stock-market troubles were widely known. If that were not bad enough, the A's attendance declined. After winning pennants in 1929, 1930, and 1931, Mack's great team finished second to the Yankees in 1932, and the A's home attendance dipped below five hundred thousand.

Mack ran short of cash. In September 1932 he sold Al Simmons, Jimmy Dykes, and Mule Haas to the White Sox for $100,000. A year later he peddled George Earnshaw to the White Sox for $20,000, sold Lefty Grove, Rube Walberg, and Max Bishop to the Red Sox for $125,000, and sold Mickey Cochrane to the Tigers for $100,000. In 1935 he sold Jimmie Foxx to the Red Sox for $150,000. Mack got (and gave) a few journeyman players as part of the deals, but he was forced to sell his best players under financial duress. The Depression was the perpetrator of this crime, and it ruined one of the greatest teams in history. Mack, a paragon among baseball owners, continued to own and manage the Athletics through 1950. But he had to operate on a shoestring, and the A's were dreadful, finishing in the first division only once in Mack's final seventeen seasons.

* * *

In 1930, however, most Americans were still working, still optimistic. Thanks to progress during the 1920s, many Americans considered themselves prosperous, urbane, and tolerant. But by today's standards, the America of 1930 was poor, prudish, rustic, and cruelly prejudiced.

Comparative income figures are hard to come by, but in Washington, D.C., the average salaried federal worker made $2,209 a year—$15,714 in 1988 dollars, a little better than half of today's average. A Ford coupe cost $495, a Ford station wagon $640. One of every four Americans lived on a farm. One home of every three lacked electricity, and three of every five lacked telephone service.

U.S. Customs agents seized a copy of James Joyce's *Ulysses,* which had been mailed from Paris to a New York publisher, on grounds of obscenity. As Congress debated the Hawley-Smoot Tariff Bill—an economy-killer that was enacted and signed in 1930—Senator Reed Smoot of Utah argued for a provision requiring the Customs Bureau to censor imported books. An ally, Senator Coleman Livingston Blease of South Carolina, railed against *Diversey,* a novel by MacKinlay Kantor about Chicago mobsters. Blease called the book "the dirtiest thing I have ever read" and proved it by reading passages such as:

"I can shoot the buttons off your God damn pants."
"God damn . . . bastard!"
"Holy jumping Jesus Christ!"

Senator Blease turned to his colleagues. "Can you believe it?" he asked. Several spectators left the gallery in shock.

America, North and South, was segregated by law and custom. Even in many white intellectual circles, black Americans were considered inferior. They were given inferior education, relegated to menial jobs, and subjected to racial jokes and other forms of ridicule.

Blacks had been barred from major and minor league baseball since 1887. The ban, though unofficial, was strongly supported by Commissioner Landis. While Bill Terry hit .401 for the New York Giants in 1930, Willie Wells of the St. Louis Stars led the Negro leagues at .404. Satchel Paige pitched for Negro league teams at Birmingham and Baltimore. Josh Gibson, eighteen, broke into Negro league baseball with a bang: He hit one ball over the roof of Yankee Stadium and another over the center field fence at Forbes Field in Pittsburgh.

A 1930 *Sporting News* interview illustrated the casual racism of the time. The subject was Gabby Street, manager of the Cardinals and a native of Alabama. The writer, Harry T. Brundidge, asked Street where he got his nickname. "Down South," Street replied, "if you see a black boy, and want him, and don't know his name, you yell, 'Hey, Gabby.' It works in St. Louis, too, and if you don't believe it, try it. To me, all black boys have been 'Gabby,' and I got my nickname from the use of that word, and not, as is commonly believed, because I am a chatterbox."

Hitler's National Socialists were gaining popularity in Germany and Mussolini's blackshirt fascists ruled Italy, but events in Europe seemed remote to most Americans. A shocked exception was Anthony Piccicuzo, a syrups and flavorings manufacturer from New York who took his wife and child to visit his grandparents in Italy. Fascist guards seized Piccicuzo and pressed him into service in the fascist infantry. U.S. diplomats were able to negotiate his release.

Women had been voting for ten years and gained additional independence in the flapper scene of the Roaring Twenties. Mary Ross, a leading feminist, looked forward to peaceable times between the sexes. "We have passed in America, I believe, the days of self-assertive and antagonistic feminism," she said. "The very word 'feminist' has come to seem a trifle archaic."

Movies burst forth in a new process called Technicolor, and featured Maurice Chevalier, Al Jolson, Charlie Chaplin, Jean Harlow, Myrna Loy, and Rin Tin Tin, whose films were called "barkies." Marlene Dietrich starred in *Blue Angel*. Greta Garbo did her first talkie, *Anna Christie,* and her first line was, "Gif me a visky, ginger ale on the side. And don't be stingy, baby." The public loved talkies, but some movie men rivaled baseball men in their suspicion of change. "People will not want talking pictures long," said Joseph Schenk, president of United Artists.

Also in 1930, Grant Wood painted *American Gothic,* Edward Hopper unveiled *Early Sunday Morning,* William Faulkner wrote *As I Lay Dying,* and Noel Coward's *Private Lives* opened on Broadway.

Sinclair Lewis became the first American to win the Nobel Prize for Literature, but the author most read by Americans was Chic Sale, a vaudeville comedian who wrote *The Specialist,* a humorous account of a country carpenter specializing in outhouses. It sold 1.5 million copies, so Sale wrote *I'll Tell You Why,* which also had to do with outhouses.

You can't beat a winning combination, and baseball had it in the power and scoring splurge of 1930. The National League had a hot pennant race, runs were pouring across the plate, and fans were pushing through the turnstiles. It must be August.

9

"Let somebody get on base and give Hack another at-bat."

Pitching to Hack

"How do you pitch to Wilson?"
    Asked the rookie up from the sticks.
"I'm up to learn the hitters,
    And know their little tricks."

"I'll tell ya," said the veteran,
    Who had pitched for many years,
"When ya' dish up Hack yer fast one
    You'd better watch your ears.

"He'll drive that agate at ya'
    Like ya' never seen before.
He'll learn ya' in a jiffy
    Not to show him speed no more.

" 'N' then y'll try t'curve him,
    'N' he'll crash one off yer shins;
If ya' keep on throwin' hookers
    He'll tear off both yer pins.

" 'N' then ya' use yer change of pace,
    He might strike out on that;
'N' perhaps he'll ride the ball so far
    You don't know where it's at.

"I'll tell ya' son," the veteran said.
    "When ya' see that sawed-off squirt;
Jes' flip one towards th' platter
    'N' take care ya' don't get hurt."

—L. H. Addington in *The Sporting News*, September 4, 1930

Sparky Adams, a versatile infielder who batted .286 over thirteen major league seasons, played third base for the Cardinals in 1930. Fifty-eight years later, he still remembered Wilson's sting:

"Hack could hit a ball with his eyes shut, and he could hit it a long way. I have a mark on my shins yet. We played in to catch the man going home and he hit a line drive right at me. The grass was wet and it skidded and hit right on my shin. I didn't say nothin'. I picked the ball up and threw the guy out going home. But hurt? Oh, boy!"

With Rogers Hornsby injured and the Cubs still in the race, Wilson seized his opportunity to mark the 1930 season as his own. He was always a colorful player, a favorite of the fans, and upon joining the Cubs in 1926 he blossomed into one of the National League's top sluggers, leading the league in home runs three times between 1926 and 1929.

Yet he was never quite regarded as the best. He set a new National League record with 159 RBI in 1929 as the Cubs won the pennant. But Hornsby, his new teammate, outshone him and was named MVP. Wilson led both teams in batting in the 1929 World Series, but was given the goat's horns because of his fielding misplays in the fourth game.

Ruth's shadow largely obscured the feats of all other sluggers, Wilson included. Because Wilson's body was so odd, sportswriters—and fans—tended to see the ridiculous in everything he did. Ruth was the Bambino. Wilson was The Hardest Hitting Hydrant of All Time. Ruth's carefree and undisciplined behavior enlarged his legend. Wilson's carousing diminished his. Ruth, of course, played in New York, Wilson in Chicago, the eternal Second City.

Like Ruth, Lewis Robert Wilson had a deprived childhood. He was born in the steel-mill town of Elwood City, Pennsylvania, which was named in honor of the man who invented barbed wire. His mother died when he was eight and his father was a lush, so he was raised—and taught baseball—by the proprietor of the boardinghouse where young Wilson and his father lived.

Wilson was a rowdy and rebellious student. He left school at sixteen, still in the sixth grade, and became a laborer, pounding hot rivets with a sledgehammer at a locomotive works. He was living alone by his seventeenth birthday.

But he could play ball. Although some scouts—including John McGraw—were skeptical, a scout who saw Wilson playing for Portsmouth, Virginia, of the Blue Ridge League in 1923 described him this way: "Wonderfully looking boy if he does not get fat. The report is he has bad legs. It's not true or he could not cover the ground as he does."

Wilson hit .388 for Portsmouth. He had batted .356 and .366 in two previous minor league seasons, so McGraw was finally persuaded to buy him. He hit .295 in his rookie year, with ten homers in 107 games, and picked up his first and most enduring nickname—"Hack," after a prominent wrestler of the day, George Hackenschmidt.

McGraw farmed Wilson to Toledo in 1925, telling him to learn the strike zone and promising to bring him up the following spring. But the Giant office inadvertently left Wilson exposed to the annual draft of minor league players, and the Cubs picked him up for $5,000. He jumped to instant stardom, but only Chicago fans cared. Here's what it was like to compete with Babe Ruth (asterisk means led league. Ruth tied for the American League RBI championship of 1928. Wilson tied for the National League home run championships of 1927 and 1928.)

	H	R	HR	RBI	BA
1926					
Babe Ruth	184	139*	47*	145*	.372
Hack Wilson	170	97	21*	109	.321
1927					
Babe Ruth	192	158*	60*	164	.356
Hack Wilson	175	119	30*	129	.318
1928					
Babe Ruth	173	163*	54*	142*	.323
Hack Wilson	163	89	31*	120	.313
1929					
Babe Ruth	172	121	46*	154	.345
Hack Wilson	198	135	39	159*	.345

No one could measure up to Ruth—not even his own teammate Lou Gehrig. Although the Yankees were out of the 1930 pennant race by early August, Ruth was still chasing his own record of sixty home runs. "If I hit fifteen homers this month, I'll beat it," he said.

But it was Wilson who set chase for Ruth's record. He hit three against the Phillies on July 26. He connected again on July 29, August 2, August 3, and August 5. The Cubs were breathing down the Dodgers' necks, and forty-five thousand fans crowded Wrigley Field for a doubleheader against the Boston Braves August 10. Wilson homered three times, bringing his total to 39, as the Cubs swept. Chicago's pitching had been weak, but Charlie Root shut out the Braves on three hits in the opener, and Pat Malone—Wilson's most boisterous drinking buddy—pitched a five-hitter in the nightcap.

As Wilson caught fire, the Dodgers buckled. They won the opener of a series at St. Louis August 9 to run a winning streak to four games. The next day Babe Herman, of all people, started a spectacular triple play. With Jim Bottomley on second base and Chick Hafey on first, George Watkins hit a screamer to right. Both runners took off, but Herman leaped, caught the drive, and threw a strike to Jake Flowers at second base to double up Bottomley. Flowers's relay caught Hafey. But the Cards won the game in the ninth inning, and the next day they swept Brooklyn behind pitchers Burleigh Grimes and Bill Hallahan. Hallahan struck out twelve.

The Dodgers limped into Chicago, still in first place. Wilson greeted them with a homer and the Cubs swept four games to take first place. The Giants came to Wrigley Field, and the Cubs took them three out of four games, extending their lead to five games. Charlie Grimm was out with a spike wound and Riggs Stephenson suffered a leg injury, but Wilson made up the slack.

In thirty-one August games, Wilson hit thirteen homers and drove in an extraordinary fifty-three runs. On August 19 he connected off Sugar Sweetland of the Phils to tie Chuck Klein's National League record of forty-three homers, set just the year before. Klein, playing right field for the Phils, acknowledged Wilson's achievement with a little wave.

A week later Wilson broke the record with a flourish. Sheriff Blake, a fellow West Virginian, was pitching for the Cubs, young Larry French for the Pirates. In the top of the seventh, Lloyd Waner lined to center field. Wilson fell down, and the ball skipped past him for an inside-the-park homer—shades of 1929. Back on the bench, Wilson called his shot with this apology to Blake:

"Sheriff, it seems like things always happen to you that never have happened before. That belly-buster couldn't have occurred behind any other pitcher. But for your sake and for the pride of West Virginia, I'm going to get that home run back with a legitimate homer. And in this very inning."

Wilson did it. He already had singled home two runs in the fifth and driven in another with a sacrifice fly. His homer provided the icing in a 7 to 5 Chicago win.

Today a new National League home-run record would be big news, but Wilson's feat was barely mentioned. Ruth's record of sixty was all that counted.

But Wilson was leading the Cubs' pennant charge. Two days after hitting the record-breaking homer, Wilson strained his back with a big swinging strike against the Cardinals and had to leave the game. The Cards won in the twentieth inning on a hit by Andy High. Wilson sat out the next day—the Cubs won in thirteen innings—and then returned with two homers and six RBI as the Cubs romped, 16 to 4.

Wilson did everything a popular ballplayer was supposed to do. After hitting a homer and three singles in a late August game, he went to a radio station for an interview, then to Chicago's Municipal Tuberculosis Hospital, where he visited with children until nearly 10:00 P.M. He spent plenty of time in speakeasies, too, but as his manager, Joe McCarthy, said, "What am I supposed to do? Tell him to live a clean life and he'll hit better?"

Charlie Grimm recalled Wilson as "the key man."

"He made the money for us, and never mind the two fly balls he lost in the sun in the 1929 World Series," Grimm told sportswriter Ed Wilks. "He was vicious with the bat. The word would go along in the dugout when we needed runs, 'Let somebody get on base and give Hack another at-bat.' "

Wilson's August explosion was no fluke; he hit ten homers in the September stretch drive, driving in forty-one runs during the season's final five weeks. "I never saw a guy win games the way he did that year," McCarthy said later. "We never lost a game all year if he came up in the late innings with a chance to get a hit that would win it for us. . . . No tougher player ever lived than Hack Wilson."

Wilson had small hands and was one of the first sluggers to use a thin-handled bat.

Woody English played shortstop for the Cubs in 1930 and had a pretty good year himself, batting .335 and scoring 152 runs, many of them courtesy of Wilson's slugging. In 1988 English fondly recalled his colorful teammate:

"He broke more bats after he struck out: He'd take the bat by the big end, and hit the little end on home plate and it would fly. Did you ever see him? He was a wonderful guy, a colorful guy. He was a short heavyset guy. Had a red neck—not much neck at all. He could hit that ball, that long ball.

"The Elgin Watch Company in Elgin, Illinois, right outside Chicago, was giving away a watch for every home run hit in certain ballparks. Nice little watches. I gave them all away—to my grandparents, my brother. That's the year Hack Wilson hit his fifty-six. Wilson had a diamond watch made up for his wife, for hitting all those homers."

To be sure, Wilson did not lack for a supporting cast. Here's the heart of the Cub lineup for 1930—*without* the injured Hornsby:

	H	R	HR	RBI	BA
Woody English, SS	214	152	14	59	.335
Kiki Cuyler, RF	228	155	13	134	.355
Hack Wilson, CF	208	146	56	190	.356
Riggs Stephenson, LF	125	56	5	68	.367
Gabby Hartnett, C	172	84	37	122	.339
Charlie Grimm, 1B	124	58	6	66	.289

This time, Wilson *did* outhit Ruth. Here are the 1930 numbers for the Babe and Lou Gehrig:

	H	R	HR	RBI	BA
Babe Ruth	186	150	49	153	.359
Lou Gehrig	220	143	41	174	.379

The Cub pitching wasn't much, but the hitters ripped the opposition. Hornsby returned, and on September 6 the Cubs once again showed their muscle. Playing at Forbes Field, the Pirates led 12 to 8 after seven innings. But the Cubs scored four runs in the eighth and six in the ninth, two of them on Wilson's forty-seventh homer. He had three hits; Hornsby had two, including a triple.

That kept the Cubs on top. The Giants stumbled, losing three straight to the Boston Braves, but on September 6 they swept Boston 13 to 1 and 7 to 2. Bill Terry homered in the opener, Mel Ott had three hits, and Fred Fitzsimmons pitched nine good innings and rapped out two hits of his own. The rabbit ball was alive and well. Buster Chatham of the Braves hit a hot grounder to Fred Lindstrom, the Giants' third baseman. It hit him and knocked him cold.

The Cubs were on top. New York's sweep pulled the Giants into second place, tied with the Cardinals, who had come from nowhere.

Gehrig had set the major league RBI record with 175 in 1927. Wilson broke it September 27, pounding his fifty-first and fifty-second homers, both with a man on, as the Cubs beat the Giants 5 to 2 at the Polo Grounds. Once again, the press gave Wilson's achievement only passing mention. Runs batted in were not considered very important back then. They weren't tabulated until 1920, and as late as 1930 *The Sporting News* did not include them in box scores.

But there was still the pennant race. Four teams were bunched near the top, and all of them had devastating lineups. The National League was embroiled in one of the closest and most explosive finales in history. Wilson would play a big role. So, in their own ways, would Joe McCarthy, Rogers Hornsby—and, of course, the equally ambitious men of the Brooklyn Dodgers, New York Giants, and St. Louis Cardinals.

10

"I thought Branch Rickey was a little bit too tight."

"Baseball virtually is dead in St. Louis," Joe Vila wrote in the New York *Sun* of Wednesday, July 16, 1930. "The Cardinals, shot to pieces, have dropped out of popular favor. The owners of the team are resorting to doubleheaders on Sunday at home in desperate efforts to defray expenses. President Breadon would like to experiment with games at night if the other National League clubs would consent."

Vila was right. The Cardinals, National League champions just two years before, were playing poorly and drawing crowds of less than four thousand. When Sam Breadon, the Cardinal owner, tried doubleheaders on Sundays, rather than the traditional weekday twin bills, the idea *did* appear desperate, though it soon became standard throughout the major leagues. Night baseball, of course, was beyond the pale.

The same edition of the *Sun* carried a lively account of the previous day's doubleheader between the Cubs and Dodgers at Ebbets Field—a scene that drew a sharp contrast with the baseball torpor in St. Louis. Ebbets was jammed with thirty thousand fans. Hundreds more sat on steel rafters in the grandstand. Police turned away ten thousand fans and chased more off Bedford Avenue rooftops overlooking the playing surface. Firemen were called in to force the gates closed against the press of eager humanity.

Those who got in were treated to quite a show. Pat Malone, Chicago's best pitcher, stopped the home team in the opener, 6 to 4. The nightcap was the kind of free-for-all that gave Ebbets its special flavor. Brooklyn's Del Bissonette tried to stretch a triple into a homer; Gabby Hartnett, Chicago's catcher, tagged him out; Bissonette was carried off the field, unconscious.

Umpire Bill Klem called Brooklyn's Wally Gilbert out on a close play. Fans threw giant firecrackers onto the field and fired pop bottles at Klem. The old arbiter wouldn't move out of harm's way, but was not hit. One bottle barely missed Hartnett as he ducked into the visitor's dugout. Ushers ejected the offending fans.

Charlie Root, the Chicago pitcher, drilled the Brooklyn pitcher, Dolf Luque. Umpire George Magerkurth dashed from first base to home plate to prevent a fight. Luque was not fazed. He stopped the Cubs 5 to 3 for a split.

The Cardinals had plenty of punch—who didn't, in 1930? But their pitching was thin. Sam Muchnik, who covered the Cardinals for the St. Louis *Times,* recalled a significant trade:

"On June the fifteenth, 1930, I was in the Alamac Hotel in New York. The Cardinals were there. Roy Stockton and I were in Sam Breadon's suite having a few highballs. Mr. Breadon always had some scotch. Where he got it I don't know. He was a good host. He asked me what I wanted to drink and I said, 'bourbon and soda.' He said, 'No, you'll like scotch. It's better for you. Scotch and water.'

"I kept on telling him, 'Why don't you try and get Burleigh Grimes from Boston?' I don't know how many games we were behind then. Quite a few. He said, 'Oh, I can't get Grimes. I've been trying to get him.'

"Finally he disappeared. Went into another room. He came back and he said, 'Well, I got you Burleigh Grimes.' I said, 'Who'd you give up for him?' He said, 'Fred Frankhouse and Bill Sherdel.' That was just before the trading deadline, at midnight.

"I remember standing at the door of the Alamac downstairs and Frankhouse came back from a picture show. I said, 'You'd better pack your bags.' He said, 'Why?' I said, 'You've been traded to Boston.' He was very much surprised."

In Grimes, the Cardinals got a good pitcher and a tough competitor. Frankie Frisch, the Cardinal second baseman, used to say that his most frightening experience as a hitter was when Grimes threw at him on a three and oh count. Grimes denied it. "It was three and one," he told sportswriter Bob Broeg.

At thirty-six, Grimes was the youngest of the four surviving spitball pitchers—the *legal* spitballers, that is. Reminiscing in a 1988 interview, Woody English, the Cub shortstop, remembered Grimes as a brushback artist:

"He was tough, Burleigh Grimes. Throw at you? He'd throw a *spitball* at you. He chewed slippery elm, you know. That's where he used to get the spit on the ball. One day I'm playing third base and Grimes is pitching. A ball was hit down to me and I got a hold of that wet spot, and I threw that ball nine miles over Grimm's head. You remember Ed Burns with the Chicago *Tribune?* Oh, he was a character. Anyway, the next day instead of writing 'Cubs Win' or 'Cubs Lose' the headline was, 'English Sets World Record for Throw in the Upper Stands.' "

Al Lopez remembers Grimes:

"Grimes just threw spitters all the time. He had great control and he could make that thing go any way he wanted to. He'd break it inside or break it outside, break it down. He was a great spitball pitcher and a great competitor.

"A spitball breaks sharper than a curveball. When you're hitting you can see the ball spinning on a curveball, so you can stay with it. A spitter kind of slides off his fingers and it breaks sharper."

Grimes shared the Cardinal pitching glory with Bill Hallahan, a fast-balling lefthander who was farmed out six years in a row because his control was poor—so poor that he was called "Wild Bill." Branch Rickey, who worked under Breadon as the Cardinals' general manager, initially heard of Hallahan from an old catcher who saw him pitching for the semipro Corona Typewriter team in Groton, New York. Hallahan finally made the Cardinals in 1929, and in 1930 he won fifteen games and led the league in both strikeouts and walks.

Like many ballplayers before and since, Hallahan always played with a chaw in his cheek. "I'll tell you about that wad of tobacco," he told sportswriter Lee Allen years after his retirement. "I never chewed off the field or in winter. But when I reported for spring training, into my jaw it went. It was almost like part of my uniform."

Two casual personnel moves also helped the Cardinals. As the 1930 season began, they traded outfielder Wally Roettger to the Giants for infielder Eddie Farrell. Both were journeymen. The Giants threw in George (Showboat) Fisher, an outfielder up for a second try in the major leagues after falling short with the Washington Senators.

The Cardinals wanted to farm out Gus Mancuso, a young catcher. But Commissioner Landis ruled that Mancuso had run out of options; if the Cards sent him down again, they'd lose him. Reluctantly, they kept him. Thus cast as a designated albatross, Mancuso hit .366. Fisher, one of history's more notable single-season flashes, did even better: .374, more than enough to make up for his poor fielding.

Still, the Cards played lackadaisical baseball. On August 9 they were in fourth place, just one game over .500, and twelve games behind the league-leading Dodgers. They returned home from a dreary road trip that included fourteen losses, ten of them by one run. The Cardinal manager, Charles (Gabby) Street, fined several players for what *The Sporting News* called "indiscrepancies."

Street was mad. "I am tired of having persons tell me we have the best team in the National League, and then watch it lose games which should be won," he said. "Most of the boys are hustling and giving all they can, but there are a few who are not taking the game seriously. They are not thinking baseball and I am tired of continually seeing throws made to the wrong base and rallies snuffed by dumb plays on the sacks."

Breadon liked that talk and signed Street to manage again in 1931. But the Cardinals had more than a sharp manager. They had Branch Rickey.

Rickey was a devout Methodist, a teetotaler, an avid supporter of Prohibition, and a catcher who flunked out of the major leagues partly because he refused to play on Sundays. He worked his way through the University of Michigan's law school by coaching the baseball team. In 1912 he was approached by Robert Lee Hedges, owner of the St. Louis Browns. Hedges wanted a general manager who could implement his theories of "multiple ownership"—a major league team owning minor league teams and using them to develop talent.

Hedges had the right man. Legend to the contrary, Rickey didn't *invent* the farm system, which went back to the late nineteenth century. But he cultivated and expanded it in a way that revolutionized baseball and laid the groundwork for today's system of player development.

Before Rickey—indeed, well into Rickey's career—most minor league teams were independently owned. A player who signed with a minor league team was bound by the reserve clause just as if he had been signed by a major league team. The majors and minors had an annual player draft that was supposed to give players an opportunity to move up, but clever minor league owners were able to hang on to promising players well into their careers. The Baltimore Orioles, then the class of the International League, kept Lefty Grove for five seasons before finally selling him to the Philadelphia Athletics for one hundred thousand dollars in 1925. Grove wasn't impatient, because the Orioles, a prosperous championship team, paid higher salaries than some major league clubs. (The Orioles joined the American League in 1954 when the St. Louis Browns moved to Baltimore.)

The Cardinals hired Rickey away from the Browns in 1916. Neither St. Louis team had won a pennant in the twentieth century, and the Cardinals had just gone through bankruptcy proceedings. Rickey had a sharp eye for young talent—so sharp that minor league club owners, when offered money by Rickey for a young prospect, learned to call wealthier clubs such as the Giants, who respected Rickey's judgment and could outbid him.

The Cardinals were too poor to carry out Rickey's dream of establishing a farm system. But Sam Breadon, the Cardinal owner, solved that problem by persuading the Browns to rent him use of their ballpark, Sportsman's Park, for $20,000 a year. Breadon sold the Cardinals' rotting old park for $275,000, and Rickey was off to the farm.

According to Rickey's biographer, Murray Polner, the Cardinals by 1928 owned seven minor league teams, controlled 203 minor league players, and were signing talented youngsters from another Rickey innovation—tryout camps. The 1930 Cardinals included at least three stars scouted by Rickey himself and developed in the Cardinal farm system. Sunny Jim Bottomley and Chick Hafey are in the Hall of Fame. Ray Blades isn't, but as a platoon player he posted a pretty good year, hitting .396.

Bottomley, thirty, had been the Cardinal first baseman since 1923 and was the National League's MVP in 1928. His heir apparent, Ripper Collins, was one of several promising Cardinal farmhands in 1930. Playing for Rochester, Collins led the International League in batting (.376), runs batted in (180), hits (235) and triples (19). Collins hit 40 homers, but didn't come close to the league championship; Joe Hauser of Baltimore hit 63. Hauser was thirty-one and had been demoted after playing five seasons with the Athletics. His 63 homers did *not* earn him a return trip to the major leagues—nor did the 69 homers he hit in 1933 for Minneapolis of the American Association.

Among other future Cardinal stars, Joe (Ducky) Medwick, eighteen, batted .419 for a bottom-rung farm club in 1930, and Jay Hanna (Dizzy) Dean, nineteen, won twenty-five games playing for St. Joseph of the Western League and Houston of the Texas League.

Rickey didn't develop players just for the Cardinals. He also developed them for sale to other clubs. Sid Keener of the St. Louis *Star-Times* estimated that the Cardinals pocketed more than $2 million between 1922 and 1942 from the sale of players—big money for that era. Rickey sold stars like Dean, Hafey, and Medwick for high prices, and he sold countless minor leaguers for as little as one hundred dollars each.

He pocketed 10 percent of the proceeds—that was part of his contract. More important, he kept the Cardinals afloat. Today St. Louis is an enthusiastic baseball city, with the Cardinals near the top in attendance year after year. But that was not so in the twenties and thirties—even in Cardinal glory years. Here's how Cardinal home attendance compared with that of their leading rivals during the first four Cardinal pennant seasons—years when Cardinal attendance should have been enthusiastically growing:

	1926	1928	1930	1931
Cardinals	668,428	761,574	508,501	608,535
Cubs	885,063 (4th place)	1,143,740 (3rd)	1,463,624 (2nd)	1,086,422 (3rd)
Giants	700,362 (5th)	916,191 (2nd)	868,714 (3rd)	812,163 (2nd)
Dodgers	650,819 (6th)	664,863 (6th)	1,097,339 (4th)	753,133 (4th)

Local support was so poor that Breadon tried to move the Cardinals to Detroit in 1933. Other club owners turned him down, but Breadon's pessimism was well founded. In 1934 the Cardinals fielded the famous Gashouse Gang—Frankie Frisch, the Dean brothers, Medwick, Collins, and Pepper Martin. The Gashousers stormed from behind to edge the Giants for the pennant on the final day of the season—and drew all of 325,056 fans to Sportsman's Park, an average of 4,222 a game. The Tigers, American League champions, drew almost three times as many fans—919,161.

With that kind of support, the Cardinals could have folded into eternal poverty, as did the St. Louis Browns, Boston Braves, Philadelphia Athletics, and Washington Senators. Instead they made money and won pennants, thanks to Rickey's farm system.

Rickey accomplished it over the ferocious objections of Commissioner Landis, who thought farm systems robbed smaller cities of locally owned minor league baseball—a precious heritage, in Landis's view, although in fact many independent minor league franchises folded, particularly during the Depression.

At the major league meetings of 1929, held in Chattanooga, Tennessee, Landis announced that he intended to destroy farm system operations. He openly attacked Breadon and Rickey. "You have raped the minors!" said Landis. To no avail, Breadon showed him statements from minor league executives who endorsed farm system operations. "You've gone out of your way to hurt my business," Breadon said. A year later Rickey had his turn at the podium and told the owners—and Landis—that farm systems ensured the health of minor league teams, many of which were undercapitalized, mismanaged, and vulnerable to the Depression.

Landis couldn't kill "chain-store baseball," as he called it, without support from the club owners, many of whom wanted to emulate Rickey's system. By 1930 the Athletics, Browns, Cubs, Giants, Reds, Tigers, and Yankees had established small farm systems of their own. Major league club owners were tired of bidding against each other for minor league stars.

Today owners accuse each other of overpaying players; in the twenties and early thirties they worried about overpaying minor league teams for prospects. In July 1930 the Senators, still trying to catch Connie Mack's Athletics, paid Newark a reported $75,000 for pitcher Carl Fischer. He won one game in 1930, forty-six in his career. The Senators were not a wealthy franchise, and one dollar in 1930 was the equivalent of about seven dollars in 1988, making Fischer a $525,000 bust.

The Yankees paid $135,000 for infielders Lyn Lary and Jimmy Reese—a premium price for ordinary players. They paid $35,000 for Jim Weaver, who didn't stick in the major leagues. They paid $150,000 for Frank Crosetti, who was worth more than his share of that big price, and Jack Saltzgaver, who turned out to be no more than a utility infielder. Unproven players are always a risk, and even the wealthy Yankees came to admire Rickey's system of signing them cheap, off the sandlots, and letting the cream rise to the top as captives of your own minor league system. In 1932 the Yankees hired George Weiss, a successful minor league operator, to set up a farm system modeled on that of the Cardinals.

As with night baseball, uniform numbers, radio broadcasts, and other intrusions of the modern world, farm systems were condemned by baseball traditionalists, led by Landis. On July 10, 1930, the New York *Sun*'s Joe Vila wrote of "a crisis . . . in the minor league field."

". . . In desperation, ball games at night under electric lights have been resorted to, but as the novelty wears off the sale of tickets steadily diminishes," Vila wrote. ". . . Chain-store ownership, practiced by several big-league clubs, is another evil . . . Commissioner Landis deserves praise for attempting to break up combinations in restraint of baseball competition, in view of the desperate plight of the minors, which threatens the foundations of the game."

Rickey kept building the Cardinal farm system, and Landis kept trying to thwart him. The Cardinal chain reached thirty-two teams with six hundred players. At one point all eight teams in the Nebraska State League were affiliated with the Cardinals. Landis was always on the lookout for transgressions of the complex rules governing the control of minor league players, and in 1938 he declared seventy-four Cardinal farmhands free agents, including Pete Reiser, who signed with the Dodgers and led them to a narrow pennant victory over the Cardinals in 1941.

Breadon was embarrassed by Landis's allegations of wrongdoing and refused to renew Rickey's contract when it expired in 1942. Ironically, Rickey paraded his own brand of virtue by unsuccessfully urging Breadon to forbid brewery sponsorship of Cardinal play-by-play broadcasts. History was not with Rickey on that one; he lived to see the Cardinals become a subsidiary of Anheuser-Busch. By that time, however, Rickey had made more lasting history on his own. Cut adrift by the Cardinals, The Mahatma switched to Brooklyn as general manager of the Dodgers. It was a providential move. Rickey signed Jackie Robinson in 1946 and brought him up to the Dodgers in 1947, breaking baseball's color bar. No one, not even Rickey, would have made that initial step in St. Louis, which retained more than a breath of Southern attitudes.

Even during the Depression, the Cardinals paid Rickey about fifty thousand dollars a year, plus 10 percent of the team's impressive take from the sale of players. Yet Rickey mercilessly squeezed his own players.

Sam Muchnik, the St. Louis sportswriter, particularly recalls Rickey's stinginess with the ballclub's money:

"I knew Rickey but I wasn't too hot for him. He was the greatest guy in baseball for forming the minor leagues. There's no question about his baseball ability. But I think he took advantage of a lot of the ballplayers who weren't too educated, as far as paying them and so on. He'd have a ballplayer in and talk to him and before you knew it the ballplayer would be willing to pay the Cardinals."

In a wide-ranging interview in 1988, Al Lopez said that Rickey's penuriousness may have swung the pendulum sharply in reaction once players won free agency:

"Branch Rickey was one of the smartest men in baseball. He picked up players all the time. He made a lot of smart moves in baseball. But I personally didn't care that much about Branch Rickey. I thought that he was a little bit too tight. He didn't treat the players as well as they should be treated. I thought the cause of these salaries today was the way he paid some of the players."

Robert L. Burnes covered St. Louis baseball from 1935 until his paper, the *Globe-Democrat,* folded in 1986, whereupon he undertook three books, a radio sports show, and regular columns in two weekly newspapers. Burnes's column, *The Bench Warmer,* graced the *Globe-Democrat* for decades. Burnes reminisced about Rickey while covering a Cardinal game on a blistering St. Louis Sunday in 1988:

"Jim Lindsey was a good relief pitcher for the Cardinals in 1930 and '31. Making, I guess, $3,500 for the season. He came in to negotiate a contract for 1932. He sat down in Rickey's office. They're negotiating, and the phone rings. Rickey said, 'Yeah, Horace, I'll have some players for you. We're going to make some changes.'

"He hung up. A minute later it was Barney Dreyfus calling from Pittsburgh. Rickey said, 'Yeah, you need a righthanded relief pitcher. I'll get somebody for you.' And he hung up again.

"Lindsey said, 'I don't know whether you're kidding or not but I can't risk it.' So he signed for $3,550. He got a fifty-dollar raise after being the best relief pitcher in the National League in 1931. Rickey's secretary, Mary Murphy, was making those phone calls from the outer office.

"Oh, he was cold-blooded. But more cold-blooded was Sam Breadon. He was cold-blooded, heartless, inflexible in negotiating salaries. They traded players rather than give them a thousand-dollar raise."

(The "Horace" in Burnes's anecdote was Horace Stoneham, owner of the New York Giants. Barney Dreyfus owned the Pittsburgh Pirates.)

11

"They drove me to a secret hideaway and forced cups of raw whiskey down my throat."

In early August of 1930, three teams were still in hot pursuit of the National League pennant. The standings looked like this on the morning of August 10:

	W	L	Pct.	Games Behind
Brooklyn Dodgers	66	42	.611	
Chicago Cubs	62	44	.585	3
New York Giants	61	46	.570	4½
St. Louis Cardinals	54	52	.509	11
Pittsburgh Pirates	50	55	.476	14½
Boston Braves	50	57	.467	15½
Cincinnati Reds	45	57	.441	18
Philadelphia Phillies	35	70	.333	29½

No one viewed the Cardinals as contenders. To win, they would have to exceed the closing dash of the "Miracle Braves," who came from last place to win the 1914 pennant. Still, twenty-one thousand St. Louis fans turned out to watch the Cards take on the Dodgers in one of Sam Breadon's newfangled Sunday doubleheaders on August 10. They were treated to a Cardinal sweep as Burleigh Grimes stopped Brooklyn 8 to 2 and Bill Hallahan fanned twelve in a 4–0 shutout.

At Wrigley Field, forty-five thousand Cub fans happily watched the numbers from St. Louis as they were posted on the scoreboard, and cheered their own heroes, notably Hack Wilson. He hit three homers and drove in seven runs, powering the Cubs to a doubleheader sweep of the Boston Braves. Brooklyn's lead shrank to one game over the Cubs, three and one-half over the idle Giants, and nine over the Cardinals. Down at the bottom of the standings, the Phillies reared their heads for a day, sweeping the Reds 18–0—a rare shutout for Weeping Willoughby—and 4–3. Chuck Klein and Lefty O'Doul, the Phil sluggers, had six hits each.

The Cardinals beat the Dodgers on Monday and again on Tuesday to complete a four-game series sweep. They then won three of five games from the lowly Braves. But the pennant still seemed to be out of reach. Indeed, the Cardinals had to hustle to stay in the first division. The Pittsburgh Pirates pulled even with them, winning fifteen of twenty games as Lloyd Waner, Pie Traynor, and pitcher Steve (Swede) Swetonic came back from injuries. Swetonic won four games in a row, just in time to fill the starting slot left by Heinie Meine, who checked into a hospital for treatment of infected tonsils. "My health is more to me than athletic ambitions," Meine told his teammates. The 1930 season hadn't done much to satisfy the rhymer's ambitions anyway—six wins, eight losses, a 6.15 ERA.

In Traynor and the Waner brothers, the Pirates had three future Hall of Famers in their lineup. Ray Kremer won twenty games with a 5.02 ERA, boosted by these hitters:

	H	R	HR	RBI	BA
Lloyd Waner, CF	94	32	1	36	.362
Paul Waner, LF	217	117	8	77	.368
George Grantham, 2B	179	120	18	99	.324
Pie Traynor, 3B	182	90	9	119	.366
Adam Comorosky, RF	187	112	12	119	.313
Gus Suhr, 1B	155	93	17	107	.286
Dick Bartell, SS	152	69	4	75	.320

Erv Brame, a pitcher and pinch hitter, batted .353 for the Pirates. Catchers Rollie Hemsley and Al Bool combined for 91 RBI. But this was 1930. The Pirates' team batting average of .303 was sixth in the league, and their average of 5.79 runs a game ranked fifth—just where the Pirates finished in the standings.

The Cardinals had more muscle. Check these guys:

	H	R	HR	RBI	BA
Showboat Fisher, RF	95	49	8	61	.374
Gus Mancuso, C	83	39	7	59	.366
Ray Blades, LF	40	26	4	25	.396
Ernie Orsatti, 1B	42	24	1	15	.321
Andy High, 3B	60	34	2	29	.279

Not a bad bench, eh? Here's the starting lineup:

	H	R	HR	RBI	BA
Taylor Douthit, CF	201	109	7	93	.303
Sparky Adams, 3B	179	98	0	55	.314
Frankie Frisch, 2B	187	121	10	114	.346
Jim Bottomley, 1B	148	92	15	97	.304
Chick Hafey, LF	150	108	26	107	.336
George Watkins, RF	146	85	17	87	.373
Jimmie Wilson, C	115	54	1	58	.318
Charley Gelbert, SS	156	92	3	72	.304

With a .300 hitter at every position and four more on the bench, Manager Gabby Street faced a delicious dilemma: plenty of guys to pinch hit *with,* but—except for the pitcher—nobody to pinch hit *for.*

The St. Louis pitching rotation offered skill and variety. Wild Bill Hallahan, a fastballer, won 15 games and led the league in both walks and strikeouts. Burleigh Grimes won 13 games with his spitball, and veteran Jesse Haines won 13 with his knuckleball. The fourth starter was Flint Rhem, of Rhems, South Carolina. Rhem won 20 games in 1926, drank himself out of the league in 1929, and came back in 1930 to win 12 games—most of them during the pennant drive.

The Cardinal defense was superb. Chick Hafey and Taylor Douthit were fast, skillful outfielders, and with Frisch and Gelbert around the keystone the Cards led the league in double plays.

Although the Cardinals of the 1930s acquired a rural and hardbitten Gashouse image, Frisch and Gelbert came from privileged backgrounds. Frisch was the son of a wealthy New York linen manufacturer. He graduated from Fordham University, where he captained the baseball, basketball, and football teams, and was a second-team All-American at halfback. His college background gave Frisch one of baseball's most memorably alliterative nicknames—"The Fordham Flash."

Gelbert, the son of a veterinary surgeon, played halfback for Lebanon Valley College in Pennsylvania. Late in a game against Brown in 1927, Gelbert ran thirty yards for one touchdown and passed thirty yards for another to give Lebanon Valley an upset victory. It was big stuff back then to beat an Ivy League team, and Gelbert won All-American mention. Gelbert played four strong seasons for the Cardinals, but on a hunting trip after the 1932 season he accidentally shot himself in the foot. He was twenty-six. The injury forced him out of baseball for two years, opening the way for Leo Durocher to gain fame as shortstop of the 1934 Gashouse Gang.

Hafey and Frisch, who slid headfirst, were fast and daring baserunners. As fast and daring, that is, as common sense allowed in 1930, when it usually made more sense to play safe and wait for the next hitter to drive you home. The league's best baserunner was Chicago's Kiki Cuyler, who stole 37 bases. No one else stole more than 18. Detroit's Marty McManus led the American League with 23.

Still, Frisch had learned the value of speed from John McGraw, and he described it in a 1930 interview with F. C. Lane of *Baseball Magazine:*

"Speed has been shoved into the background by slugging. That's all well enough, so far as it goes. But speed still remains a good deal more important in baseball than most people think. Speed not only magnifies the offense, but weakens the opposing defense. A fast man can beat out many an infield hit that a slow man would never make. Opposing fielders know this. With a fast man at bat, they often have to hurry the play. Hurried plays have a habit of turning into misplays."

The Cardinals won twenty-three of their thirty-two games in August, climbing into the race. The Dodgers lost nineteen of twenty-seven and fell to fourth place. "The Brooklyn team was all but ruined," reported *The Sporting News.* "The club seemed through, shot, completely washed up, totally out of it so far as this year's pennant race is concerned." The team was exhausted, having played forty straight days, with doubleheaders on eight of them.

But Brooklyn came back, winning eight straight. All four contenders were thundering at bat. On August 14 Bill Terry, Babe Herman, and Chuck Klein all were batting above .400. The Cardinals were getting good pitching from Flint Rhem, Burleigh Grimes, and Bill Hallahan, the Giants from Fred Fitzsimmons, Carl Hubbell, and Bill Walker, and the Dodgers from Dazzy Vance, Dolf Luque, and Ray Phelps.

No one was pitching well for the Cubs, but they went East in first place thanks to the hitting of Wilson, Hartnett, Cuyler, and company. The correspondent covering the Cubs for *The Sporting News* predicted they'd win despite this assessment of their pitching: "Just what the pitchers are going to do on the Eastern jaunt is something that nobody cares to think about. On a law of average basis, they should settle down and do something worthwhile, but they probably won't."

In fact, Chicago's Pat Malone and Guy Bush pitched well against the Dodgers, but the Cub attack was stifled by superb Brooklyn pitching. Ray Phelps shut out the Cubs 3–0, Dolf Luque shut them out 6–0, and Dazzy Vance—whom the Cubs had beaten four times—struck out thirteen, beating Chicago's Bush 2–1. A homer by Wilson provided the only Chicago run of the series.

Meanwhile the Cardinals carried a seven-game winning streak into the Polo Grounds. In a battle of old spitballers, New York's Clarence Mitchell, thirty-nine, beat St. Louis' Burleigh Grimes, thirty-six. Bill Terry got three hits in the 2–1 victory.

In the second game, the Giants led 3–1 with two out and two on in the Cardinal eighth. Frisch hit an easy grounder to Fred Lindstrom at third base. He caught it, but was blinded by the sun as he turned to throw, and held the ball. With the bases loaded, Bottomley hit a fly ball to right. Mel Ott caught it, but first it nicked the front of the upper tier. That was a home run under the ground rules of the Polo Grounds, and the grand slam won it, 5–3.

Hafey, who had been out with a cracked rib, came back with a three-run homer as the Cards won the third game of the series, 5–4, the Giants leaving fourteen runners on base against Hallahan and Lindsey. Manager Street won the game with strategy John McGraw would have loved, had his team not been the victim. With the score tied and two out in the Cardinal seventh, Sparky Adams stole second base; Frisch singled him home. The Giants tied it up again, but in the Cardinal eighth, with one out and Hafey on first, Street called a hit-and-run. Jimmie Wilson singled to left, and Hafey made it safely to third. Street quickly called another hit-and-run—with a runner on third base! Gelbert grounded to Hughie Critz at second base, and Hafey scored the winning run easily.

Flint Rhem outpitched Carl Hubbell to win the series finale, 5–2.

On Friday, September 12, the Cardinals went to Boston and took two out of three from the Braves over the weekend. The Cubs went to Philadelphia, where Hack Wilson stroked a homer, two doubles, and two singles in a 17–4 romp. The Phils won the next day on a pinch-hit homer by Lefty O'Doul, who had been out with an injury. After sitting out Sunday in mandatory observance of the Sabbath, the Phils won the opener of a doubleheader on another O'Doul homer; the Cubs took the nightcap on Wilson's fiftieth of the season. The Pirates swept two from the Giants, and the Dodgers vaulted into first place by beating up on Cincinnati. The race stood this way on the morning of September 15:

	W	L	Pct.	Games Behind
Brooklyn Dodgers	83	60	.580	
St. Louis Cardinals	82	60	.577	½
Chicago Cubs	81	60	.574	1
New York Giants	77	65	.542	5½
Pittsburgh Pirates	74	67	.525	8
Boston Braves	67	78	.462	17
Cincinnati Reds	55	84	.396	26
Philadelphia Phillies	48	93	.340	34

The Dodgers beat Cincinnati again to extend their lead to a full game and their winning streak to eleven games. They began accepting applications for World Series tickets. For three games, $19.80 bought a box seat, $16.50 got a reserved seat in the grandstand.

On September 16 the Cardinals came to Brooklyn for three games. The Dodgers were hot, but they were playing without their fine center fielder, Johnny Frederick, who had pulled a hamstring, and their left fielder, Rube Bressler, who had broken a finger as he tried to make a difficult catch. To even things out, misfortune hit the Cardinals. The night before the opener of the series, one St. Louis pitcher disappeared, and another suffered an accident.

The vanishing pitcher was Flint Rhem, fresh from his sixth straight win but still occasionally referred to in the press as Bad Boy Rhem because of his drinking habits. Rhem didn't return to his hotel room the night before the first Brooklyn game and did not show up at the ballpark the next day. He reappeared a day later and immediately was pressed by newsmen as to his whereabouts.

"He was befuddled," recalled his roommate, Bill Hallahan. Tongue in cheek, a writer asked Rhem if maybe he had been kidnaped. Rhem liked that excuse and spun a tale appropriate to the gangster era. He said he was standing outside the hotel minding his own business when a big, black limousine pulled up. A passenger beckoned to him, Rhem said, and when he stepped alongside the car its occupants pulled guns and forced him to get in. He said they drove him to a secret hideaway and forced cups of raw whiskey down his throat. O cruel fate. "Imagine kidnaping Flint Rhem," said Hallahan, "and *making* him take a drink!"

On the night of Rhem's disappearance, Hallahan and Ray Blades decided to take in a movie. Hallahan recalled the incident almost a half-century later:

"We were staying at the Alamac Hotel, Seventy-first and Broadway. We walked from there to Forty-second Street. Went to a movie. When we came out, probably 11:00 P.M., we thought we'd get a cab. Blades got in. I got in and pinched my hand in the door. My right hand, across the fingers. Back at the hotel, Doc Weaver applied heat and cold. Did it ever hurt! Rickey came in and asked if I could pitch. I said, 'I pitch with my left hand, Mr. Rickey.'

"That same night, somebody said they wondered where Rhem was."

The next day, Hallahan pitched with two fingers of his right hand packed in salve. "I had the catcher throw the ball lightly," he said. Hallahan had a no-hitter for 6⅔ innings. But the Cards had as much trouble with Dazzy Vance, who fanned eleven. Ebbets Field was jammed, the National League's premier fastballers were dueling, and the game was a rare classic of pitching and defense, with Dodger bumbles thrown in.

Babe Herman stopped a Cardinal rally in the fourth with a brilliant catch. In the Cardinal sixth, Sparky Adams got a hit (he had four for the day), made it around to third base, and—with two out—tried to steal home. He had it stolen, but Vance cut short his windup and threw at Chick Hafey, who was batting. It hit him: Dead ball, batter to first, runner back to third. George Watkins, the next batter, fouled out. "Vance just lobbed the ball and Hafey stood there and let the ball hit him," Adams recalled. "I was across the plate when the ball hit him. If he had moved out of the way . . ."

In the Dodger eighth, Mickey Finn took a hit-and-run pitch; the runner, Harvey Hendrick, was out at second. Finn then singled, tried to stretch it and crashed into Charley Gelbert, the Cardinal shortstop. Gelbert was knocked cold; Finn was safe but woozy. He tottered off second base; Hallahan, the Cardinal pitcher, picked up the loose ball and tagged him out.

With Gelbert out, Adams moved from third to short for the Cardinals, and Andy High took over at third base. In the Cardinal tenth, High doubled, went to third on Hallahan's bunt, and scored on a single by Taylor Douthit.

But the Dodgers trailed by only a run and had one chance left. Glenn Wright led off the Brooklyn tenth with a double to the left-center gap. Del Bissonette walked, and Harvey Hendrick sacrificed the runners to second and third.

Jake Flowers pinch hit for Mickey Finn, and Hallahan walked him intentionally, hoping to set up a double play. The pennant race turned on the next play. Here's how Roscoe McGowan described it in the *New York Times:*

"Al Lopez blazed a drive to Sparky Adams's right, which bounded away from the Cardinal shortstop and it seemed a certainty that at least the tying run would be scored.

"But here came one of the fastest double plays on record. Adams recovered the ball, tossed to Frankie Frisch, and the Fordham Flash rifled it to Bottomley to end the game so suddenly that the fans scarcely registered it was over."

In 1988 interviews, Lopez and Adams remembered the play well. Lopez described it this way:

"I hit a line drive, one hop. It hit him in the chest and bounced up. He picked it up and threw it to Frisch, and they doubled me at first base. I thought I hit the ball real good but I hit it right at him. If Charley Gelbert would have been playing I don't think he would have been playing in that spot. But Adams was trying to protect the double play."

Sparky Adams gave his version:

"The catcher, Lopez, hit one of those low line drives. It hit in front of me, and it took a bad hop. I dived, and with my bare hand I got it and threw to Frisch, and we got a double play."

Ebbets Field, recalled Hallahan, lapsed into sudden silence: 1–0, St. Louis; the race was tied. The Giants meantime shoved the Cubs back, 7–0, on a three-hitter by Hubbell.

The next day, with the Cardinals and Dodgers tied at 3 and two out in the Cardinal ninth, Dolf Luque walked Gus Mancuso. Charley Gelbert scratched a single, and Manager Street called on Andy High to pinch hit. He doubled again; the Cards won and took over first place. Grimes won the next day, 4–3, to complete the sweep. The Giants beat the Cubs two games out of three, Wilson hitting two homers in the only Chicago victory. The Cards had a two-game lead with seven to play.

The Cards went to Philadelphia, the Dodgers to Pittsburgh. Chuck Klein hit his thirty-seventh and thirty-eighth homers for the Phils, but the Cards scored five runs in the seventh to win, 7–3. Next time out it was St. Louis, 15–7, with the usual kind of balanced Cardinal attack—a double, three singles, and four RBI for Gus Mancuso; a double and two singles each for Jim Bottomley and George Watkins; two hits each for Taylor Douthit, Sparky Adams, and Frankie Frisch.

Connie Mack and several of his players came to scout the Cardinals in the series finale, the Athletics having clinched the American League pennant. The Phillie ace, Fidgety Phil Collins, was working against the Cardinals' Flint Rhem.

The game exemplified the ferocious slugging of 1930. The Cards knocked out Collins with six runs in the third inning and added five in the fourth. But Rhem couldn't hold that 11–0 lead. Klein got four hits, and a substitute catcher, Tony (Pug) Rensa, hit a grand-slam homer. The Cards had to keep hitting, and they did: St. Louis, 19–16.

The Cardinals retained enough breath to beat the Pirates two straight and clinch the pennant. Altogether they won thirty-six of their last forty-six games, twenty-one of their last twenty-five. As the *Spalding Baseball Guide* put it, "The Missourians made a demoniacal rush in the last half of the campaign that had the whole nation gasping." The Cardinals batted .314 as a team—third in the league— and scored 1,004 runs, a National League record that still stands even though the schedule has been lengthened from 154 games to 162. In 1988 the New York Mets led the National League with 703 runs; in 1987, a strong hitting year with a rabbit ball in play, the Mets led the league with 823 runs, and in team batting average at .268.

Dizzy Dean, nineteen, came up from the minors in September, and Street let him pitch the season finale. He beat the Pirates, 3–1, and said it was too bad he wasn't eligible to pitch in the World Series. "Gee, I'll bet a lot of St. Louis people wish I was pitching every game," he said.

Back in St. Joseph, Missouri, Dean gave local writers this assessment of big league pitching: "I don't recall seeing any better than myself. I told Gabby I could win him twenty or thirty games next year. And to tell the truth I don't think I will be beaten. I've got a 16-year-old kid brother that I'm going to take to camp next year, so I've got to kind of coach him up on a few pointers about the majors. Next to me, I think he will be the greatest pitcher in the world." With Diz and Paul, the Cardinals had a future.

The Cubs finished second, two games out; the Giants third, five games out; the Dodgers fourth, six games out. Terry nailed down his .401 batting average, and in the season's last game Wilson drove in two runs to reach 190, a major league record that is now considered virtually untouchable. The highest RBI total of the last four decades, in either league, was 153 by Tommy Davis of the Los Angeles Dodgers in 1962.

All that remained in the American League was the race for the batting championship between Al Simmons of the Athletics and Lou Gehrig of the Yankees. Simmons sat out the last game and wound up at .381. With Babe Ruth pitching the whole game for the Yankees—and winning—Gehrig went three for five against the Red Sox but fell short at .379. You'd think a guy could hit better than that.

With President Herbert Hoover watching, Lefty Grove won the 1930 Series opener for the Athletics, 5–2, as Al Simmons and Mickey Cochrane homered. Seven runs wasn't much for a game in 1930, particularly between teams with the muscle of the A's and Cardinals. But the World Series turned the Year of the Hitter on its head. The *Reach Official Base Ball Guide* put it this way:

"The 1930 World's Series will go down in history as providing some of the most demoniacal pitching in history. Connie Mack's two beaux ideal of the peak, George Earnshaw, righthander, and Robert Moses Grove, lefthander, did all of the pitching in five of the six games played."

Earnshaw took the second game, 6–1, as the Athletics pounded Flint Rhem. The Series moved to St. Louis, where Bill Hallahan shut out the A's 5–0. Rube Walberg, Bill Shores, and Jack Quinn shared the pitching for Philadelphia. The Cards beat Grove 3–1 in the fourth game behind Jesse Haines, described by the *Reach Guide* as "the grim-visaged and veteran right hander."

With the Series tied at two games each, Mack picked Earnshaw to start the fifth game, while Gabby Street started Burleigh Grimes. Earnshaw was lifted for a pinch hitter in the eighth and Grove relieved, although he had pitched eight innings the day before. The game was scoreless going into the ninth, when Jimmie Foxx homered with Cochrane on base. Grove pitched two scoreless innings for the win.

After a day off for travel, Earnshaw started the next game, too.

Al Simmons and Jimmy Dykes homered for Philadelphia, and Earnshaw pitched a five-hitter for an easy 7–1 victory.

The World Championship was the Athletics' fifth, then high in the major leagues, though the Yankees would soon leave poor Connie Mack far behind. In 1930, of all years, team batting averages for the Series were among the lowest on record—.197 for Philadelphia, .200 for St. Louis.

The Series was broadcast nationwide, with telegraphic reports to Canada, the West Indies, and Mexico. "Even newspapers in far off Japan had representatives at the series and came out with extra editions for the base ball lovers of Nippon," the *Reach Guide* said. (According to Paul Dickson, author of *The Dickson Baseball Dictionary*, baseball was often written as two words until the 1940s.)

Compared with player salaries, World Series shares were much more significant than they are today. The A's took home $5,038 each, while the losing Cards got $3,536. That made quite a nest egg for the first year of the Great Depression.

12

"I should like to see the spitball restored and the emery ball, too."

Hack Wilson's landmark hitting of 1930 inspired F. C. Lane of *Baseball Magazine* to heraldic prose. This testimonial to Wilson's heavenly status appeared in the February 1931 issue of *Baseball:*

". . . For many years the National League has cast an envious eye upon the unrivalled exploits of that great champion of the American circuit, Babe Ruth. From time to time the National has thrust forward a champion to battle Babe at his pet specialty. All have fallen short of Babe's best. But now, in Hack Wilson, the National League has a champion that has made the whole world sit up and take notice. Fifty-six homers is much better than Babe's average performance. It falls only four short of his record for all time.

"Yes, the National League has a real champion in this one-time boilermaker who became a Home Run King."

Wilson's remarkable 1930 season did appear to place him as Ruth's successor, if not his equal. Not even Ruth had ever driven in 190 runs. Wilson was thirty, five years younger than Ruth, and his slugging had improved every year since 1926, his first season with the Cubs.

There was no official Most Valuable Player award in 1930, but *The Sporting News* and the Baseball Writers Association of America conducted separate MVP polls of sportswriters. Bill Terry won the *Sporting News* poll, with Frankie Frisch second and Wilson third. Wilson won the BBWAA poll, with Frisch second and Terry third. That was the one to win, because it carried a thousand-dollar award. Bill Deane of the National Baseball Library at Cooperstown combined votes in the two polls to arrive at an unofficial MVP. The winner was

Wilson with 111 points, followed by Frisch with 107 and Terry with 105. (The American League winner was Joe Cronin with 100 points, followed by Al Simmons with 85 and Lou Gehrig with 68.)

Wilson was on top of the world. He performed off-season on the vaudeville stage with teammates Gabby Hartnett, Kiki Cuyler, and Cliff Heathcote. Haberdasheries hired him to model the latest men's fashions. Wilson loved the attention, as Edward Burns wrote in the Chicago *Tribune:*

"After his first matinee Hack thought he could dance better than Terpsichore and Bo-Jangles Bill Robinson combined and that he possessed the voice of a nightingale, much sweeter than Caruso's ever was. As the act went on, Wilson's superiority complex increased to the point where the presence of his three pals irritated him and he wanted them to hide behind the piano while he was doing his stuff.

"In his extra-curricular appearances he received additional adulation while demonstrating what the well-dressed man should wear. Sometimes, though he had been signed on merely as a mannikin, Hack would drift off into a song and dance. Never a day went by that he didn't autograph a gross of baseballs, but this never seemed to remind him that he was just a star ball player who was the big man of the day."

Back home in Martinsburg, West Virginia, Wilson was greeted as a hero. A crowd led by the mayor met him at the railroad station, a brass band led a parade in his honor, and the townsfolk gave him a big silver cup and a new Buick.

Wilson looked forward to another big year and signed a contract for thirty-three thousand dollars. In fact, however, his wings were clipped before he ever took another swing. Much as the owners liked the record attendance of 1930, they could not stand the imbalance between hitting and pitching. No one had made more money off the home run than Jacob Ruppert, owner of the Yankees, and even he wanted less hitting.

"I should like to see the spitball restored and the emery ball, too," Ruppert said. He added this scornful comment about a proposal designed to boost hitting even more: "Why, they have suggested someone hitting for the pitchers. Now, isn't that rich?"

Old-timers spoke scornfully of the hitting barrage. Joe Tinker of Tinker-to-Evers-to-Chance fame said pitchers weren't following through properly. "Maybe it's the lively ball," Tinker told John Kieran of the *New York Times*. "Pitchers are afraid to get off-balance like that for fear they'll get killed when the ball comes back at them. When they throw these days, they have to be prepared to duck."

The National League changed one rule. A ball that bounced into the stands had been counted as a home run in the National League, but as a ground-rule double in the American League. Beginning in 1931, it became a ground-rule double in both leagues. More radical proposals, such as moving the pitcher closer to the plate or restoring the spitball, were pushed aside.

But the ball was changed. No one pretended that the two leagues were using identical balls. In 1930 the National League ball was livelier; in both leagues, the stitches were low, almost countersunk, which kept pitchers from getting the kind of grip they needed to throw sharp breaking pitches.

For 1931, both leagues raised the stitches, and the National League took some of the jump out of its ball. Officials acknowledged the change in explaining a sharp decrease in slugging in 1931. In late August of 1931, John A. Heydler, president of the National League, said the reduced scoring resulted from "the new ball with raised stitches and a heavier cover."

The change was drastic in the National League, mild in the American. In 1930 the eight National League teams scored a record 7,025 runs. In 1931 scoring dropped by 21 percent, to 5,537. American League scoring declined by 5 percent, from 6,670 runs in 1930 to 6,354 in 1931. The American League regained its position as the league with the most slugging, and the ball was at least partially responsible.

At mid-season 1931, William Harridge, president of the American League, predicted that the two leagues would adopt a uniform ball for 1932. They finally did just that, although they didn't get around to it until the major league meetings in December 1933. They chose the American League ball, which was considered livelier, and they made no bones about their purpose—to increase scoring so attendance would pick up from its Depression lows.

So in 1931 National League hitters were suddenly faced with

better pitching—a result of higher stitches—and a ball that lacked the carry of the rabbit on which they had feasted a year before.

Al Lopez recalled the change:

"Bill Terry was a great hitter. I was talking to him at Cooperstown about the lively ball we had in 1930. It was a real good ball. I liked that ball.

"In 1931 they came in with a dead ball and the averages went way down. In 1930 Bill Terry hit .401 and the following year he hit .349.

"It killed Hack Wilson. Just murdered Hack Wilson. In 1930 Wilson hit 56 homers and hit .356 and drove in 190 runs. In '31 he hit 13 homers, .261 percentage, and 61 RBI. Was that because of the ball? No question about it. Hack was more of a right-center field hitter in the Cubs' ballpark. When they came in with a dead ball it was just an easy fly ball."

As if that were not enough, Wilson also suffered from an unwise managerial change. William Wrigley, Jr., owner of the Cubs, was displeased at his team's loss of the 1929 World Series and its failure to win the pennant in 1930. For 1931, he decided to fire his manager, Joe McCarthy, and replace him with Rogers Hornsby. Word leaked, and the change was made during the final week of the 1930 season. "I have always wanted a World's Championship team," Wrigley said, "and I am not sure that Joe McCarthy is the man to give me that kind of a team."

Wrigley was firing a smart, flexible manager in favor of an unpopular and inflexible disciplinarian. The move didn't hurt McCarthy, who was quickly hired by the Yankees, for whom he won eight pennants in sixteen seasons. But it cost the Cubs dearly.

"Hornsby never chewed tobacco or smoked or drank anything at all, and he expected all his ballplayers to live that way," recalled Charlie Grimm. "He didn't know how to handle men. We were not allowed to smoke in the clubhouse, not allowed to eat in the clubhouse. Wilson wasn't used to that. Neither one of them liked the other."

Hornsby believed that a player's eyes would deteriorate from overuse and should be reserved for baseball. "We couldn't read," recalled Woody English, the shortstop. "We couldn't have newspapers. He wanted your mind on baseball, I guess. He was real strict that way. But Hornsby, he liked to play the races. He always had a *Racing Form* in his hip pocket." Hornsby also liked pinball, and the Cubs had a pinball machine in their clubhouse. But no soda pop was allowed.

Wilson started slowly in 1931. He had a few bursts of slugging, but never approached his form of 1930. Hornsby benched him from time to time, partly because he wasn't hitting and partly as punishment for his carousing. On September 5 Wilson and Malone hit the town after a loss in Cincinnati. They then went to the train station for the trip home to Chicago. Two sportswriters were on the platform, and Malone got into a fight with them. According to Wilson's biographers, Robert S. Boone and Gerald Grunska, Wilson didn't participate, although he watched with apparent approval.

The Cubs suspended Wilson for the rest of the season. On December 10, 1931, they traded Wilson and Bud Teachout, a pitcher, to the Cardinals for Burleigh Grimes. Wilson had taken a lot of criticism for his batting decline, and Branch Rickey rubbed it in with a contract offer of $7,500—a 77 percent cut. Wilson balked, and a month later the Cards traded Wilson to the Dodgers for minor league pitcher Robert Parham and $45,000. The Dodgers signed Wilson for $16,500.

Wilson's comedown was one of the steepest in baseball history. He was only thirty years old in 1931. He suffered no injury. Yet his hitting declined precipitously. The Cubs nevertheless led the National League in runs scored, but they finished a distant third as the Cardinals ran away with their second straight pennant.

J. Roy Stockton of the St. Louis *Post-Dispatch* visited Wilson at his Martinsburg, West Virginia, home after the 1931 season and found him sweating through a workout in a makeshift gym Wilson had built in his basement. The fallen slugger gave Stockton this explanation:

"It must have been a combination of things. Probably the ball had something to do with it, but it couldn't make that much difference. Then, possibly, I was trying too hard to live up to my new contract and my 1930 record. Even in the spring exhibition games I found myself fussing and swearing because I couldn't get hold of the ball. It wouldn't carry for me and I was missing more swings than usual.

Naturally, after my good year of 1930, the fans were expecting me to do something every time I went to bat and even the spring exhibition crowds razzed me pretty hard. That bothered me and I kept on getting the old razzberries all year.

"... Some people said I was a batting flop because I was carousing around too much. That was all wrong. I went out occasionally, but not as much as I did the year before, when I was hitting all those home runs. You have to do something for recreation, but I was in condition to play every day. They told me at Chicago that I'd have to quit this and that, but I'm not signing any pledges."

Wilson denied that he and Hornsby feuded, but said Hornsby, unlike McCarthy, made him take pitches on two-and-oh and three-and-one counts. "It just seemed that every time that situation came along, the pitcher would give me one that I thought I could have socked, and I had to take it," Wilson said. "And that didn't help my temper or my confidence any."

Wilson had a pretty good year for Brooklyn in 1932—23 homers, 123 RBI, .297. But the Dodgers finished third, and Wilson was out of the headlines in favor of his old team, the Cubs, and his old manager's new team, the Yankees, who squared off in the 1932 World Series.

Hornsby's gambling ruined his career with the Cubs. He was a heavy horse player; a lawsuit in 1927 brought out the fact that the Rajah bet $327,995 on the horses between December 1, 1925, and March 1926. Betting on horse races was legal, so Hornsby's gambling did not affect his baseball career. However, during the 1932 season Hornsby borrowed about $11,000 from some of his players to repay debts. Commissioner Landis conducted a well-publicized investigation, and though he found no wrongdoing on Hornsby's part the Cubs fired him on August 2, 1932.

They replaced him with his opposite—Charlie Grimm, the cheerful, banjo-playing first baseman. Grimm led the Cubs to the 1932 pennant, and they took on the Yankees—Joe McCarthy's Yankees— in the World Series. If anyone doubted that Babe Ruth would forever personify the home run, the Babe dispelled that doubt in the Series' third game with his dramatic "called shot" homer. Whether Ruth really called it is in dispute, but never mind; it is part of the legend.

As for Hornsby's popularity among the Cub players, they voted him not a penny of World Series money, although he had managed the team for almost two-thirds of the season.

Wilson's career declined steeply after 1932. He wound up with the Phillies, who released him on September 4, 1934. He still holds the major league record for RBI in a season (190) and the National League record for home runs (56). But while Ruth is remembered for his called shot homer, Hack Wilson is recalled for a piece of outfield buffoonery.

Playing for the Dodgers—the Dolorous Dodgers—in the lag end of his career, Wilson was panting in the infamous right field of Philadelphia's Baker Bowl, where he had been chasing shots off that short wall through a long, hot afternoon. Legend has it that he was badly hung over and dozed on his feet during a pitching change. Glenn Wright, the Dodger shortstop, related the story this way to Eugene Murdock:

"One of my duties as captain was to remove the pitcher on orders from the bench. Well, this day at Philadelphia they were knocking Walter Beck all over the lot, and I went in to take him out. But he was mad at himself and wouldn't give me the ball. Finally, he turned and fired it against the metal rightfield fence. Our right fielder, Hack Wilson, was daydreaming out there, but when he heard the ball rattle off the fence, he hopped on it and fired a strike to second base. Then seeing no one running he came charging in to see what was going on. When he learned what had happened he was ready to murder Beck. I had to keep them apart. From that time on it was Boom Boom Beck."

Baseball Magazine, which had so enthusiastically compared Wilson with Ruth, took a philosophical view of Wilson's decline. "Many a wiser man than Hack Wilson has drowned his sorrows in the flowing bowl," the magazine said. Wilson's drinking consumed his life. His wife divorced him in 1938.

Wilson remarried, wandered from job to job, and wound up in Baltimore, where he died a pauper in 1948. He was forty-eight years old. Babe Ruth had died just three months before. Ruth's funeral was held in St. Patrick's Cathedral. His body lay in state in the lobby of Yankee Stadium, and more than eighty thousand people came to see it; many of them wept.

Wilson's body was unclaimed for three days. Then Ford Frick, president of the National League, wired $350 to pay for a funeral in Baltimore, which was attended by about fifty people. His body was sent by hearse from Baltimore to Martinsburg. Wilson's lodge brothers, fellow members of the Benevolent and Protective Order of the Elks, drove to Baltimore for the funeral and accompanied the hearse back to Martinsburg. Wilson's body was laid out for viewing at a funeral home, and about one thousand Martinsburg residents came to see it. Two hundred attended his funeral and burial. Ten months later, a memorial service was held. Joe McCarthy, Charlie Grimm, Kiki Cuyler, and a few other players attended.

McCarthy addressed the small crowd. "I know you will say a fervent prayer for the great Hack," he said. "And may God rest his soul." McCarthy unveiled a granite tombstone, ten feet high, with crossed baseball bats at the top and this inscription:

ONE OF BASEBALL'S IMMORTALS,
LEWIS R. (HACK) WILSON RESTS HERE

The first election to the Baseball Hall of Fame was held in 1936, and Ruth was one of five players elected. He got 215 votes, seven fewer than Ty Cobb. Wilson was passed over year after year. He was finally elected to the Hall of Fame in 1979, largely because of that great year in 1930—as fine a season as any batter ever put together. But he is remembered as well for the ugly bookends of his career— two fly balls lost in the sun as the Athletics stunned the Cubs in the 1929 World Series, and the ludicrous relay of Boom-Boom Beck's angry throw off the Baker Bowl wall five years later.

Anyhow, say some skeptics, who cares what anybody did in 1930? Wasn't that the year the whole *National League* batted .303?

After Wilson's final game with the Cubs in 1931, a fan wrote this to the meter of "Old Ironsides." It appeared in the Chicago *Tribune,* and was reprinted in Wilson's biography, *HACK,* by Robert S. Boone and Gerald Grunska.

Old Hack

Aye, tear our tattered hero down!
    Long has he been on high,
And many an eye has danced to see
    His homers split the sky.

Around him rang the grandstand's shouts
    And burst the bleachers' roar—
The pudgy one's terrific drives
    Shall sweep the clouds no more.

He had a splendid record
    Which topped his every foe,
But "Freedom's" price was very high,
    So now our Hack must go.

But whether he knocked a homer
    Or whether he weakly fanned,
He always showed us what he had,
    So give the boy a hand.

PART II

1968: The Year the Pitchers Took Revenge

13

"We white and black players respect what Dr. King has done for mankind."

On Thursday, April 4, 1968, the Reverend Dr. Martin Luther King was shot to death in Memphis, Tennessee, as he leaned over the balcony of his motel room to talk to Jesse Jackson, a young colleague who was standing below.

The summer before, blacks looted stores and burned buildings in Detroit, Newark, and other cities. King's assassination sparked a new wave of rioting. Among the cities worst hit were Baltimore, Chicago, Kansas City, Cincinnati, and Washington, D.C. From the U.S. Capitol, congressmen could see fires burning throughout the city's large black neighborhoods, which touched upon the Capitol area itself.

Four days before, President Lyndon B. Johnson had addressed the nation on television about the Vietnam War—an issue even more divisive than the struggle for civil rights. There is "division in the American house," Johnson said. For the sake of unity, he said, "I shall not seek and I will not accept the nomination of my party as your president."

Now Johnson had to deal with the second consuming crisis of the 1960s—the struggle of American blacks for equality, and the violence that it sometimes engendered. He declared Sunday, April 7, a national day of mourning in honor of the fallen civil rights leader.

King's funeral was Tuesday, April 9. William Eckert, baseball's commissioner, wired Mrs. King his condolences and expressed hope that "all of us can carry out the goals" of her late husband. Eckert also called major league owners, urging them to postpone season openers. Some didn't like it, but every opener was postponed. The last team to fall into line was the Los Angeles Dodgers—the very team that, as the Brooklyn Dodgers, had broken baseball's color line on opening day twenty-one years before.

The Pittsburgh Pirates had eleven black players, more than any other team in baseball. Joe E. Brown, the team's general manager, canceled the team's Sunday exhibition game against the Yankees, scheduled for Richmond, Virginia. But the Pirates were scheduled to open the season Monday at Houston, and Brown said it was up to the Houston Astros' management to decide whether to play or postpone the games scheduled for Monday and Tuesday.

The Pirates' black players met, voted not to play either game, and told Brown. They then met with their teammates, and the whole team ratified their decision. Roberto Clemente, a Puerto Rican, and pitcher Dave Wickersham, a white, issued a statement saying, "We are doing this because we white and black players respect what Dr. King has done for mankind." First baseman Donn Clendenon, a black, said, "I knew him well and considered him a close friend. Dr. King talked me into attending Morehouse College in Atlanta, and I taught school with his sister, Christine." Clemente said he also was friendly with King, who visited the outfielder's home in Puerto Rico. The games in Houston were postponed.

The riots spread to 125 cities, and many were not one-day outbursts. The Oakland Athletics came to Baltimore and, to avoid the riot areas, stayed at a motel ten miles outside the city. Cincinnati outlawed the sale of liquor and imposed a curfew from 7:00 P.M. to 6:00 A.M., confining the Chicago Cubs to the Netherland Hilton Hotel. It was a restless place; trapped with the Cubs were two hundred bowlers, attending a tournament of the American Bowling Congress. "I feel just like a prisoner confined to a hotel instead of a cell," said the Cubs' Ron Santo.

The morning after King's funeral, troops marched outside D.C. Stadium, home of the Washington Senators. Six had died in the extensive rioting in Washington, and entire blocks were destroyed by fire. "People were wary and frightened," reported *The Sporting News,* afraid of driving through the black neighborhoods around D.C. Stadium. "Last year, it took the Senators months of hard work to get the fans back to the point where they no longer feared for their safety," the newspaper continued. ". . . Now that anxiety has returned." Reluctantly, the Senators announced that they would play their home games in daylight until further notice.

The Senators had sold 45,000 tickets for their opener, but only 32,063 fans showed up. Although fear of the neighborhood was widespread in Washington, the stadium itself was an oasis. "The big fear out at the stadium was that Frank Howard might lose his grip on the bat," one columnist wrote.

Vice-President Hubert H. Humphrey, subbing for President Johnson, threw out two balls. Rod Carew of the Minnesota Twins was spiked in a dash for the souvenirs, which were caught by Hank Allen, a utility player, and Nellie Fox, a coach, both of the Senators. Humphrey visited manager Jim Lemon in the Senators' dugout, then crossed the field and paid his respects to Cal Ermer, the Twins' manager. With Johnson stepping aside, everyone assumed that Humphrey would run for president, competing for the Democratic nomination with Senators Eugene McCarthy of Minnesota and Robert F. Kennedy of New York, who were running in opposition to continued U.S. involvement in Vietnam. The fans booed Humphrey in a good-natured way. "Don't worry, Cal," the vice-president told Ermer. "They're booing me, not you."

Minnesota's Dean Chance outdueled Camilo Pascual of Washington, 2–0. After the game, Chance gave Humphrey an autographed baseball and said, "I'm going to register and will vote for you."

President Johnson and other authorities called out twenty thousand soldiers and thirty-four thousand National Guardsmen to help police the disturbed cities. Many of the Guardsmen were young men who had signed on to fulfill their military obligations without risking the draft. One of them was Private First Class Edwin A. Brinkman, twenty-six, a member of the District of Columbia National Guard and veteran shortstop for the Washington Senators. Geographically, at least, it wasn't a bad combination; the D.C. Armory is a short walk from R.F.K. Stadium, which in early 1968, before the tragedy that took Robert Kennedy's life, was still called D.C. Stadium.

Brinkman recalled the odd mixture of military and baseball duty during an interview in 1988, when he was a coach for the Chicago White Sox:

"From spring training, we went to Louisville to play three games prior to the season opener. On Sunday, after the game, we flew back into Washington, and there was a sergeant at the airport waiting for me, to notify me that I had to go to the Armory right away. So my wife took my luggage back to my house and I went to the Armory.

"On opening day in Washington I was at the ballpark. But I had my Army uniform on. I was on duty over there. I was up in the stands. The National Guard motor pool was in the parking lot outside, and I was one of many Guardsmen in charge of protecting the motor pool.

"There was always something going on in those days. I was doing a lot of National Guard duty. I would rejoin the club. I would try and get myself back in shape a little bit, and about the time I would be ready to play I'd have to go for something else—a demonstration against the war or something. They would call me at home and I'd have to go down. They would call me on the road and I'd have to fly back. Then I had my normal weekend drills and summer camps and all those things. I just wanted the thing to be over with so I could settle down and get back to a normal life. Play some ball."

In 1968 Pfc. Brinkman managed to play in seventy-seven games. He batted .187. Ron Hansen filled in for him and batted .185. The Senators finished dead last, largely because their pitching was weak—a staff ERA of 3.64, highest in baseball. In 1930 no team—and only nine *pitchers*—had an ERA that *low*. America had changed and so had baseball.

14

"Hey, Denny, how come you took the last piece of pie?"

As Denny McLain saw it, the Boston Red Sox would have enjoyed no "Impossible Dream" in 1967 had he not suffered a freak injury. "We win it easy in '67 if I can pitch in the month of September," McLain said.

"I had won seventeen games going into September and all I got to do is win one ballgame, maybe two, and that's it. I had won twenty the year before. There was no reason for us not to win it. We lose by one game. My inability to pitch was the bottom line."

Those are not the words of a cocky young pitcher—which McLain surely was—but of a forty-four-year-old man whose baseball star fell as rapidly as it rose, and whose life after baseball has included 902 days in prison. McLain has erred. He says so himself. He has been humiliated. That, too, he acknowledges. Twice he considered suicide; both incidents are related in his autobiography (*Strikeout: The Story of Denny McLain,* The Sporting News, St. Louis, 1988). He flays himself in print for inflicting hardship on his wife, Sharyn, and their four children.

But humble he is not. His account of the incident that decided the 1967 American League pennant race may irritate Red Sox fans. After all, the Red Sox survived the loss of their young slugger Tony Conigliaro, who was beaned on August 18. The Bosox went into the final two days of the season trailing the Minnesota Twins by one game. Twice they came from behind to beat the Twins, as Carl Yastrzemski capped a Triple Crown season with a homer, a double, five singles, and a crucial throw from left field. In two games, the Twins retired Yaz once.

That pennant race was the closest in American League history, and McLain looked back upon it from a different perspective—his own. To him, the crucial date was September 18. The Red Sox, Twins, and Tigers were tied for first place, with the White Sox a half-game back. The Red Sox came to Detroit for two games and knocked out McLain in the second inning of the opener. He angrily kicked a locker in the clubhouse, hurting his left ankle and two toes. That night he fell asleep watching television. A noise in the garage startled him, and he got up from the couch suddenly. His left foot was asleep, and he somehow aggravated the injuries.

McLain did not pitch again until the final game of the season. It was the nightcap of a doubleheader against the California Angels, and if the Tigers won it they would tie for the pennant with the Red Sox, who had finished their season finale two hours before. McLain lacked his usual stuff, and the Angels won. Boston's "Impossible Dream" came true, and the Tigers and Twins just missed.

McLain missed two starts because of the injury, and he was a terrific pitcher. Had he pitched two more games—or had he been on top of his game in the finale—Detroit might well have mooted Boston's climactic victory. Another player might have said, "Well, you have to hand it to the Red Sox," might have pointed out that Al Kaline, Detroit's veteran star, broke his hand and missed twenty-six games.

But not Denny McLain. As an athlete—if not a diplomat—you can't fault him. To win, you have to think of yourself as a winner. McLain's cocky and foolish self-indulgence may have ruined his life, but when it came to pitching, his brash self-confidence served him well. McLain, interviewed from his Fort Wayne, Indiana, home in September 1988, put it this way:

"You have to be brash and intimidating on the mound. You have to think that you are the best there is for those particular couple of hours. If you expect to lose, you will. The easiest thing in the world to do is to lose. I believed that you had to do whatever is necessary to win, and that started with a good mental outlook. You had to be very positive about what you were doing."

The Tigers faced a test in 1968. They were loaded with talent, but some people thought they were jinxed—or that they jinxed them-

126

selves. In the heat of the 1967 pennant race, Dick Williams, Boston's rookie manager, made the kind of put-down statement that could have come back to haunt him.

"I don't worry about the Tigers," Williams said. "They always manage to find a way not to win." The Tigers did indeed lose, and Detroit fans went into the 1968 season almost afraid to hope. In Detroit, Governor George Romney threw out the first ball and joined an opening-day crowd of 41,429. "This has got to be it, Mayo," Romney said to Mayo Smith, the Tiger manager. "It" meant the pennant, something missing in Detroit since the wartime season of 1945.

Denny McLain had no such doubts. Watson Spoelstra, veteran baseball writer for the Detroit *News,* asked McLain in February 1968 about the Tigers' chances. "Nobody in the league comes close to us," McLain said. "We should win by six or seven games if we get off to a good start and nobody falls off any couch." McLain said he had strengthened his right arm and shoulder with an off-season bowling regimen—fifteen or sixteen lines a day, shades of Chuck Klein in 1930—and was seeing better with the help of contact lenses.

"I just know I'll have a good year," McLain said. "I can feel it. I've got to prove something to some people." One of them may have been Jim Campbell, the Tiger general manager, who had called McLain "a brash young kid."

Earl Wilson, a twenty-two-game winner in 1967, pitched the '68 opener for the Tigers, but McLain got his name in the papers by bringing his sheepdog, named Pepsi in honor of the soft drink that McLain consumed in huge quantities. Clubhouse attendant John Hand barred Pepsi from the clubhouse. "You're welcome," he told McLain, "but your dog stays out." The Tigers bowed, 7 to 3, to the Red Sox.

Detroit then won nine straight games. McLain pitched seven good innings twice, the official wins going to relief pitchers. He notched his first win April 21 as Detroit swept the White Sox in a double-header. Eddie Stanky, the feisty White Sox manager, tried to revive the jinx, saying, "The Tigers better win big or they won't win at all." But Stanky's voice was fading as his team sank into the second division. Anyway, it looked like the Tigers *might* win big.

The Detroit pitching staff was allowing fewer than two earned runs a game, and the team was rallying from behind. On April 17 the

Indians led 3 to 2 with two out in the Tiger ninth, one man on base, and two strikes on the Tiger cleanup hitter, Willie Horton. He homered. Al Kaline celebrated his two thousandth major league game with a homer. It was Kaline's sixteenth season, and he wanted a pennant. "I'm picking the Tigers to win because of Kaline," said Tony Kubek, the Yankee shortstop turned television sportscaster.

Mayo Smith, the Detroit manager, was delighted with his pitching. Other managers were delighted with their pitching, too. The season was like 1930 turned on its head; ordinary pitchers were overpowering, and star hitters appeared futile. In frustration, a number of hitters went to eye doctors.

Larry Shepard, manager of the Pittsburgh Pirates, said, "I have a hunch we might own three twenty-game winners this season—Bunning, Veale, and McBean." Herman Franks of the Giants said he might have four—Juan Marichal, Ray Sadecki, Mike McCormick, and Gaylord Perry.

Cleveland's pitching was the best of all. With the season twenty-eight games old, the Indian staff had nine shutouts and a team ERA of 1.98. Steve Hargan pitched fourteen straight scoreless innings, and he was the team's fifth starter, behind Luis Tiant, Sudden Sam McDowell, Stan Williams, and Sonny Siebert. Tiant pitched four straight shutouts. In three straight outings, McDowell struck out fourteen Yankees, sixteen Athletics, and ten Orioles. Never before had a pitcher fanned forty men in three games. Jack Sanford, the Cleveland pitching coach, viewed his five starting pitchers with pride. "Every one of them is capable of winning twenty games," he said.

But there were not enough wins to go around. Nobody was hitting. Bob Veale of the Pirates gave up only eight runs in his first five starts, four of them complete games. But the Pirates scored only four runs, and Veale was oh and three. Yastrzemski, the defending American League batting champ, was hitting .250. "He's trying to carry the burden all by himself because the team is not hitting," said coach Bobby Doerr. Among the teammates not hitting was George Scott, a .300 hitter in 1967 who couldn't get his average up to .100. Dick Williams benched him. "I wish he would hit," the manager said. "He's a lot of fun to have around when he's hitting. I hate to see him moping around like this."

The Red Sox were without their pitching ace, Jim Lonborg, who broke his leg in an off-season skiing accident, but Jose Santiago moved into Lonborg's role. Among his first four starts were a two-hitter, a three-hitter, and a four-hitter; he was three and oh with an ERA of 1.08. Bill Hands of the Cubs, never known as a strong finisher, struck out the side in the ninth to beat the Mets.

Fastballers like McLain and McDowell won, and so did slowballers like Phil Ortega of the Washington Senators, who threw thirty-two changeups while shutting out the Indians. His pitching coach, Sid Hudson, was astounded. "Six to eight changeups is high and ten is tops," Hudson said. "I've never seen a performance like that."

Even the National League's doormat expansion teams, the New York Mets and Houston Astros, were showing pitching strength. They played each other for six hours and six minutes on April 15. In the sixteenth inning, the Astrodome's saucy scoreboard flashed this message: "I told you baseball wouldn't replace sex." In the bottom of the twenty-fourth, a Met infielder missed a ground ball with the bases loaded; Houston won, 1–0, behind pitchers Don Wilson, Jim Ray, and Wade Blasingame. Tommy Agee and Ron Swoboda of New York were each oh for ten at bat; Houston's Bob Aspromonte was oh for nine.

The Mets came home to play the Giants and were greeted by a crowd of 52,079. The Giants loaded the bases in the first inning, but New York's rookie phenom, Jerry Koosman, struck out Willie Mays and went on to win, 3–0. The shutout was one of seven for Koosman, tying the record for a rookie pitcher. He wound up with nineteen wins. His teammate Tom Seaver had been voted Rookie of the Year in 1967, and Koosman almost made it two Mets pitchers in a row; Johnny Bench of the Reds edged him by one vote.

Fans and players were anxious to see another Met rookie, Nolan Ryan, who struck out eighteen batters in seven innings of minor league work in 1967 before sitting out the rest of the season with a sore arm. Ryan's first pitch in a spring exhibition game was a swinging strike. Rube Walker, a Mets coach, was watching with two sportswriters. "Boys, let me tell you something," Walker said. "That pitch had a little hurry on it."

Ryan made his first appearance of the season in the Houston Astrodome. He struck out the side in the first inning and struck out four more in the next two innings. "He threw me three hellacious pitches," said Rusty Staub, Houston's best hitter. "I couldn't even make an offer at one."

A blister on a finger of his pitching hand sent Ryan to the showers, and the bothersome injury persisted. The Mets' trainer, Gus Mauch, who formerly worked for the Yankees, recalled that pickle brine had helped a couple of Yankee pitchers with similar problems, so he stopped by a delicatessen and got Ryan a bottle of the stuff. "I can smell the brine when I'm pitching," Ryan said. "Look, no blisters. That stuff really works." He threw his first complete game, beating the Cardinals, 4 to 1, and raising his strikeout total to thirty-six in twenty-six innings.

The Mets were just a year away from their first pennant, but first they had to overcome the clownish reputation they had acquired since their debut in 1962. Tom Seaver, their studious young right-hander, was particularly anxious to build team pride. He faced a test one day when a green balloon floated near the mound.

Seaver reached for the balloon. It drifted out of his reach, then drifted close again. He reached once more, and once more it floated away. Seaver turned his back on the green plaything, and shortstop Bud Harrelson stepped on it and stuffed it in his pocket. "I wasn't going to touch it after that," Seaver said of his second grab for the elusive balloon. "I would have missed it. Do you think I'd want to be known as a Met who couldn't catch a balloon? That's the image we're trying to erase."

The Mets lacked hitting, but even teams that should have been hitting could not. The Pirates boasted one of baseball's strongest lineups, with Roberto Clemente, Willie Stargell, Matty Alou, Manny Mota, Bill Mazeroski, and Donn Clendenon. On Sunday, May 12, Pittsburgh scored two early runs and beat the Phillies, 2–1. The Pirates then lost successive 1–0 shutouts to Nelson Briles and Steve Carlton of the Cardinals. John Hallahan, the Pirate equipment manager, was putting away bats after the game and said, "Maybe I ought to burn some of these bats." The idea inspired several Pirate pitchers, who filled a wheelbarrow with bats, pushed it to the bullpen, doused the bats with gasoline from a tractor, and set them afire. It worked—or at least something worked. The next night, Clemente hit a two-run triple in the third inning and Stargell singled him home.

* * *

The 1968 All-Star Game was billed as a symbol of all that was modern in baseball. It was played at night, in the Houston Astrodome, on artificial turf. Willie Mays led off the home first with a single, advanced to second on a wild pickoff throw, took third on a wild pitch, and scored on a double play.

Whatta rouser! The National League didn't score again, and the American League didn't score at all. At one point twenty straight American League batters were retired. Mays was voted the game's most valuable player, perhaps because the writers couldn't decide among the NL's six shutout pitchers—Don Drysdale of the Dodgers, Juan Marichal of the Giants, Steve Carlton of the Cardinals, Ron Reed of the Braves, and Tom Seaver and Jerry Koosman of the Mets. Koosman finished the game by striking out Carl Yastrzemski, rounding out the game's strikeout total at twenty.

McLain pitched two scoreless innings for the American League. He was already the talk of baseball with a record of sixteen and two. He beat the Senators 12 to 1 on May 10 to put Detroit in first place to stay; they led at the All-Star break by nine and one-half games.

McLain was young, opinionated, and loquacious, and his comments made headlines. Detroit's two daily newspapers, the *News* and *Free Press,* were on strike, and Billy Hoeft, who had pitched for the Tigers a decade before, said the Tigers would win if the strike lasted, because sportswriting tended to dampen team morale. In *The Sporting News,* Joe Falls of the *Free Press* commented, "The Tigers haven't won a pennant for 23 years, which must mean we've had some terrible sports writers around here for 23 years."

The newspaper strike lasted most of the season, and McLain, asked about it twenty years later, said that the blackout of critical sportswriting in Detroit affected the team "in a very positive way."

But the Tigers did not play in secret, and McLain was not reticent. Spoelstra of the *News* and Falls of the *Free Press* continued to cover the Tigers for *The Sporting News.* Detroit radio and television stations covered the team, and so did other Michigan papers, so McLain's comments were recorded and repeated. The more he won—and the more he said—the more attention he got from the national press, particularly with his team in first place.

Tiger Stadium was—and is—a hitter's ballpark. McLain yielded thirty-five homers in 1967, tops in the majors. He gave up five in his first five games of 1968, and said, "I hate this place. It's a bandbox. But I've got to pitch here and I'll make the best of it."

Not too bad. But when a few fans booed Tiger stars Al Kaline and Norm Cash, who, like most hitters, were slumping, McLain put his foot in it.

"The Detroit fans are the biggest front-running fans in the world," he said. "I think the fans helped us to lose the pennant last year. There were certain guys on this club who didn't want to go out and play last year because of the abuse. I don't care if I get booed here the rest of my life. Detroit is a great town. I like it. I've bought a home and have roots here. But the fans in this town are the worst in the league. . . . If they think we're stupid for playing this game, how stupid are they for watching us?"

McLain's comments raised a furor, and he quickly explained that he was referring to only a few fans. "Mr. Campbell wants me to be a diplomat," he said of the Tiger GM. "I'm doing my best." He made no secret of his desire for a big raise. "I think $100,000 is a beautiful figure, but I'm not halfway there yet," he said.

McLain was making $30,000—the equivalent of roughly $102,000 today, since a dollar in 1968 bought as much as $3.40 could buy in 1988. He spent money like a millionaire. "When you can do it out there between the white lines," he said, "then you can live any way you want. Me? I like to travel fast—and always first class. Why, there's no other way to go, is there?"

Actually, first class was new to McLain. He grew up in Harvey, Illinois, a south-side suburb of Chicago. To support the family, his father worked two jobs. He played the organ and taught Denny how to play. When Denny was fifteen, his father suffered a fatal heart attack while driving to watch his son pitch a high school game. Denny's mother remarried, and young McLain did not get along well with his mother and stepfather. He earned spending money by running numbers.

McLain had the kind of fastball that attracts scouts, and in 1962 the White Sox signed him, giving him a bonus of ten thousand dollars—which he quickly spent on a new car for himself and another for his mother. He was to get another seven thousand dollars based on his progress, and he didn't take long to get started, pitching a no-hitter in his first professional game. That was in Harlan, Kentucky, of the all-rookie Appalachian League. McLain regarded Harlan as a poor hick town. He was moved up a notch to Clinton, Iowa, close enough to Chicago so McLain made several unauthorized visits home to court his girl friend. His manager caught him and fined him.

His pitching was erratic. In the spring of 1963 the White Sox had three bonus pitchers. Under the rules then in force, they had to keep a "bonus boy" on the major league roster or make him available to other teams through the annual player draft. The White Sox could not afford to go into a season with three unseasoned pitchers. They kept Bruce Howard, who turned out to be a journeyman pitcher, and Dave DeBusschere, who turned out to be a star—in the National Basketball Association. DeBusschere gave up on baseball, though not until after the 1963 season.

McLain became available for the eight-thousand-dollar draft price, and the Tigers claimed him. He pitched superbly in the minor leagues, and the Tigers called him up in September 1963. He beat the White Sox 4 to 3 in his first big league start and hit his only big league homer. After the season McLain married Sharyn Boudreau, daughter of Lou Boudreau, who earned a spot in the Hall of Fame as a shortstop and manager for the Cleveland Indians, and later became an announcer for the Chicago Cubs.

In 1964 McLain started to get a taste of first-class life. A sportswriter wrote about his huge consumption of Pepsi-Cola, and Pepsi signed him to a PR contract. He blossomed into stardom in 1965, winning sixteen games, and his off-season value increased. Everything about McLain bespoke the friendly, cocky, gregarious athlete. He strutted on the field, and wore his baseball cap tilted low over his forehead. He was tough-kid handsome and he talked fast. He went on and on about money, show biz, endorsements. A Detroit bar hired him to play the organ. He began to get speaking engagements. He started a business or two, assuming his name would carry them to profitability.

He learned to fly an airplane, borrowed a Lear jet at the 1968 All-Star break, flew to Las Vegas with Sharyn, and gambled all night. The next afternoon he flew to Los Angeles so he and Sharyn could tour Disneyland, and from there they flew to Houston for the game.

He pitched his two innings, showered, and was back in the air before the game was over, en route to Las Vegas for another night at the casinos.

In the mid-1930s another Tiger pitcher, Schoolboy Rowe, interrupted a radio appearance with a memorably innocent question to his sweetheart: "How'm I doing, Edna?" McLain was not that kind of bumpkin, but he was naively attracted to shady con artists. He seemed blind to any human avarice besides his own, and unaware that his celebrity value was no stronger or more durable than his right arm. He hired an agent to handle his bookings and a lawyer to manage his money. Instead, the lawyer stole his money, or so McLain contends. He appeared on television with the Smothers Brothers and Ed Sullivan, and he saw more Hollywood ahead. He didn't sleep much, except on nights before he pitched. He spent his days making appearances or playing the organ or talking deals on the telephone.

Pat Dobson was a young relief pitcher with the Tigers in 1968 and a close friend of McLain's. Dobson blossomed into a twenty-game winner with the Baltimore Orioles in 1971. In 1988 he was the pitching coach for the San Diego Padres and recalled McLain in an interview:

"Dolph is what we called him, Dolphin, because he was such a fish playing cards. We played poker and we used to beat the heck out of him. He was the largest of fishes—a dolphin.

"We had a card game in Oakland one time. He was drawing light on the hand. He drew light about sixty or seventy dollars. He and Jim Northrup split the pot. When you split a pot, playing high-low, you give the other guy your lights and then you split what's in the pot. But he told Northrup that he wasn't light that money. He said, 'That's my money.'

"Northrup came over the bleeping bed. Pennies and cards were flying. Northrup was going to punch him out, but Jim said, 'I'm not going to mess with you now. We're going to win the pennant. As soon as the season's over I'm going to kick the bleep out of you.' Did Northrup do it? No. He cooled off.

"Denny would give you the shirt off his back, but don't let him borrow money from you. You'd never see it again. He was one of those guys, if he made $35,000 he'd spend $45,000. If he had $100 he'd spend $110.

"He was a good guy, no doubt about it. He got in with the wrong people. He got in over his head. With the notoriety he had, he got out of his realm. He'd meet people he shouldn't have been hanging around with. They got enamored of him just because he was Denny McLain. And he ended up getting screwed by it. He was out of his class, out of his range. He was better off with us, his teammates.

"He was always one of those guys who was going to try to make a dollar without working. Playing the organ! Oh, he was bad. He was terrible! Sheckie Greene got all over him on the 'Tonight Show' about that, and Denny said it was an easy way to make a buck. He was always like that, and it was a shame that he was. With all the job opportunities that he had in Detroit, that son of a gun could be a wealthy guy. But Denny didn't want to work. Work from nine to five? There was no bleeping way that he was going to do that. Dolph would a lot rather play cards.

"They ought to pin a medal on Sharyn, his wife. She's a great girl."

Dobson's description of McLain matches the pitcher's description of himself. However, his autobiography is not a mea culpa, because McLain does not confess guilt, only bad judgment and poor selection of friends and business associates. To be sure, he says, he gambled and made book. But he insists that he was innocent of the crimes for which he was convicted in 1985—racketeering, conspiracy to commit racketeering, extortion, and possession of cocaine with intent to distribute.

His conviction was overturned on appeal. Facing the prospect of a new trial, McLain and his lawyers negotiated a plea agreement. On October 18, 1988, he pleaded guilty to federal charges of racketeering and possession of cocaine with intent to distribute. The government agreed to drop charges of extortion and conspiracy.

Jim Northrup, the Tiger right fielder in 1968 and a teammate of McLain's for six years, recalled his colorful colleague during an interview in 1988. Twenty years after the Tiger pennant year of 1968, Northrup was still involved with baseball and Detroit, dividing his time between announcing duties on cable TV broadcasts of Tiger games and working as a manufacturer's representative, selling products to the auto industry.

"Denny always played by his own rules, and I think he probably truly, honestly believes he's not guilty of anything. He believes it. Oh, he does! Whether he's right or wrong.

"That's just the way Denny has always been. He's the kind of guy, you'll be at the dinner table with him, and everybody will be there, and he'll take the last piece of pie. When it's all gone you'll say, 'Hey, Denny, how come you took the last piece of pie?'

"He'll say, 'I didn't take any pie.' And you'll say, 'I saw you eat it.'

"He'll say, 'I swear to God, I didn't take the last piece of pie.' And he would believe that he didn't!

"That's the exact mentality Denny's always used for everything. It's gotten him in a lot of trouble. It doesn't make him a bad guy. He's a good guy. He's tried hard. I know he's trying very, very hard now to make a living for his family. To stay straight. He has no intentions of fooling around—I hope—once this is over.

"When we were playing ball he always played by his own rules. He wanted to fly his airplane and he would do it. There were times he didn't travel with the team. Of course the management finally made him do that. But he thought why should he? As long as he showed up, pitched, and won, that was all. That was his responsibility.

"He was a very young person. He was thrust in the limelight very fast, and it was tough to cope with. He was playing [the organ] at Vegas. He was playing here. He was playing there. He met a lot of people at a very tender age without any experience. He believes everybody and trusts everybody and he never thought that there would be anything wrong. He gambled. He loved to gamble. And he didn't think he was doing anything wrong. Denny just believes that when he does things, as long as he's doing them with no malicious intent, it's OK."

McLain crashed even before his brushes with the law. In 1970 Commissioner Bowie Kuhn suspended him for consorting with gamblers. The Tigers suspended him for dousing two sportswriters with buckets of water. Then Kuhn suspended him again, this time for carrying a gun. McLain blames Kuhn. He says he never took bets on baseball and kept the gun in his car, for self-defense only. Whatever he had done, it didn't pay off. He made lots of money, in baseball and out. Yet by June of 1970 he owed more than four hundred thousand dollars, and he declared bankruptcy. A sore arm pushed him out of the major leagues in 1972, and his business pursuits in subsequent years landed him in prison.

Nineteen-sixty-eight was a year of youthful assertion—of demonstrations, strikes, protests, and styles designed to set the younger generation apart from its elders. Hit movies included *The Graduate* ("Where have you gone, Joe DiMaggio . . ."), the Beatles' *Yellow Submarine,* and Stanley Kubrick's *2001: A Space Odyssey,* which to older viewers appeared to be straight science fiction but to younger, hipper fans was understood as an impressionistic portrayal of an LSD trip.

High school and college students began using four-letter words in conversation with members of the opposite sex. Miniskirts were in fashion. So were marijuana and sex; virginity was no longer something every young woman wished to claim. The economy was still surging on President Johnson's "guns and butter" program. Gasoline sold for thirty-four cents a gallon, and continued prosperity was taken for granted. Few foresaw the inflation and recession that would follow.

McLain was only twenty-four in 1968, and he was certainly an independent young man. But little about him reflected the youthful ferment of the 1960s. He played the organ, not the electric guitar. He was not the kind of fellow you found wearing a tie-dyed shirt or picketing in behalf of someone else.

The major leagues had precious little of that. Baseball usually provides a window on American culture, but the shade was down in 1968. Hawk Harrelson of the Red Sox wore his hair long and put on Nehru jackets, and Ron Swoboda of the Mets shocked his teammates with a string of love beads, but most ballplayers were wrapped up in the conservative code of their profession. Major league ballplayers are young princes, and few princes enlist in revolutionary causes. Ballplayers avoided Vietnam by joining the National Guard, not by declaring themselves conscientious objectors or skipping off to Canada or Sweden. In 1968 roughly one-third of major league players had to take time off for weekend drills, National Guard summer camp, or some other kind of part-time military duty.

Just before spring training, Jim Fregosi, star shortstop of the California Angels, went on a USO morale-building trip to military hospitals in Guam, Okinawa, Japan, and the Philippines. He was shocked by the severity of the wounds suffered by many servicemen, and said that they complained about a shortage of sports news in the newspapers available to them. "They can hardly find them because of all the stories on the demonstrators," Fregosi said. "I had a Marine come up to me and say, 'Just give me two more good Marines and we'll stop all that nonsense.' "

On the other pressing social issue of the era, however, major league baseball was a pioneer, and ballplayers were far ahead of their countrymen. In 1968 black Americans were demonstrating, even rioting, against persistent racism and lack of equal opportunity. From today's vantage point, it is easy to say that baseball was slow to integrate. But when Jackie Robinson joined the Brooklyn Dodgers in 1947, the notion of giving a black an equal shot at a big job was almost revolutionary. The Supreme Court decision outlawing school segregation was still seven years ahead. Congress waited until the 1960s to enact laws granting blacks equal job opportunities, equal access to restaurants and other public facilities, and a guaranteed right to vote. Housing segregation wasn't outlawed until 1968.

By then baseball was thoroughly integrated, and many of its brightest stars were blacks and Latins. Most of the Detroit players were white, but three of the team's most valuable men were black—slugger Willie Horton, pitcher Earl Wilson, and utility man Gates Brown, who enjoyed a spectacular 1968 season as a pinch hitter. Pat Dobson recalls playing with some of his future Detroit teammates in Southern minor league cities, when hotels and restaurants were still segregated:

"Gates and Mickey Lolich and I and a lot of other guys played together in the Carolina League. When we went on the road they'd take the black guys to the other side of town. We'd say, 'That's a lot of horsebleep, that they have to do that.'

"The fact that we had been through the minor leagues together for five or six years made a lot of difference. We knew each other pretty well. We had been through things like that together. We had a lot of mutual respect for each other.

"That Tiger team was probably as cohesive a group on and off the field as you'll ever want to see. We were together all the time. On the road it was nothing for us to go out and there'd be ten or twelve guys together in some bar, black and white, shooting the bull together and talking about baseball.

"I probably learned as much about baseball off the field as on it. I hung around guys like Earl Wilson and McLain, and we'd talk about pitching, about how to pitch to hitters."

McLain was a naif about life and a layabout when it came to most kinds of work, but as a pitcher he was all business. He made the big leagues on the strength of his fastball, but as a rookie he worked to learn a good overhand curveball and a changeup under the tutelage of Frank Lary, a veteran pitcher, and Charlie Dressen, the Tiger manager.

In 1967 the Tigers hired Johnny Sain, who is probably the most honored pitching coach in baseball history. As a pitcher, Sain won twenty or more games four times. In 1948 he and Warren Spahn pitched the Boston Braves to a pennant and were immortalized in a rhyme that described the team's thin pitching rotation:

> Spahn and Sain,
> And two days of rain.

The Yankees hired Sain as pitching coach in 1961. He stayed three seasons, and the Yankees won three pennants. He went to the Minnesota Twins in 1965; the Twins won their first pennant. The Tigers hired him in 1967, and by 1968 the Tiger pitching staff had rounded into shape. Some managers considered Sain too independent, but as Casey Stengel once said, "You couldn't say that he ruined the staff anywhere."

McLain credits Sain with teaching him a slider that filled out his assortment of pitches. Sain credits McLain with dedication and hard work. Sain talked about McLain in the late summer of 1988 from his home in Illinois:

"Denny McLain was a real student of pitching and the game. Denny originally threw a fastball, curve, and a change. He learned to throw a slider-type control curve. They call it a slider, but the original slider is more like a fastball that runs a little bit. I call this particular pitch a hard curve. It is a control pitch. It's a pitch you can throw any time you want to. You can throw it when you're behind on the hitter, when the count is two and oh or three and one. That makes it an important pitch. Most batters are looking for a fastball on that count, and if you just do a little something to the ball, in lots of cases you'll be effective.

"It took Denny about a year to learn this particular pitch. Al Downing learned it in one day with the Yankees, and Whitey Ford in just one afternoon. That was in 1961, you remember, when Whitey won twenty-five games.

"When Denny added this other pitch, that gave him a complete assortment. He knew how to use them. Charlie Dressen was the manager in Detroit before I went over there. He was hard against the slider. Charlie died, you know, during the season in 1966. One day in '68 Denny was pitching in the bullpen, and he threw a good pitch like that—a slider, or hard curve, or some people call it a slurve—and he took his cap off and put it over his heart and looked up and said, 'You've got to forgive me, Charlie.'

"That was Denny. He had a sense of humor. He was all business on the mound. He was a great competitor. He could rise up and *do it.* In '68, in a very important game, he struck out Reggie Smith, Yastrzemski, and Harrelson. The tying run was on third and the winning run was on second. He rose to the occasion. He threw some outstanding fastballs in that situation.

"He could do that. He also threw an outstanding change. He did that an awful lot, like on two balls no strikes and three and one. He would do this with his other pitches, too.

"You know one time he jokingly said he was going to open up a restaurant and name it The Upper Deck, because they hit quite a few home runs off him. But mostly solo home runs. If a home run would beat him, they didn't hit the home run. That's the difference in a Spahn or a McLain. Consistent pitchers. They're able to get the hitter out when they need to get him out.

"A flake and a playboy? That side didn't show. Nobody liked success any more than he did. Think of the pressure he went through to win the thirty-one games. Every game was a World Series game. If he didn't have something unique he couldn't have done it. Denny was always just tops in his field. Preparing himself to pitch and learning to pitch and the whole bit."

McLain looked back on 1968 from his home in Fort Wayne, Indiana. It was September 1988, and McLain was just home from a publicity tour promoting his autobiography, *Strikeout.* At the time, his lawyer was negotiating with the government in an effort—ultimately successful—to protect McLain from a retrial that could have resulted in an additional prison sentence.

"The bottom line was I never walked a lot of guys. In '68 my control became better. I think with experience you have a tendency to relax more out there. You don't have the pressures, the tension of having to win a job.

"I picked up the little slider from Sain. I had a difficult time mastering that pitch, but once I got it, it was terrific. I had a good curveball, and changeup, and I threw sidearm a number of times during a ballgame. I was an 80 percent fastball pitcher. How fast? They said I consistently threw in the low to middle nineties.

"My out pitch? The fastball. You've got to remember, too, on occasion you don't have that good fastball. You'll have a different out pitch. Might be a slider. Might be an overhand curveball. Could be a changeup. Could be anything on a given night. But a majority of the time it certainly was the fastball.

"I had a full assortment. I played with a good ballclub. I had a good catcher, Bill Freehan. He knew how I wanted to pitch, and all he had to do, basically, was sit there. When you get a good groove and get good rhythm going the game can be real, real easy. It all boils down to rhythm."

15

"Gibson's got some kind of vicious desire. . . . Hell, he'd challenge Michael the Archangel, if he had to."

Bob Gibson had reason to expect a quick start in 1968. He was the best pitcher on the best team in baseball. At least, that's the way it looked, after the Cardinals' world championship showing of 1967. Gibson liked to pitch in the cool weather of April and May, and his arm, which tended to ache from the strain of his fastball pitching, was rested from a winter of ease.

His leg was healed, too, from an injury that had become a legend— yet another Gibson legend—among his teammates. On July 15, 1967, Gibson started against the Pirates. The Cards were in first place by four games, and Gibson was their leading pitcher with a record of ten wins, six losses.

The Cards took a 1–0 lead. Gibson didn't allow a hit for the first three innings. Roberto Clemente led off the fourth with a sharp line drive that hit Gibson in the right leg, below the knee. Players and fans close to the field heard a loud CRACK—ball against bone. Gibson collapsed in pain.

Bob Bauman, the Cardinal trainer, rushed out. Gibson said, "Just put a little tape on it, Doc, and I'll be ready to go again." Bauman was surprised. So was everyone else who saw—and heard—the accident.

Gibson went to his stretch and pitched. He walked Willie Stargell. He retired Bill Mazeroski on a fly ball. He went to a full count on Donn Clendenon, then threw ball four—and fell down as the leg gave way. Gibson himself described what happened in an interview with Neal Russo of the St. Louis *Post-Dispatch:*

"There was some sting when I got hit, but right after that it didn't hurt, so I figured I could keep pitching. On that last pitch, my leg felt as if it had been hit again, in the same spot. . . . The bone was broken when I got hit. The break was there, and when I twisted my weight on the leg with that last pitch, the two parts of the bone popped loose."

Gibson's account sounds clinically routine, but the incident made a strong impression on other players. Dal Maxvill, the Cardinal shortstop who later became the team's general manager, described it this way to Roger Angell of *The New Yorker*:

"That was the most extraordinary thing I ever saw in baseball—Gibby pitching to those batters with a broken leg. Everyone who was there that day remembered it afterward, for always, and every young pitcher who came onto our club while Gibson was still with us was told about it. We didn't have too many pitchers turning up with upset stomachs or hangnails on our team after that."

Gibson's teammates wondered if they could hold first place without him. Nelson Briles, twenty-four, was moved from the bullpen into Gibson's starting slot and won nine straight games. Dick Hughes, a rookie at twenty-nine, won sixteen, and a skinny young lefthander named Steve Carlton won fourteen. Gibson came back in September to win three more games. The Cardinals won the pennant by ten and one-half games and were favored to beat the Boston Red Sox in the World Series.

Because of his aching elbow, Gibson liked four days off between starts. To rest his arm, he didn't throw between starts, as most pitchers do. With Carlton, Briles, Hughes, and Ray Washburn, the 1967 Cardinals had a deep pitching staff, so Manager Red Schoendienst could have used Gibson just twice. But Gibson was such a great money pitcher—such a *winner*—that it was inevitable he would start three games, if the Series went to seven.

At Fenway Park, Gibson won the first game, 2–1. He got three days of rest, then won the fourth game, 6–0, in St. Louis. Briles beat the Red Sox in game three, so the Cards had a commanding lead of three games to one. But the Red Sox kept their "Impossible Dream" alive by winning the fifth and sixth games.

The finale pitted Gibson against Jim Lonborg, the Red Sox ace. Both had pitched two complete-game victories, and both were working on two days' rest. The game was no contest. Gibson pitched a three-hitter, hit a home run, and won, 7–2. Lonborg was knocked out in the seventh inning. Gibson wound up the Boston ninth by striking out slugger George Scott. In three games Gibson yielded only fourteen hits, tying a World Series record set by Christy Mathewson in the dead-ball year of 1905.

Later, Joe Torre, a strong hitter for the Atlanta Braves in 1968, described Gibson's three Series wins. "I watched him in the last World Series and he was so great that he even struck me out while I was watching the tube," Torre said. He later became a Cardinal teammate and friend of Gibson's. After Torre became manager of the Braves in 1982, he hired Gibson to coach Atlanta's young pitchers— not so much on how to *pitch,* Torre explained, as on how to *win.*

World Series heroics were not new to Gibson. In 1964 he lost his first World Series start to the Yankees. He came back four days later to beat the Yankees 5–2, and three days after that he started the seventh game. The Cardinals gave him a 6–0 lead, but Mickey Mantle hit a three-run homer for New York in the sixth inning. Johnny Keane, the St. Louis manager, visited the mound. "I'll go get 'em," Gibson told him.

Gibson was tired, but Keane left him in. "I wasn't going to take him out," he said. "I had a commitment to his heart." The Cardinals had a four-run lead going into the ninth, and Gibson, though laboring, had a few good fastballs left. He struck out Tom Tresh. Clete Boyer homered. He struck out John Blanchard—Gibson's thirty-first strikeout in that Series, a World Series record. Phil Linz homered. Gibson got Bobby Richardson on a pop fly for the final out.

Gibson had great pitching tools, and after 1964 he refined them. In 1965 he won twenty games for the first time. In 1966 he won twenty-one and posted an ERA of 2.44; the trend toward dominant pitching was under way in both major leagues. He was walking fewer batters and striking out more.

Tim McCarver, now a baseball broadcaster, caught Gibson for seven seasons, from 1963 through 1969. In 1988 McCarver's memories of Gibson remained vivid:

"It seemed like in 1967 and '68 everything came together as far as his control was concerned. His control was almost perfect. He could put the ball in a space of about four inches on the outside part of the plate with his slider or his fastball. Any time you wanted it. Plus he was so consistent with that pitch the umpires started giving him pitches just off the plate. Almost unreachable for righthanded hitters. When a lefthander came up he would raise it about six inches and put it right on the hands.

"His stuff was already established. Your stuff is more or less God-given. It's corraling it that makes the difference. He had an exploding fastball and a sweeping slider. His fastball sailed, almost like a natural slider. That was his best pitch."

If a hitter leaned over the plate, Gibson moved him back. In fact, the three top pitchers of the National League in 1968—Gibson, Don Drysdale of the Dodgers, and Juan Marichal of the Giants—all had superb control, and all hit a lot of batters.

In a filmed interview, Curt Flood, the Cardinal center fielder, recalled talking with Gibson about Babe Ruth's "called shot" home run in the 1932 World Series. Flood, quoting Gibson:

" 'If a guy stood in front of home plate when I was pitching and pointed where he was going to hit my next pitch, I would throw the next pitch in his left ear and out his right ear.' "

Gibson's competitive drive and his frightening pitching demeanor are legendary. He did not speak to opposing players, even when they were teammates on National League All-Star teams.

The 1982 *Baseball Research Journal* quoted McCarver this way:

"Listen, Gibson's got some kind of vicious desire, hasn't he? Tenacious. That's what he is, tenacious. He pitches on guts. You can see it. He challenges anybody. Hell, he'd challenge Michael the Archangel, if he had to."

Legends sometimes grow with time, so in July 1988 I asked McCarver whether Gibson's reputation was exaggerated.

"No part of Gibson's competitive drive can be overplayed. You had to experience that to really believe it. He was the fiercest competitor I've ever played with, or against, or seen since. You hated him, playing against him, and loved him, playing with him. He was a teammate that guys *revered.*"

* * *

In 1968 Don Sutton was twenty-three and was establishing himself as a strong young pitcher for the Los Angeles Dodgers. Twenty years later his hair was gray, but he was still pitching and was back with the Dodgers. He talked about Gibson while preparing to undergo therapy for an injury. A few weeks later, the Dodgers released Sutton. He pitched twenty-three seasons in the major leagues and won twenty games only once. Yet he racked up 324 victories, marking him as a model of longevity and consistency.

"I remember wondering if Gibson was human. He was one of the most dominant, intimidating pitchers you'd ever see. I thought Sandy Koufax had more velocity and a better curveball. But Gibson's demeanor on the mound was such that you were fairly certain you were in a fight. You were not in a ballgame. You were in a *fight*.

"Watching him pitch, I got the feeling that he was going out of his way to make us dislike him. He wouldn't talk to you. He'd walk right by you. I'd say, 'Nice game last night.' He wouldn't even look up. I was convinced he didn't like anybody in baseball.

"You were going to have to battle for your part of the plate, for the strike zone. Even a pitcher, hitting. He drilled me. He was going to overpower you. He was going to dominate you. I thought he gave a new meaning to the term 'black power.' "

"Black Power" described a new phase of the civil rights movement that reached a peak in 1968. Many blacks had become impatient with the nonviolent tactics and integrationist goals articulated by Martin Luther King. King's assassination exacerbated their anger. These blacks, most of them young, wore their racial hostility with pride and sought no friendships among whites, whom they derided as "honkies." Policemen were "pigs"—an enemy force in black neighborhoods. The black power leaders were Malcolm X and, for the most radical blacks, Eldridge Cleaver and Huey Newton of the Black Panthers. Cleaver wrote a controversial book, *Soul on Ice* (McGraw-Hill, New York, 1968), while in prison for allegedly raping a white woman. Newton was convicted of manslaughter in the death of an Oakland policeman.

Many blacks adapted the trappings of the black power movement without advocating violence. Dashikis became fashionable. Black college students demonstrated for more black admissions and for courses in black history and culture. Lew Alcindor, soon to be Kareem Abdul-Jabbar, wore an African "dignity robe" as he left the dressing room after leading UCLA to the 1968 NCAA basketball championship, the team's second straight.

Black protests swirled around the 1968 Olympic Games in Mexico City. Militant black protestors were banned from the Games. Several black stars refused to play for the U.S. basketball team, which nevertheless won a gold medal. Lee Evans, Larry James, and Ron Freeman, all black Americans, finished first, second, and third, respectively, in the four-hundred-meter run. In a black power protest, they wore black berets to the awards presentation. They were not disciplined, but officials came down hard on Tommy Smith and John Carlos, who finished first and third in the two-hundred-meter run. They were suspended from the Games and expelled from the Olympic Village after wearing black gloves and black scarves to the awards ceremony and raising their fists in the black power salute as "The Star-Spangled Banner" was played.

The Olympic controversy prompted sportswriters to ask black ballplayers about race relations in the major leagues. Frank Robinson, the Oriole slugger, said it was high time blacks were hired as managers and in front-office positions—jobs in which he eventually pioneered. Jackie Robinson said that Willie Mays and other black stars should devote more effort to the civil rights cause. Mays replied that he spoke frequently to youth groups and contributed time to the Job Corps.

Veterans Ernie Banks of the Cubs and Lee Maye of the Indians said things had improved. "I know the brothers in other professional sports and, from what I can tell, baseball has come the farthest in race relations—with fans and players," Maye said. "But there always will be some resentment, or a quiet crack now and then, and some unfairness still exists."

Perhaps the most convincing example of progress was cited by Willie Smith of the Indians, who praised fellow black teammate Leon Wagner. "Leon keeps laughing and joking," Smith said. "He calls us spooks and white players whiteys. He brings it out into the open. This is the way it is among all the players in the game."

Wagner himself told a frightening story about his early minor league experiences. "It was bad, man, in the beginning," he said. "In Greensboro, a guy was hiding out behind the left field stands. He pointed a shotgun at me and yelled, 'Nigger, I'm going to fill you with shot if you catch one ball out here.' "

Wagner let the first fly ball drop at his feet. "Listen, man, I was only nineteen, and I was afraid to test that cat's aim," he told sportswriter Bob Sudyk. "When I got into the dugout, the manager really chewed me out. I told him about the man with the gun. They sent the cops out there and took him to jail."

Blacks had been excelling in sports ever since they were given an opportunity, and in 1968 Arthur Ashe, twenty-five, became the first black male to win a major tennis tournament. He beat Tom Okker of the Netherlands in the final of the U.S. Open. For the first time, the famed tournament at Forest Hills admitted professionals and paid prize money. But Ashe was an Army lieutenant and played tennis as an amateur. Okker got the fourteen-thousand-dollar first prize.

Public officials were aware of the symbolic importance of black athletic stars. President Johnson named Bob Gibson to his Citizens Advisory Board on Youth Opportunity.

Gibson came across to some players and sportswriters as an angry black, but he was not one to copy anyone else's way of expressing his attitudes. He was as proudly individualistic as a person can be. Gibson acknowledged in his autobiography that he had a racial chip on his shoulder. He had reason. His mother, widowed before Bob was born, worked as a laundress to raise her seven children in the black ghetto of Omaha, Nebraska. Gibson was a high school basketball star and yearned for a basketball scholarship to the University of Indiana. His high school coach wrote to Indiana in his behalf (this was 1952) but Indiana turned him down, explaining that it had filled its quota of Negroes—one.

Gibson got a basketball scholarship at Creighton University in Omaha, where he was the team's star and its only black player. The team traveled to Tulsa, Oklahoma, when Gibson was a sophomore, and he was not allowed to stay in the same hotel with his white teammates or eat in the same restaurant.

After finishing college, Gibson signed two four-thousand-dollar contracts in 1957—one to pitch for the Cardinals' farm team in

Omaha, the other to play basketball for the Harlem Globetrotters once the baseball season was over. Gibson enjoyed the basketball but not the clowning, and after one season he went along with the Cardinals' request that he stick to baseball.

The Cardinals invited Gibson to spring training at St. Petersburg, Florida, in 1958, and he walked into the team hotel, assuming a room was reserved for him. But the hotel was for whites only; Gibson was ushered out a side door and sent to the city's black section to room with a black family. Curt Flood was one of his housemates.

Gibson made the Cardinals in 1960, and gradually developed into a star, winning 13 games in 1961 and, in subsequent years, 15, 18, 19, 20, and 21. He was often unfriendly to sportswriters and uncooperative to fans seeking autographs. "I owe the public just one thing—a good performance," he said.

In 1968 Bob Addie of the Washington *Post* found Gibson looking through mail that had accumulated while the Cardinals were on the road. "Do you want to know why I get surly and bitter sometimes?" Gibson asked him. "Take a look at some of the mail I get. It's typical, but I've got some worse than that."

The letter said, "Why don't you and the other blackbirds on the Cardinals move to Africa where you belong? If you and the other darkies can't read this because of your low mentality, get one of the white players to do it."

Gibson said to Addie, "I walk on the field and I'm upset after reading mail like this. I know I snap at reporters and they call me sullen and uncooperative. It's a relief to go on the field. The pressure is in here—in these letters—the day-to-day pressure of those people on the outside. There is no pressure in a baseball game. It's clean and competitive. There is honesty in performance."

Yet Gibson was friendly to some sportswriters. Robert L. Burnes of the St. Louis *Globe-Democrat* called him "an excellent subject for an interview." And among his teammates, Gibson was, as McCarver said, more than popular. His winning attitude inspired other players. He was a clubhouse leader in the kind of playful pranks that athletes enjoy. Gibson palled around with white and Latin players as well as blacks, and said that the team succeeded partly because the Cardinal players were not divided into cliques. "We don't have three separate groups like some clubs, where the Negro guys stay together, the

Spanish guys stay together, and the white guys stay together," he wrote in his 1968 autobiography, *From Ghetto to Glory* (Prentice-Hall, Englewood Cliffs, New Jersey).

Gibson's intensity was often mistaken for hostility. Mike Shannon was the Cardinal third baseman in 1968; twenty years later he was a radio sportscaster on the Cardinal network. He talked about Gibson shortly before a Cardinal game in 1988:

"Gibson never spoke to anyone on game day, when he was pitching. He didn't speak to *anybody*. We just simply ignored him. That's the way he got himself prepared, by talking to himself and developing his tenacity. You might call it what you want—nasty or whatever—but what he was doing was concentrating. That was the great thing about Gibson. I don't think that Gibson wanted to *win* so much. He despised *losing*. There's a difference. He took winning in stride. It was no big deal to Bob. He expected it. What he despised—I mean *despised*—was losing.

"When he was a youngster he was a scrawny little kid. He was sickly. Got his butt kicked every day. As a freshman in high school he was something like five nine and weighed 120 or 125 pounds. Three or four years later he was six one, 175 pounds. Once Gibson grew up, it was kind of like time for him to kick the bully on the block.

"Bob Gibson is not a fellow who dislikes human beings. But he doesn't want any human being to beat him. When he beats you he's fine. Go out to dinner with him, sit down, think he's the nicest guy in the world. But prior to him beating you, you don't want to be around him.

"That team was unbelievably cohesive. The phenomenal thing is, almost everyone on that team is successful in life after baseball. Start with me at third. I got into this radio business. The shortstop was Maxvill. He's the Cardinal general manager. The second baseman was Javier. He does extremely well in his home country. He's a very big man down there. Gibson is in radio here in St. Louis, and in business back in Omaha.

"McCarver you know about. Lou Brock and Curt Flood are doing well. Just about everywhere you look the people off that ballclub are very successful. Very high-quality, high-character people. We'd go out at night to a restaurant or a bar. There'd be twelve, fifteen of us!

Hack Wilson, Rogers Hornsby, and Kiki Cuyler (left to right), *batting stars of the 1930 Chicago Cubs. This picture was taken just a couple of days after Hornsby succeeded Joe McCarthy as Cub manager during the final week of the 1930 season. The smiles didn't last long: Wilson and Hornsby feuded, and Wilson never again approached his achievements of 1930, when he hit 56 homers, drove in 190 runs, and batted .356. (Library of Congress)*

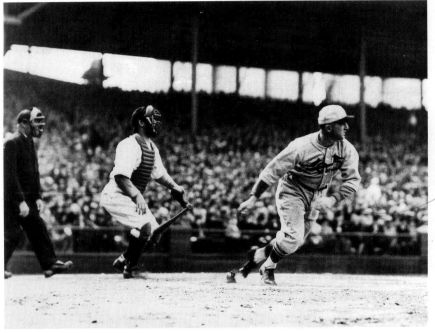

Three future Hall of Famers open the 1930 season at Wrigley Field. Bill Klem is the umpire, Gabby Hartnett the Cub catcher, and Frankie Frisch of the Cardinals the batter. (Library of Congress)

Babe Herman and Hack Wilson compare their sticks during a timeout in the 1930 season. Babe hit .393 that year and did not win the National League batting crown! Bill Terry did with .401.

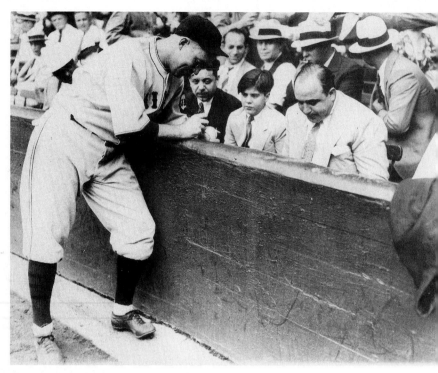

This is the picture that outraged Commissioner Landis. Here's the original caption transmitted with the picture by the Associated Press on September 9, 1931:

AL CAPONE TAKES HIS SON TO THE BALL GAME

Surrounded by his watchful lieutenants, Chicago's gang chief and his 12-year-old son, Al Jr., get Gabby Hartnett of the Cubs to autograph a baseball just before the Cubs defeat the White Sox, 3 to 0, in a charity games before 35,000 spectators at Comiskey Park, Chicago, Sept. 9. Pictures of Capone before the public are not frequent, and a pose with his son is rare. He affectionately calls the boy "Sonny." Note the watchfulness of one of his bodyguards directly behind him. A pop-corn vendor evidently rubbed his shoulder and he looks ready to protect his chief.

Babe Ruth was known to breakfast on steak, eggs, potatoes, and gin with orange juice, but to kids he was a Quaker Puffed Wheat man. (The Ted Patterson Collection, Craig Daniels. Courtesy of the Quaker Oats Company)

Carl Hubbell won seventeen games in 1930 but complained that manager John McGraw wouldn't let him throw a fastball. (The Ted Patterson Collection, Craig Daniels. Reprinted with the permission of General Mills, Inc.)

Sparky Adams, the Cardinal infielder, started the double play that turned the 1930 pennant race. He recalled it in 1988 at the age of ninety-three. (The Ted Patterson Collection, Craig Daniels)

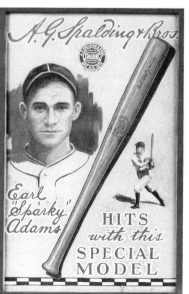

Oh Yes, The "A's" Did Win The World Series

Judge Kenesaw Mountain Landis, czar of baseball, proves it (not that anyone had doubts) by awarding championship medals at Shibe Park. Photo
shows Landis presenting medal to Al Simmons, stellar slugger, who captured American League batting honors last year. At present Washington
club is battling to keep "A's" out of third series.

WATCH THIS BULLETIN FOR LATEST NEWS

*Before the television age store windows used to
display news pictures like this one. That's Lefty
Grove looking straight at the camera from the
second row. (The Ted Patterson Collection, Craig
Daniels)*

*Al Lopez broke in as a catcher with the Brooklyn
Dodgers in 1928. In 1930 he batted .309,
catching 126 games for the likes of Dazzy Vance
and Dolf Luque.*

Mike Shannon, Steve Carlton, and Tim McCarver. Carlton was twenty-three years old in 1968. In 1971 he won twenty games for the first time, and the Cardinals traded him to the Phillies for Rick Wise. (St. Louis Cardinals)

Branch Rickey with two of his favorite props: a cigar and a telephone. (St. Louis Cardinals)

Bob Gibson and Orlando Cepeda exchange high-fives. Gibson's competitive fire made him a favorite of teammates, and the bane of opponents. (St. Louis Cardinals)

Bob Gibson won the Cy Young Award in 1968, with his microscopic 1.12 ERA. He also recorded 268 strikeouts, only 62 walks, and 13 shutouts in 304.2 innings of work. (St. Louis Cardinals)

Denny McLain, the brash thirty-one-game winner of 1968, and Denny McLain the up-and-coming entertainer who between starts flew his own airplane to nightclub engagements.

Bill Freehan hugs Mickey Lolich as the lefthander completes a magnificent 4–1 triumph over the Cardinals in the deciding seventh game of the 1968 World Series. He recorded three wins for the series, twenty-seven innings pitched, twenty-one strikeouts, and an ERA of 1.67.

With his distinctively high leg kick, Juan Marichal went 26–9 in 1968. He also racked up a 2.43 ERA, 218 strikeouts, and only 46 walks in his league-leading 325.2 innings pitched. Here he is pictured during his 1963 no-hitter against the Houston Colt 45s.

Pitching against the Phillies on June 8, 1968, Don Drysdale broke Walter Johnson's record by completing 58⅓ consecutive shutout innings. Drysdale finished the 1968 season with a 2.15 ERA and 8 shutouts.

Black, white, Latin, it didn't matter. There wasn't any color. There wasn't any language barrier. We didn't even think about it. They were teammates!"

Shannon was right about Gibson's sickly childhood. In 1964 his mother, Mrs. Victoria Bolden, gave this account to the *New York Times:*

"He was born sick. And he got sicker. He had rickets, hay fever, asthma, pneumonia and a rheumatic heart. I hardly let him out of the house until he was four years old.

"I never thought he'd make it. Neither did he. When he was three and a half he got pneumonia. He was so weak we had to carry him into a hospital, bundled in a blanket. I'll never forget that moment. His oldest brother, Leroy, was holding him. Bob looked up at Leroy and asked, 'Am I going to die?' Leroy looked down and said, 'You'll make it. And when you come home I'll get you a baseball glove and bat.' "

In 1968 Gibson had an impressive cast of teammates. Three of the team's stars—Gibson, and outfielders Lou Brock and Curt Flood—were black. Two others—first baseman Orlando Cepeda and second baseman Julian Javier—were Latin. It was hard to remember that only twenty-one years before, the Cardinals had threatened to strike rather than play against Jackie Robinson, and the city of St. Louis had been considered so Southern in attitude that the Cardinals had hesitated to follow Brooklyn's lead in scouting and signing black players.

Stan Musial often said that the Cardinals' reluctance to recruit blacks cost the team several pennants in the late 1940s and 1950s. The fear that St. Louis fans would not support an integrated team turned out to be groundless. The last all-white Cardinal champions drew 1,061,807 home fans in 1946. The team moved to its new riverfront ballpark, Busch Stadium, in 1966, and in both 1967 and 1968 the Cardinals of Gibson, Brock, Flood, Cepeda, and Javier drew more than 2 million at home.

The team was solid. A one-sided trade brought the Cardinals right fielder Roger Maris, who was unhappy with the Yankees despite his home-run record. He fit in well with the Cardinals and, though he no longer could hit with consistent power, played his usual all-around game—good hit, good field, good run. Maris had talked of retiring, but changed his mind. "What makes it possible to continue is the feeling on this Cardinal club," he said. "Everybody pulls for everybody else. It's a great club, close to a perfect club."

Another deft trade brought Cepeda, whom the Giants found expendable because they didn't trust his injured knee (it healed) and because they could play only one man at first base, and his name was Willie McCovey. In 1967 Cepeda hit twenty-five homers for the Cardinals, led the league in RBI, and was voted the National League MVP.

McCarver was considered the National League's best catcher, although in 1968 rookie Johnny Bench gave him a run. Javier and Dal Maxvill made up a superior double-play combination. The Cardinals needed a third baseman, and after acquiring Maris in 1967 they made one out of their right fielder, Mike Shannon.

Red Schoendienst played nineteen years in the major leagues, sixteen of them with the Cardinals. A graceful fielder and a sharp switch-hitter, he was the National League's reigning all-star at second base for most of his career. Schoendienst was named Cardinal manager in 1965. He managed the team for thirteen seasons, including the pennant years of 1967 and 1968. He then became a Cardinal coach. In 1988 he was sixty-five years old and still coaching. Pouring sweat from his daily session of hitting practice ground balls to the infielders, Schoendienst sat in the Cardinal dugout before a July 1988 game and talked about his championship team of twenty years before:

"Mike Shannon was our right fielder so we had to move him. He had enough guts so we thought he could play third. We took him down to spring training early. I hit him a lot of ground balls. I would hit B-Bs down to him at third base. He'd dive and try to come up throwing. He was just a tough ballplayer. He got big hits for us, along with Maris in right field and Cepeda. We had Flood, who could run down that ball in center field, and Lou Brock. We had a lot of speed in the outfield. Brock led off for us. He could steal bases, he could hit with power. He could *run*.

"We needed a first baseman bad and we were fortunate to get Cepeda. They called us 'El Birdos' because of Cepeda, but I think Joe

Schultz, my third-base coach, was the one that gave El Birdos their name.

"Roger Maris, from the Yankees, knew how to play. He was a real good ballplayer. He'd move the runner around.

"We had Maxvill at shortstop. The two most underrated ballplayers I've seen in baseball were Maxvill and George Kurowski [the Cardinals' third baseman for most of the 1940s]. They could play hard. They knew how to play. Maxvill got big hits for us. Outstanding shortstop. Knew how to win.

"We had Javier playing second, a good second baseman. Tim McCarver was the catcher. He helped the manager so much. He understood the game. How to pitch to everybody. Once you went over the hitters, you knew he remembered it. He got along good with the pitchers. It helps to have a great catcher like that.

"Tim caught every day for years and years, so I figured I'd better give this guy a little rest. We got John Edwards that year, and he did an outstanding job. Fatigue is a big thing in this game. A lot of times when you're not hitting it's because you're getting a little tired, especially after the All-Star Game. The time to rest them is before, so you won't wear them out and they'll be ready the last six weeks of the season. Say with an off-day tomorrow, you can give him today off. He gets two days off and only misses one game.

"The competitive spirit on the ballclub grinds down in the last month or six weeks of the season. You're bearing down. You're a game out, or a game in front. Clubs that aren't in the race are bringing up young guys. You can't play your young guys out of the minor leagues. You've got to go with what you have.

"That ballclub I had in '67 and '68, they all knew how to play. They had the experience. Once they were out on the ballfield they were hard players. They worked hard. They were a good bunch of guys. Put 'em out and let 'em play."

As the 1968 season opened, Gibson was pitching well. But that powerful Cardinal lineup wasn't hitting. Gibson lost to Ferguson Jenkins, the Cub ace. He edged Bob Veale, the Pirate fastballer, 2–1. He beat the Houston Astros 3–1 in eleven innings, and he stopped Tom Seaver and the New York Mets 2–1 in ten innings. Woody Fryman of the Phils edged Gibson 1–0 in ten innings, Gaylord Perry of the Giants beat him 3–1 in ten, and Larry Dierker of the Astros defeated him 3–2. Gibson yielded the Dodgers one hit and no runs in eight innings, but he left for a pinch hitter and the Dodgers wound up winning, 2–0, behind Don Drysdale. Through nine starts in April and May, Gibson was never knocked out, never hit hard. He allowed seventeen runs, only twelve of them earned. His ERA was 1.33. He won three games and lost four.

Gibson didn't complain, at least to the press. He reminded writers that the Cardinal hitters had supported him in the past. Gibson was a pretty good hitter himself, but wasn't connecting. He tried switch-hitting, which he had done in college and the minor leagues. "I've got to do something about that nasty slider they throw me," he said.

Behind superb pitching, the Cardinals won fourteen of their first nineteen games. But they then dropped eleven of thirteen and slipped to fourth place, three games out of first. In one stretch of eight games they scored only eleven runs, losing seven of the contests. On May 23 they stranded fifteen runners and lost to the Dodgers in eleven innings, 3–2.

Cepeda, Shannon, and McCarver, supposedly the team's power hitters, were not contributing. In one stretch of twelve games, Cepeda left twenty-seven runners on base. Schoendienst benched all three power hitters. Lou Brock was neither hitting nor running; in the season's first forty-five games, he stole only five bases.

"When's the next bat day at the ballpark?" cracked Schoendienst. "Maybe we can do better with those Little League bats. We'd better lock up our own." In both leagues, other managers were saying much the same thing.

16

"You show me a pitcher who can't throw inside and I'm going to show you a loser."

For much of his career, Don Drysdale, for all his skill and fortitude, was The Other Guy on the Dodger pitching staff. He won the Cy Young Award in 1962, but for the next four seasons he was overshadowed by a teammate and friend named Sandy Koufax.

Koufax and Drysdale epitomized the shift from power to pitching that began in the early 1960s. No team changed more radically than the Dodgers. In cozy Ebbets Field, the slugging Dodgers won six pennants between 1947 and 1956. They moved to Los Angeles in 1958 and won a pennant in 1959 while playing at Los Angeles Coliseum, with its absurdly short left field wall—252 feet from home plate.

In 1962 the Dodgers moved to spacious Dodger Stadium, and Maury Wills stole 104 bases, breaking Ty Cobb's record of 96 and beating Jackie Robinson's best mark by a margin of almost three to one. Almost overnight, the Dodgers switched their emphasis to speed, pitching, and defense. To be sure, much of this resulted from a gradual change in personnel; Walt Alston, the manager, would have welcomed a few sluggers.

But the Dodger changes reflected changes that were taking place throughout baseball. Ballparks were bigger, defensive play had improved, pitching was better, and sluggers were vulnerable to the wider variety of pitches that many pitchers had learned to throw. Two years after Roger Maris hit sixty-one home runs in 1961 to break Babe Ruth's record of sixty, baseball enlarged the strike zone to restrict slugging.

The Dodgers were quick learners. In 1962 they tied for first place and lost a playoff to the San Francisco Giants; the Dodgers would have won outright had Koufax not lost time with a finger ailment. They won pennants in 1963, 1965, and 1966, even though their hitting was feeble. "I hate to lose to them," said pitcher Al McBean of the Pirates. "It's like being beaten by a Triple-A team. . . . Those Ping-Pong hitters getting all that money. They aren't even big leaguers."

But they had a couple of big leaguers in Koufax and Drysdale, the team's number one and number two men. Take a look at their records from 1962, the first year at Chavez Ravine, through 1966, Koufax's final year as a pitcher (asterisk means led league; CY means Cy Young Award, which then was given to only one pitcher in baseball, not one in each league as it has been since 1967):

	Koufax			*Drysdale*		
Year	W	L	ERA	W	L	ERA
1962	14	7	2.54*	25*	9	2.83 CY
1963	25*	5	1.88* CY	19	17	2.63
1964	19	5	1.74*	18	16	2.18
1965	26*	8	2.04* CY	23	12	2.77
1966	27*	9	1.73* CY	13	16	3.42

No one else—not even Lefty Grove—ever won five straight ERA championships. When Koufax retired after the 1966 season to avoid permanent injury to his arthritic left elbow, the Dodgers sank from first place to eighth. Drysdale's record in 1967 was thirteen and sixteen, but in thirteen of his losses the Dodgers scored a total of fifteen runs.

By 1968 Drysdale was the team's only survivor from Ebbets Field, and he longed for the good old days. "We had some hitters in Brooklyn, I'll tell you that," he told an interviewer in early 1968. "Any time I was five runs down, I expected to win it—with Duke Snider, Gil Hodges, Roy Campanella, Jackie Robinson, Carl Furillo, Pee Wee Reese, Jim Gilliam, and all the rest."

But Big D, as other players called him, had adjusted. "Every time I go out there, I'm trying to pitch a shutout," he said. "If I give up a run, I hope we'll get one. If I give up two, I'm hoping we'll get two."

That was the right attitude for the Dodgers, particularly in 1968. Drysdale lost three of his first four decisions. Then the Dodgers got a run for him, and he won, 1–0. Next time out they got him another run, and again he won, 1–0. He came up against Gibson May 22. Neither starter allowed a run, but after Gibson went out for a pinch hitter the Dodgers scored twice: 2–0, Los Angeles.

Drysdale's fourth straight shutout was a laughter, 5–0. Writers scurried to the record books and found that the record for consecutive shutouts was five, set by Doc White of the White Sox in 1904. Here it was nearly a half-century after the lively ball supposedly put offense on top to stay, and the sudden rise of pitching, personified by Drysdale, was threatening an ancient record from the dead-ball era.

Drysdale had the perfect setting as he went after his fifth straight shutout on May 31. The Dodgers were playing at home against their arch-rivals, the Giants. To tie White's record, Drysdale would have to get by Willie Mays and Willie McCovey. A crowd of 46,067 came to Dodger Stadium for the spectacle, and the fans got their money's worth.

The action, appropriately, came in the ninth inning. The Dodgers led, 3–0; three outs to go. But Drysdale lost his usually superb control. He walked McCovey on a three-and-two pitch, yielded a single to Jim Ray Hart, and walked Dave Marshall. Bases loaded, nobody out.

Dick Dietz, a catcher and righthanded batter, took Drysdale to two and two. Drysdale threw an inside pitch. It hit Dietz on the left elbow. What a way to end the pursuit!

But it did not end. Without hesitation, the home-plate umpire, Harry Wendelstedt, called "Ball three!" Dietz, he said, hadn't tried to get out of the way, as the rules require a batter to do in order to be awarded first base. The rule is firm, though rarely invoked, and the call depends entirely on the umpire's judgment. Dietz and Herman Franks, the Giant manager, argued long and hard; Franks was thrown out of the game.

In an interview twenty years later, Drysdale, a broadcaster for the Dodgers, recalled that pitch to Dick Dietz:

"I threw a slider. Dick went into the pitch and the ball hit him. As soon as Wendelstedt called him back I knew why, because I knew the rule.

"Hodges and I used to lay in bed at night and read the rule book. We'd figure out ways to beat the rules. We'd get that book, *Knotty Problems of Baseball,* and we would lay in bed and he'd say, 'OK, here's one. What would you do here?' We'd read the Blue Book. The rules of baseball as far as ownership is concerned. The option rules and all that.

"So as soon as he called it, I knew what it was. I don't know what Dietz was trying to do. But I know he went in and he didn't make a real legitimate attempt to get out of the way. It's not a call that's called a lot. But I've seen a couple of calls that are not even in the rule book.

"Herman Franks, my God, he ranted and raved, and he got kicked out. Even to this day, he'll say, 'Ah, Goddam, if it wasn't for that Wendelstedt . . .' And I say, 'Bull, Herman, if you were such a great manager, you still had the bases loaded and nobody out. How the hell did we get you out?'

"That call made the count three and two. He fouled off a pitch or two after that. There was no room for air. I couldn't work on him. He hit a shallow fly ball to left. The next guy hit a ground ball to Parker, and he forced the guy at the plate. The next guy popped up to Parker and the game was over." (Wes Parker was the Dodger first baseman.)

Drysdale was a pitcher's pitcher, a strong fastballer who believed in using every tool in the box. One tool, exemplified by the controversial pitch to Dietz, was the brushback—this great control pitcher led the league in hit batsmen five times, and hit more batters than any other pitcher of the twentieth century. Another was the greaseball or spitball. Drysdale, a friendly and cheerful man, laughs and shakes his head when you ask him whether he threw any kind of illegal pitch, but testimony around the league is unanimous on the side of guilt—or credit, from a pitcher's viewpoint.

Tim McCarver, the Cardinal catcher turned baseball broadcaster, recalled an encounter with Drysdale and the Dodger catcher, John Roseboro:

"I remember a home run I hit off Drysdale. I think it was the only one I got off him. It wrapped right inside the foul pole at Dodger Stadium. I came up the next time, and Roseboro winked at me, and he said, 'That last one was a wet one that didn't wet.' "

After the Cubs fell victim to one of the shutouts in Drysdale's streak, Leo Durocher, the Chicago manager, urged the umpires to search him for grease. The umps refused. "I won't file a formal protest," said Durocher, "but I'm going to get myself ten spitball pitchers."

Drysdale pitched a sixth shutout to break White's record, but one record remained: Walter Johnson's string of 55⅔ consecutive scoreless innings, set in 1913. On June 8, 1968, Drysdale faced the Phillies. Once again, the limelight was friendly—an enthusiastic Los Angeles crowd of fifty-five thousand. Gene Mauch, the Phils' manager, stacked his lineup with six lefthanded hitters and coached third base himself to keep an eye on the big Dodger ace.

If he could stop the Phillies for 2⅓ innings, Drysdale would have the record. He walked Johnny Briggs in the first inning, but got out of the inning with the help of a fine play by shortstop Zoilo Versalles. Drysdale put down the Phils quickly in the second inning, tying Johnson's mark. Leading off the Philadelphia third, Roberto Pena grounded out. The fans gave Drysdale a big hand. He retired the next two batters and walked toward the dugout, bathed in applause.

But Augie Donatelli, the plate umpire, stopped him. The fans saw the little umpire talk to Drysdale. They saw Drysdale talk back. Then Donatelli took off Drysdale's cap—he almost had to jump to reach it. He looked at the cap, reached up, and felt Drysdale's hair. The fans booed. Drysdale disappeared into the dugout.

He came out for the fourth and stopped the Phils again. In the Philadelphia fifth, Tony Taylor and Clay Dalrymple led off with singles, Taylor reaching third. Drysdale brushed Pena back and then struck him out, but Howie Bedell flied to left field and Taylor scored after the catch. That broke Drysdale's streak of scoreless innings at an amazing 58⅔. The Phils knocked him out in the seventh, but the Dodgers won.

Record keepers have since stopped counting partial innings in pitching streaks, so Drysdale's scoreless streak is in the books at 58 innings even. In 1988 Orel Hershiser of the Dodgers pitched 59 straight scoreless innings to break Drysdale's record. Drysdale was on hand broadcasting the game and cheering Hershiser on.

After Drysdale's record-breaking game, sportswriters asked Donatelli what the inspection was all about. He said he warned Drysdale against throwing a greaseball and told him to keep his hands away from the back of his head. Drysdale, he said, assured him that the only substance on the back of his head was sweat.

In retirement, Donatelli gave a more vivid account twenty years later:

"I said, 'Don, you're throwing the greaseball.' He said, 'Oh, no, Augie, I'm not throwing a greaseball.' I was standing about three feet from him at least. I said, 'I smell the Vaseline from here.' He said, 'Oh no, you don't mean that.' I said, 'The hell I don't.'

"It got in a discussion where I had to do something. He's a big guy, six six or six seven. I reached up and grabbed his cap and came down with a handful of Vaseline. And it smelled. He said, 'All right, what do you want me to do?' I said, 'Don't go any higher than your shoulders [with your hands].' He didn't, and the Phillies got [knocked] him out of there."

Drysdale, relaxed in a hotel room in St. Louis while awaiting his broadcasting chores for the evening, also was interviewed in 1988:

"I was walking off the mound when the inning was over. Augie Donatelli was the home-plate umpire. As I got by the foul line at third base, why, Augie came over and Goddam, he jumped up and he grabbed my cap and he's running his fingers through my hair.

"I said, 'Augie, what the hell are you doing?' He says, 'I'm checking you.' I said, 'For what?' He said, 'Don't worry. Just shut up. I'm checking you.'

"I said, 'Well, Goddam, Augie, usually when someone rubs their fingers through my hair I get a kiss with it.' He said, 'Get the hell out of here. You're OK with me.' And after the game was over, there was never a word."

At that point, I told Drysdale about Donatelli's account. Drysdale laughed uproariously.

"I don't remember Augie saying that. I tell you what. It startled me so much because I didn't know what he was doing. He caught me completely off guard when he grabbed my cap. I don't remember him saying that, but if he said so, maybe he did.

"Did I use Vaseline? No. I didn't. Vaseline! How the hell do you smell Vaseline to start with? Did I ever use it? No.

"You know what? I used to do a commercial for Vitalis. Herman Franks and I did it, at Candlestick Park. Herman comes running out of the dugout yelling 'Greaseball!' Running at the umpires, and they get in a hell of an argument. It was really a conversation piece. People would say to me, 'Hey, you still using that greasy kid stuff?' Because that was part of the commercial. As a matter of fact, at a couple of old-timers games when I pitched, why Durocher or Mays brought out a pillow that was a Vitalis pillow. Maybe Augie was thinking back to that—'Greaseball, greaseball!'

"No, I threw sinkers and things like that. Legal pitches.

"I'm not a record-conscious person. I didn't really think anything about the shutout streak until after the fourth game, in Houston. When I went out, I tried to work a game. We didn't score runs. We knew that. If you gave up three runs you were probably going to get beat. I broke down every game. I tried to take it pitch by pitch, hitter by hitter, and inning by inning. So when I got the first shutout it was no big deal. I had had shutouts before. The second one was no big deal. You look at the pitchers I beat and damn sure they could turn around and beat my ass one to nothing as well as I could beat theirs. Gibson, and Bunning, and Fergie Jenkins, Larry Dierker, and Larry Jackson.

"After the fourth game the writers evidently got up there in the booth and said, 'That's four shutouts in a row. What the hell! What's the record on that?' Then they came down and said, 'You're only one away from Doc White.'

"I said, 'Who the hell was Doc White?' And they said, 'Back in 1904, with the White Sox.' I said, 'Well, so be it.'

"Then it went on. The last game I was conscious of it. But it was nothing like the media coverage when Pete Rose was going for his record. We didn't have the media coverage at that time that they have today. Today everything is on cable television. You got ESPN out there. You got many more writers covering the ballclubs now, especially in LA and major cities like that.

"After it was over, Mr. O'Malley gave my wife a beautiful strand of fifty-eight pearls, and the two-thirds was the locket, made out of diamonds and emeralds."

The pitchers of 1930 and 1968 express scorn and distress at the current restrictions on throwing at hitters—or, as pitchers express it, pitching inside. Surprisingly, hitters from those past seasons also disdain the present rule, under which a pitcher is warned when he first throws at a batter, and ejected and fined for a second such pitch. No one speaks better for the old practice than Don Drysdale:

"You show me a pitcher who can't throw inside and I'm going to show you a loser. I don't advocate knocking a hitter down. I don't advocate hitting a hitter. I hit a lot of hitters, but my fastball tailed. It moved in to a righthanded hitter. If I'm thinking 'inside' and you're guessing with me, thinking 'outside,' and you start diving over that plate, and I'm coming inside, you've got one hell of a chance of being hit. It's just that plain and simple.

"You have to move a hitter off the plate. The toughest pitch for a hitter to hit is the pitch down and away from him. That down and away pitch is your out pitch. If you give that hitter a false sense of security so that he never anticipates a pitch being thrown inside, then he'll be diving outside to take away that pitch, which should be an out pitch for you. They'll go out and take away your out pitch! What the hell have you got left?

"So you have to pitch inside. If intimidation works, let it be an ally. I think intimidation is a word that can be used in all professional sports. Hell, it's used in the business world. I've gone into an office where the darn guy behind the desk is sitting up higher and in a bigger chair, and you're sitting in a lower chair.

"One day in San Francisco Frank Secory was umping behind the plate. Mays was hitting. Willie was the type of hitter who would go down on anything close. He would go down because he wasn't going to take any chances whatsoever. That was no disrespect to the pitcher. It was just the way Willie was.

"But that incites the fans. 'Jesus Christ, he's knocking Mays down!' That's why they think that Mays and I had these great battles through the years. Hell, Willie and I are best of friends. We laugh about it. I don't think I ever hit Mays. You couldn't hit him. Oh, boy, he was quick as a cat.

"I'm pitching to Mays and I throw a pitch that's up and in, and he goes right flat on his ass. Roseboro catches the ball and throws it back. Secory comes out and he says, 'That's fifty dollars.'

"I said, 'For what?' He says, 'For knocking Mays down.' I said, 'Frank, Jesus Christ. The ball wasn't even close. Roseboro caught the ball. He never had to get out of a crouch.'

"He said, 'That's all right. It's fifty dollars. No more of that.'

"So he started to walk away. I said, 'Frank, come here a minute.' He said, 'Yeah? What do you want?' I said, 'Make it a hundred, because the next son of a gun pitch is going in the same spot.'

"He just looked at me and walked back. I threw the next pitch in the same damn spot and Mays had the *biggest* swing at it and fouled it right straight back.

"I looked at Secory and he looked at me. I just shrugged my shoulders and kind of spread my hands a little bit. And I never got fined.

"Today they've put this false sense of security into hitters. They go into the batter's box today in a way that you wouldn't even think of doing twenty-five or thirty years ago. A stance. An approach to the plate. Calling time. Digging a toehold. And then saying, with a motion, 'OK, now come on and pitch.' Why holy Christ, you do that to Gibson he'd bury you! Remember what Dizzy Dean said. When a hitter was digging a hole, he said, 'Just make it deep enough so you fit in it.'

"The things today I see, I shake my head. I've seen guys swing hard and fall down. I've seen guys swing hard and fall across the plate. You didn't used to do that. Uh-uh. Uh-*uh*.

"We used to have a clubhouse meeting and somebody would say, 'How do you pitch to so and so?'

" 'Knock him on his ass. He don't like that.'

"If you said that today in a meeting your own club might file a grievance against you. I say that tongue in cheek, but it wouldn't surprise me. That's how much the game has changed."

17

"That's some kind of game but it's not baseball. Not in the eyes of the old-timers."

The pitching dominance of 1968 was an offshoot of the same root that produced the hitting splurge of 1930. Different as the two seasons were, Babe Ruth planted the seed for both.

Ruth's record of 60 home runs in a season stood for thirty-four years, but it was not for want of trying that so many challengers fell short. Jimmie Foxx hit 58 homers in 1932 and Hank Greenberg hit 58 in 1938. No National Leaguer touched Hack Wilson's record of 56.

Lots of homers were hit—lots more, in fact, than in the Ruthian era. Ruth was Superman. In 1927 he hit about one out of every seven homers hit in the whole American League (60 for Ruth, 439 for the league). Wilson, Foxx, and Greenberg couldn't quite fly, but for one season each they could leap tall buildings in a single bound: Wilson hit one of every sixteen National League homers in 1930 (56 out of 892), Foxx one of every twelve AL homers in 1932 (58 out of 708), Greenberg one of every fifteen AL homers in 1938 (58 out of 864).

In 1930 the major leagues rang up 1,565 homers, a new record that roused cries of anguish about home-run overkill. Not until 1940 was that record broken. Since then, it's been broken over and over again. By today's standards, the hitters of 1930 were Ping-Pong players. They pasted hell out of the ball and scored runs in bunches, but the home run was far less of a weapon than it became in later years. In 1930 baseball was split between a few power hitters like Ruth and Wilson and a lot of contact hitters like Bill Terry and Charlie Gehringer. But the pursuit of power was gaining. By 1950 virtually every team played home-run baseball.

As homers increased, you would expect scoring to increase, but it didn't. To oversimplify just a little, the trend in baseball has been more and more homers, countered by fewer and fewer hits mixed with more and more strikeouts. For example:

	Homers per game	Hits per game	Strikeouts per game	Runs per game
1930@	1.27	20.74	6.43	11.1
1940	1.27	18.61	7.32	9.36
1950	1.67	18.24	7.73	9.7
1960	1.72	17.34	10.37	8.63
1961*	1.91	17.55	10.47	9.06
1962+	1.85	17.59	10.84	8.92
1968−	1.23	15.82	11.78	6.84
1980	1.47	18.12	9.6	8.58
1987#	2.12	18	11.92	9.45
1988	1.51	17.27	11.13	8.28

@The Year of the Hitter
*The year the American League expanded and Roger Maris broke Ruth's record.
+The year the National League expanded.
−The Year of the Pitcher.
#Like 1930, a rabbit-ball season.

In 1930 Hack Wilson led the major leagues in strikeouts with 84. In 1962, the last season before baseball lengthened the strike zone to restrict slugging, 84 strikeouts would have ranked him sixth from the top—on the Chicago Cubs! Thirty major leaguers struck out more than 84 times in 1962. The Big Swing was worth it for a guy like Harmon Killebrew of the Minnesota Twins, who countered his 142 strikeouts and .243 batting average with 48 homers and 126 RBI. But you can't say the same for the National League leader, Ken Hubbs of the Cubs—129 strikeouts, .260 batting average, 5 homers, 49 RBI. (Killebrew drew 106 walks, Hubbs 35. Give that man the take sign!)

A recent year, 1987, draws the comparison even more starkly. A rabbit ball boosted hitting in 1987, just as it did in 1930. But the hitters played the rabbit differently. In 1930 they punched it through the gaps and off the walls. In 1987 they swung for glory. Hack Wilson struck out 84 times in 1930, and Glenn Davis of the Houston Astros struck out 84 times in 1987. Wilson led the majors. Davis finished *eighty-third;* Rob Deer of Milwaukee was the leader with 186 strike-outs.

To be sure, those big swingers do sometimes connect. To repeat, Wilson's 56 homers in 1930 amounted to one of every sixteen in the NL. In 1987 Andre Dawson of the Cubs and Mark McGwire of the A's led their respective leagues with 49 homers each, the highest totals in a decade. But Dawson hit only one of every thirty-seven National League homers (49 out of 1,824), McGwire one of every fifty-four in the AL (49 out of 2,634).

The home run has become a democratic article, sort of like a second car. Trouble is, the more homers you hit, the fewer men seem to be on base—and that's not a joke. Bill James and other knowledge-able baseball analysts conclude that baseball switched to a home-run strategy because it became more difficult to score by stringing sev-eral hits together. In other words, players began swinging for homers in the line of duty. Hey, guys, it's for the *team.*

Maybe, but listen to Al Lopez, major league catcher from 1930 through 1947, major league manager from 1951 through 1965, again in 1968 and 1969, and member of the Baseball Hall of Fame:

"We had guys who made contact with the ball more than they do today. We had big guys. Hack Wilson was a strong guy. Hornsby was a great hitter. Bill Terry was a great hitter. Babe Herman and Lefty O'Doul were great hitters. They made contact with the ball. Today, I think, everybody's swinging from their heels. They're using smaller bats and they get more speed on the swing. They don't feel bad about striking out. They just walk back to the bench like they're supposed to do it.

"We didn't do that so many times. Players would get mad as hell when they'd strike out. I know I did. The most I can remember striking out in a game, the whole time I was playing, was twice. Hal Schumacher struck me out twice in the Polo Grounds. I'll always remember that. I wasn't a free swinger. They say the pitching's better now? We had some guys who were real tough pitchers. Carl Hubbell and Dazzy Vance and Dizzy Dean. My God!

"We concentrated more on making contact. Is that a better way to score runs? I think so. Some of these kids today, hell, they're bigger and stronger than we were when we were playing. They do all these exercises, they got barbells and all that kind of stuff. They're strong kids. I don't see why they should have to swing on every pitch that hard. I think if you concentrate on making contact you're going to hit home runs when you're not even trying."

Charlie Gehringer hit .320, with 184 home runs, over nineteen seasons—1924 through 1942—with the Detroit Tigers. Like Lopez, he is a member of the Baseball Hall of Fame:

"I used a stubby, thick-handled, short bat, probably thirty-four ounces. I think that works better when you're hitting against a left-handed pitcher. You can get more wood on it, so to speak. I hardly ever broke one. I've got one yet.

"I played for Cobb, who said, 'Choke up on the bat a little. Don't try to go for homers.' He never did. I more or less took his word. My homers came by accident.

"Today, a lot of the hitters seem to want to swing right from the heels, even with two strikes on them. They go all out. Of course, there are a lot of great hitters among them. But when you try to pull the ball every time you've got to guess right or you're going to look pretty silly. Just check the amount of strikeouts in the old days compared with now."

Just a couple of old gaffers, right? Listen to Don Drysdale, the Dodger pitching ace, quoted in *The Sporting News* during his remarkable shutout streak of 1968:

"It's an accepted fact that good pitching will stop good hitting, and until the batters realize what they have to do to adjust, the hurlers will dominate. Of course, the good batters are going to get their hits whether it's in a Little League park or the International Airport. The hardest to face are the ones that just go with the pitch, like the Willie Mayses, Roberto Clementes, Pete Roses, Rusty Staubs, and Gene Alleys. . . .

"Batters are stupid if they keep swinging for the fences. When they do that they're helping me as well as the other pitchers. They're just not thinking right, although I'm glad they're doing it."

The hitting drought was much in the news all season, and sportswriters sought out opinions from hitters and pitchers alike. Frank Howard of the Washington Senators was a pure slugger who did not lose his touch in 1968, leading the American League with forty-four homers. Nevertheless, Howard, too, advocated more cautious hitting—at least for most batters:

"If a man cannot hit twenty homers a season, he should not try to hit any. If a fellow has speed and just ordinary power, he will be much better off keeping the ball on the ground. That's why there are so few .300 hitters today. Too many hitters trying to go for the bomb. I'm paid to hit home runs, but I know my potential. Forty homers would be a good year for me, forty-five tops."

By the 1950s, the home run was fully democratized—"cheap"—as more and more players swung for the downs. Ruth's record was bound to fall, and in 1961 it did, to a guy named Roger Maris. The American League expanded to ten teams that year, and with the pitching thinned out and the schedule stretched to 162 games, Maris hit sixty-one homers. It could have been someone else—five other players hit forty-five or more homers that season, and Maris hit only one of every twenty-five American League home runs (61 out of 1,534). But he was the ogre who slew the Babe, and everybody hated him for it.

In 1962 the National League expanded to ten teams, and again thin pitching yielded more homers and more runs. Scoring and slugging declined a little in the American League, and scoring overall was still below the levels of a decade before, but baseball's old guard felt that Maris's desecration demanded atonement. Commissioner Ford Frick, a former sportswriter who had been Ruth's friend and ghostwriter, stated the case: "I would even like the spitball to come back. Take a look at the batting, home run and slugging record for recent seasons, and you become convinced that the pitchers need help urgently."

They got it. The Official Baseball Playing Rules Committee lengthened the strike zone, which had been tightened in 1950 to *encourage* slugging. When Ruth hit sixty homers, the strike zone was between the batter's shoulders and knees. When Maris hit sixty-one, it was between the batter's armpits and the top of his knees. Starting in 1963, it was between the batter's shoulders and the bottom of his knees.

The change could not have come at a worse time—worse, that is, for the hitters—because other factors already were tilting the balance in favor of pitching. Night baseball, resisted for so long, became common. The skeptics of 1930 were right on one point: Most batters hit better in daylight.

Fielding greatly improved. Gloves and mitts were much larger, and fields were better groomed. Charlie Gehringer, who is regarded as one of the greatest defensive second basemen of all time, quickly acknowledged the superior fielding of the modern era:

"Is the fielding better? I think so. I've seen plays I can't believe, outfield and infield. The equipment's made a tremendous difference. They make plays now on balls we could knock down but couldn't keep in the glove.

"The infields are smoother. They level out the infield at the five-inning mark. Didn't do that in our day. That's got to help, because if you get a lot of men on base, they tear up a lot of ground in front of you."

Shirley Povich began covering baseball for the Washington *Post* in the 1920s. Although retired as sports editor, he was *still* covering the game part-time in 1988, when he talked about the contrast between defensive play in the old days and that in the modern era. Povich, like many old-timers, believes that today's ballplayers are no better than their forebears, but succeed because of better equipment, conditions, and pitching strategy:

"One of the big differences in the game today is the size of the gloves. They're out there with lacrosse baskets, grabbing everything around them. They're *so* different from the old pancake gloves. You couldn't make a one-handed catch.

"I was sitting with Ty Cobb one day when he saw Rudy York for the first time, making one-handed catches. Cobb said, 'How long has he been doing *that?*' (York, a first baseman, played in the American League from 1934 through 1948.)

"So when you talk about defense, I think you have two different games. You have the little-glove game and the big-glove game. The gloves are getting bigger and bigger. The one-handed catch is preposterous, but everybody makes them. You can't miss. Why did they profane the game?

"The pitching hasn't improved man for man. It's the system. You don't face any more tired pitchers. All those old-timers were going nine innings. Now you get the manager outraging traditionalists like myself when he signs a pitcher and says, 'I hope he can give me five good innings.' If you pitched only five good innings in the old days you were a bum. Now you have long relievers, short relievers. What the batter is now facing is fresh pitching. No more fatigue.

"Yes, it works. As Red Smith would say, 'That's some kind of game but it's not baseball.' Not in the eyes of the old-timers."

The cozy old downtown ballparks, many of them with at least one short fence, were replaced by big new stadiums, most of which have deeper fences and more foul ground, so pop fouls get caught rather than drifting into the stands. Here's a breakdown of the changes by 1968. As the following list shows, the Dodgers, Giants, Cardinals, Orioles, Athletics, and Indians all moved to ballparks where home runs were harder to hit than in the teams' old parks. Only the Braves and Twins moved to friendlier home-run country. None of the ballparks built for expansion teams offered easy homers.

OLD FRANCHISES

Dodgers	From Ebbets Field, with a short right field fence, to Dodger Stadium, a pitcher's ballpark.
Giants	From the Polo Grounds, where homers down the line were cheap, to Candlestick Park, where the wind inhibits slugging.

Cardinals	From Sportsman's Park, where Musial and Slaughter feasted on the 310-foot right field fence, to spacious—*very* spacious—Busch Stadium.
Braves	An exception. Braves Field in Boston was a pitcher's park. Atlanta–Fulton County Stadium is more than one thousand feet above sea level, and the ball carries.
Twins (formerly the Senators)	Another exception. Griffith Stadium in Washington was a very tough park for power hitters. Metropolitan Stadium, where the Twins played until they moved to the Dome in 1982, had deep power alleys, but it wasn't as tough on sluggers as Griffith.
Orioles (formerly the Browns)	From Sportsman's Park to Baltimore Memorial Stadium—a good home-run park, but not as good as the old digs in St. Louis.
Athletics	Fences are average depth at Oakland–Alameda County Stadium. Lots of foul ground. A tougher home-run park than Shibe Park in Philadelphia.
Indians	The Indians used to play weekday games at League Park, a homer paradise, and use big Municipal Stadium only on weekends. In 1948 they started playing all their home games at Municipal. Feller, Lemon, Wynn, and Garcia liked Municipal just fine, and so did Tiant, McDowell, Williams, Siebert, and Hargan.

EXPANSION FRANCHISES

Mets	No cheap homers at Shea, although the fences aren't severely deep. Extensive foul ground.
Astros	The Astrodome is a very tough place to hit homers.
Senators (The expansion Senators, who later moved to Dallas.)	Deep fences at D.C. Stadium, which is now called R.F.K. Memorial.
Angels	Corners are pretty close, but fences break out sharply to the power alleys.

In the 1960s a few teams—the Dodgers with Maury Wills, the Cardinals with Lou Brock, the Athletics with Bert Campaneris—were adapting to the new conditions by emphasizing speed and taking chances on the bases: a bit of the old "scientific baseball." Stolen bases were way up from the trough of the 1950s, but the running game still had a long way to go. For example:

TOTAL MAJOR LEAGUE STOLEN BASES

1911*	3,404
1930	1,079
1950	650
1968	1,515
1987	3,585
1988	3,301

*Record total for eight-club leagues.

To sum up, the hitters of 1968 were swinging for power, in ballparks that no longer yielded easy home runs, against skilled and well-equipped infielders and outfielders. "They were home-run crazy then," recalled Whitey Herzog, who was director of player development for the New York Mets in 1968.

Pat Dobson, a young pitcher for the Tigers in 1968 who became a twenty-game winner for the Orioles, talked about the hitting style of 1968 twenty years later, when he was the San Diego Padres' pitching coach:

"At that point in time, 1968, everybody tried to pull the ball. Very few guys tried to hit the ball the other way. That made it easier to pitch. You could pitch away and they'd try to pull and they'd be out. There were more high-ball hitters then, too. If you could keep the ball down in the strike zone and you could pitch away, you definitely had an advantage.

"I think hitters have changed. I think there are more low-ball hitters now, guys who hit the ball more down in the strike zone. More guys now use the whole field. They'll go the other way. They won't give in.

"There wasn't much speed in those days. As time went on there was more emphasis put on speed. You got guys a little bit smaller in stature, guys that could run better.

"Nineteen-sixty-eight was just a time when the pitching got *that* good at the big league level. Just one of those swings where the pitching got real good."

Part of the improvement in pitching was technical. The last legal spitballer was long gone, but his illegal descendants were legion. In 1967 *Sports Illustrated* reported that "almost 25 percent of all major league pitchers are throwing the spitter, while 100 percent of all major league umpires, unable to enforce the rule against it, look the other way."

The slider wasn't new—George Blaeholder of the Browns had a pretty good one back in 1930. But a lot more pitchers had learned to throw it. Don Drysdale, who pitched for the Dodgers from 1956 until 1969, talked about the slider during the 1988 interview:

"What you're trying to do as a pitcher is keep the hitter off balance. Don't let him keep that same stride, that same motion, that same grooved swing all the time, as a golfer would. You don't want him to do that. You want to back him off the plate. You want to change speeds.

"That's why the slider, when it came into existence, gave Williams and Musial so damned much trouble. It came in just maybe a tad prior to my career. They could gauge the speed of the fastball, and now all of a sudden the slider comes to be a dominant pitch, and it is thrown harder than the curveball, and just a shade slower than the fastball, yet it has a little break to it. Here's a whole new thing coming in. All of a sudden they have to start gearing down from the fastball to the slider.

"Stan told me he used to sit and watch a pitcher, and his computer mind would think, 'What is the speed of his best fastball? The speed of anything else he may throw—curveball, or change?' Now he has to say curveball, change, or slider. There's a new element in there."

Baseball, to its glory, is a game played by people. In 1930 the major leagues were blessed with an unusual abundance of superb hitters. There was no shortage of good hitters in 1968, but the batters were overwhelmed by the pitchers—probably the greatest array of pitching talent ever to people the major leagues.

Manny Mota, a superb contact hitter, batted .321 in 1967, .281 in 1968, and .321 again in 1969. He finished with a lifetime batting average of .304 for twenty seasons, all in the National League. In 1988 Mota was a coach for the Dodgers, the team for which he played for the last thirteen years of his career. He recalled 1968, when he was with the Pirates:

"There were an awful lot of fine pitchers. There were fewer teams in the league. So the pitching was more high quality. Also, they didn't used to give as much rest between starts. There was a quality pitching staff everyplace you'd go. Every city you'd go, you'd face the four toughest guys.

"I don't take anything away from the pitchers today, but from what I see the pitching then was better than right now. Right now you see Nolan Ryan and Dwight Gooden. You can compare those guys to Gibson and Marichal, maybe. Gibson used to have super stuff.

Fastball, a slider. No change and no slow curve—nothing to hit! Like Jim Maloney. You don't see guys like that coming along now."

Mike Shannon of the Cardinals pointed out that the Met and Astro pitching staffs, so weak when those expansion teams joined the National League in 1962, had matured by 1968. The Mets had Seaver, Koosman, and Ryan; the Astros had Don Wilson, Larry Dierker, Dave Giusti, Denny Lemaster, and Mike Cuellar. The Oakland Athletics had five good young pitchers in Catfish Hunter, Blue Moon Odom, Jim Nash, Chuck Dobson, and Lew Krausse.

Attendance suffered in 1968, and the major leagues adopted two changes for 1969 designed to help the hitters. During the Year of the Pitcher, the mound was supposed to be fifteen inches high, although players unanimously say that it varied from city to city, depending upon the preference of the home team's hurlers. Beginning in 1969 it was cut to ten inches, and umpires were given a measuring device so they could enforce the rule. In addition, the strike zone was tightened. To a man, pitchers and hitters say that the shorter mound made a big difference—and that umpires essentially ignored the change in the strike zone.

Whitey Herzog, the very successful Cardinal manager of the 1980s, was director of player development for the New York Mets in the 1960s. Asked about 1968 during an interview twenty years later, he thought back and reeled off, from memory, the top eight or ten draft choices of 1968, his point being that many of them were strong fastball pitchers. Herzog elaborated:

"I can remember how high some of those mounds looked. That's a hell of a thing when you get a pitcher out there coming over the top and he's got another five inches of hill and that ball's coming down to you. That helps the power pitcher.

"I can remember in 1967 I scouted throughout the country and double-checked all the top prospects. There were some good young high school pitchers that could throw the ball in the nineties. They had some arms! I had that job for seven years, and I've never again seen that many good high school arms. High school pitchers, and they had plus–major league fastballs.

"I had fourteen pitchers at my instructional league camp with the

Mets. Eleven of them were in the big leagues the following year. Not all with the Mets, and not all at the beginning of the year, but by the end of the year they had come up. Seaver had already come up in '67. Then the following year here came Ryan, Koosman, Jim McAndrew. They could all throw the ball ninety miles an hour. When a team would come in and face the Mets and Nolan Ryan would pitch after Seaver and Koosman, people didn't think Ryan was that quick. They had already seen two guys who could throw in the nineties, and Nolan threw one hundred.

"It seems like now we've gone from the high school player to the college player. We go after more twenty-two-year-olds. I don't see the hard throwers like I used to. We baby arms, pamper them. Little League coaches let kids pitch only so many innings. Kids don't do anything anymore unless it's organized. When their arms are developing they don't throw as much as they did in those days. You really don't see as many high school kids throw the ball hard.

"Basically I always say there's two things that a young boy who's playing high school ball should do. He should extend his arm every day and his legs every day. If you don't extend your arm every day it's not going to get stronger.

"You say they changed the strike zone in '69? Well, I don't believe that. I've been in baseball since 1949. I don't think they ever changed the strike zone. I think that every umpire has a different strike zone and it's up to the hitter and pitcher to know what his strike zone is. They can tell you it's the top of the shoulders, the armpits, the knees, but you never know what it is until you get out there every night. I can't tell you what this guy's going to call tonight or that guy's going to call tomorrow night. There's no consistency in strike zones.

"How does today's pitching compare? Well, you don't hear the expression anymore, 'wild young lefthander.' Twenty years ago you'd hear, 'another wild young lefthander coming up.' You don't hear that anymore because they throw more strikes. I think it's tougher to hit today, average-wise. When you get into pro ball, rookie league, you may never see a fastball on three and two. They might throw you a change or curveball. You never used to see that, even when I was in the big leagues. The big thing was in the old days, two and oh you'd see a lot of fastballs. You didn't see a lot of straight changes and stuff.

"The fastball is the number one pitch in baseball. The location of it is what's important. The real good pitchers are the guys who on two and oh and three and one don't have to throw the fastball. They can get their change over, their slider, whatever.

"Years ago a hitter always wanted to have more walks than strikeouts. Now you see very few hitters like that. Most of them, they strike out four times more than they walk! I won't say they don't care, but they don't stress it. They just can't get the bat on the ball. It's tougher hitting out there.

"You have control pitchers today as far as strikes are concerned. I think they're better on throwing strikes. But I don't think they can throw the ball to a zone like they used to be able to. I'm talking about a Robin Roberts. If he wanted to pitch a guy high, he'd ride that ball right there.

"Look at Satchel Paige. I saw Satchel when he was old, but shit, he'd warm up with a handkerchief on the plate. And he could throw that bleep right over there, every pitch."

Herzog's opinion was largely echoed by Mel Stottlemyre, a twenty-one-game winner for the Yankees in 1968 who looked back on that season in 1988, when he was pitching coach for the Mets:

"Has pitching improved? I think the quality of pitching has not gotten any *worse*. There's not as many guys who throw quite as hard as they used to. I think more pitchers are becoming finesse pitchers. A lot of college pitchers, for instance, are encouraged to throw a lot more breaking balls. I don't think there's anything better than a good fastball. When I was in high school you didn't hear about a slider, but now your high school pitchers are trying to throw sliders and that sort of thing, and I think it takes away from the fastball down the line."

18

"It's getting pretty tough to find a .300 hitter, never mind a guy who's going to hit .340 or .350."

Gabe Paul, general manager of the Cleveland Indians, promised his pitchers a new suit for every shutout in 1968, and soon found himself a patron saint of the men's clothing industry.

Luis Tiant was the best dressed. He pitched four straight shutouts and ran his string of scoreless innings to forty-one before Boog Powell reached him for a three-run homer. The Orioles went on to beat the Indians, 6–2, but Tiant quickly renewed his mastery.

On June 23 he shut out the Tigers, 3–0, and fanned nine. On June 29 he beat the Red Sox 8–1, striking out thirteen. On July 3 the Twins and Indians took a scoreless tie into the tenth inning. Rich Reese opened the Minnesota tenth with a double, and Frank Quilici bunted safely. With runners on first and third, Tiant struck out John Roseboro, Rich Rollins, and Jim Merritt. That gave him nineteen strikeouts for the game and forty-one for three games. Joe Azcue drove in the game's only run for Cleveland in the tenth.

Tiant was from Cuba and, with Fidel Castro in power, had not seen his parents since 1961. "My father pitch for the old New York Cubans in the Negro league, but he could not play in the big leagues because he is colored," Tiant said. "I know he was better than I am because everybody in Cuba tell me."

Tiant had good stuff, but in 1968 he added another dimension by teaching himself a variety of jerky and confusing motions, all of which entertained baseball fans in the 1970s, when Tiant pitched for the Red Sox and Yankees. His natural style was herky-jerky. Tiant accentuated that by whipping his arms around, corkscrewing his body, flapping his glove, tossing his head, and looking at left or center field as he pitched. He dubbed his favorite offering "the hesitation pitch."

"The motion depends on how I feel and how I think the hitter is thinking," Tiant told sportswriter Russell Schneider. "Sometimes I do nothing but throw the ball. You can't use the motions too much or they will get used to it."

Nobody got used to it in 1968. The Indians couldn't hit—Tiant at one point sprayed the team's bat rack with perfume in hopes of getting something started—but Tiant wound up twenty-one and nine, with nine shutouts and a league-leading ERA of 1.60, the AL's lowest since 1919. For the season, batters hit a composite .168 against him, breaking yet another pitching record from the dead-ball era—the .176 batting average against Ed Reulbach of the Chicago Cubs in 1906.

Not bad, but most hitters considered Tiant Cleveland's second-best pitcher, behind Sudden Sam McDowell, whose stuff they described in reverent tones. The Indians didn't score at all for poor McDowell—with an ERA of 1.81 he wound up the season at fifteen and fourteen—but he led the league in strikeouts with 283. His only flaw, hitters said, was a tendency to use the wrong pitch at the wrong time.

Jim Fregosi, then with the California Angels, was the American League's starting shortstop in the 1968 All-Star Game. In 1988 he was managing the Chicago White Sox and still remembered that Cleveland pitching staff of 1968:

"I remember those guys back in Cleveland. They had Tiant, Sonny Siebert, Steve Hargan, McDowell. Those guys all threw ninety-plus fastballs. They had some great arms.

"McDowell had the best five pitches in the league. He had the best fastball, the best slider, the best curveball, the best changeup, and the best spitball. A smart pitcher? No. He wanted to embarrass people instead of just get them out. He'd want to strike people out and make them look bad."

Jim Northrup, a Tiger slugger in 1968, talked about the Year of the Pitcher twenty years later:

"I want to tell you something. When we went to Cleveland, they had Louie Tiant, who equaled McLain, dang near. Tiant could really blow the ball. Plus Siebert was right there behind him. And then they had

Sam McDowell, who had better speed and better stuff than all of them. Siebert had a darned good breaking ball, and so did Tiant and McDowell. Steve Hargan didn't have the breaking stuff, but he could *blow it* for five or six innings. And out of the bullpen they had another guy or two who could throw flame.

"So when you went to Cleveland you'd better get your sleep, because those guys could really throw the ball. And it was not unusual. There were an awful lot of good pitchers in baseball. I think those things come in cycles. The National League at that time had some awfully good hitters. The American League was on the downside. Some of our guys were getting a little long in the tooth—Mantle, for example.

"Every team had four good starters, maybe five. They didn't have the bullpens they have today—though they had decent bullpens—but they didn't need them, because most guys wanted to complete games. It wasn't like it is now, 'Give us five, six, or seven innings and get out of there, we've got a bullpen full of guys to come in.' Back then, most guys tried to get at least to the ninth inning. We didn't have free agency, and if you pitched the way they do today, you wouldn't make any money. You had to complete games, you had to stack up some innings, you had to strike out people, and you had to get some wins. You had better win sixteen to twenty if you were going to make good money. If you won fifteen and lost fifteen they'd figure, 'Well, that's zero. You're a zero pitcher. What makes you think you're going to get a raise?' You go fifteen and fifteen today and you get a million and a half bucks.

"The next year, 1969, we had expansion. That weakened everything, and everybody hit better. Expansion liberalized the pitching staffs. After expansion, it takes pitching a while to catch up."

The Indians wound up with a team ERA of 2.66. So did the Orioles; Dave McNally was twenty-two and ten, 1.95, and Tom Phoebus, pitching with a sore throat in raw, rainy weather, delivered the first of 1968's five no-hitters April 27, beating Boston, 6–0.

On May 8 Jim (Catfish) Hunter of the Oakland Athletics pitched the American League's first perfect game in forty-six years, beating the Twins 4–0. He struck out eleven. Harmon Killebrew fanned three times. Hunter himself squeezed home the first Oakland run in the seventh inning and singled home two more in the eighth. He was only twenty-two, but he was already a pitching craftsman. "Control, control, control," Hunter said of his perfect game. "A little pitch here, a little pitch there."

The Twins hit only four balls hard. Two were caught by Joe Rudi, one by Reggie Jackson, and one by Sal Bando. Rudi was twenty-one; Jackson and Bando were twenty-two. The Athletics were building the team that would win three straight world championships in the early 1970s. In 1968 fans and writers paid more attention to a fifty-three-year-old Oakland coach, Joe DiMaggio.

The Athletics had paid Hunter a sixty-thousand-dollar bonus in 1964 and almost found it wasted when the young farm boy's brother accidentally shot him in the foot while they were hunting. He went to the Mayo Clinic for surgery, spent a year recovering, joined the Athletics in 1965, and was a major league starting pitcher at the age of nineteen.

On July 29 George Culver of the Reds needed a shot of novocaine to deaden the pain from an ingrown toenail. Nevertheless he was ready to pitch and had a premonition. En route to the ballpark, Culver said, "I kept thinking 'no-hitter, no-hitter.' Don't ask me why. It just happened, like I was in another world." The Phillies got a run off Culver but not a hit; 6 to 1, Cincinnati.

On September 17 and 18 fans in San Francisco got a double dose. Gaylord Perry pitched a no-hitter to beat the Cardinals and Gibson, 1–0. The next day, Ray Washburn of the Cardinals returned the compliment, no-hitting the Giants, 2–0.

In an earlier two-hitter, Perry threw only seventy-seven pitches while beating the Cubs. "Almost every pitch he threw was a spitter," complained the Cubs' Ron Santo. Leo Durocher, the Cub manager, persuaded the umpires to check Perry's cap for grease, whereupon the Giant manager, Herman Franks, said, "Durocher's got a lot of guts upsetting my pitcher when he's got one who makes a career out of throwing a greaseball."

Franks was referring to Phil (The Vulture) Regan, the National League's premier reliever with ten wins and twenty-five saves. Umpires frequently inspected Regan's cap and forehead in search of Vaseline or some other substance, and on August 18 umpire Chris Pelekoudas tried to do what no umpire had dared—actually police the spitball. Alex Johnson of the Reds hit a foul ground ball; Pelekoudas called it a ball, ruling that Regan had thrown an illegal pitch. Johnson then flied out; ball two, said Pelekoudas. Johnson grounded out. In the Cincinnati ninth, Pete Rose swung and missed at strike three, but Pelekoudas called it a ball, and Rose singled. The Reds won, 2 to 1.

Before the controversial calls, Pelekoudas explained, he had checked Regan. "I could feel the Vaseline on the inner lining of Regan's cap," he said. He called the illegal pitches because of the way they broke. "We umpires talked this over some time ago," the twenty-year umpiring veteran explained. "We decided, when we see it, this is how we're going to handle it."

Pelekoudas was supported by umpire Shag Crawford, who said he also felt Vaseline inside Regan's cap. George Culver, the Cincinnati pitcher the day of the incident, said he found a tube of Vaseline and two slippery elm tablets on the ground, and turned them in as evidence. Although baseball officials were desperately seeking ways to increase scoring so attendance would revive, the prospect of actually enforcing the rule against the spitter apparently was too much. Warren Giles, the National League president, flew to Chicago, held a hearing, and ruled in Regan's favor, giving umpires an unmistakable message to lay off.

Regan was a well-mannered young man who gave of his time for charitable causes, and Giles used this character reference as an excuse for his ruling. "I know Phil Regan and have respect for him and felt a gentleman like him should be shown the consideration and courtesy of a hearing," Giles said. "Phil has told me he did not have Vaseline or any other lubricant on his sweat band, and I believe him."

Regan struck a martyr's pose, reveling in the self-righteous grief of the falsely accused. "I've got four children," he said, "and the oldest one, a girl—she's eleven—she's old enough to know what's going on. She reads about it in the paper and she sees it on TV. Last night I came home and I could see it had really affected her. She asked her mother if Daddy was cheating."

Orlando Pena, a relief pitcher for Cleveland, broke an unspoken rule of the pitching fraternity by answering honestly when a sportswriter asked him if he threw a spitter. "Sure, I throw a spitball sometimes," Pena said. ". . . A lot of guys in the big leagues throw spitballs. What the heck, pitchers have got to live, too." Pena went further, estimating that at least twenty pitchers in the American League threw a spitter or greaseball. "Boston has [John] Wyatt, [Jim] Lonborg, and [Gary] Bell," Pena continued. "Minnesota has [Dean] Chance and used to have [Ron] Kline.

"Detroit has [Earl] Wilson. McLain sometimes throws one and, boy, that guy [Larry] Sherry used it all the time. Baltimore has [Moe] Drabowsky and [Dave] McNally. California has [George] Brunet, I think, and the number one spitballer in the league, Jack Hamilton. Oakland has Blue Moon [Odom]. He has a good one. So does [Lew] Krausse. New York has [Steve] Barber and [Thad] Tillotson. When Pedro Ramos was there, oh ho. His spitball dripped tobacco juice all the way to the plate. And Whitey Ford, he used everything he could get away with."

The spitball was subject to innovation. Rusty Staub of the Astros credited one to a Dodger pitcher whom he declined to name. "He doesn't throw a spitball, he throws a toothpaste ball," Staub said. Herman Franks, the Giant manager, described pitchers who didn't use illegal pitches as "pure" pitchers. Hank Aguirre, a former Tiger ace who was winding down his career with the Dodgers in 1968, said he should be on the list. "I tried to become an impure pitcher but I couldn't master it," Aguirre said.

No one could master the Giants' pitching ace, Juan Marichal, who was so good he didn't need a spitball. In 1968 Marichal beat every team in the league. His twentieth victory, 2–0 over the Dodgers, was his sixteenth straight complete game and the ninety-fifth out of his last ninety-sixth victories, the exception being a game from which he was removed in 1966 because the Giants were leading 14–2, and manager Herman Franks decided Marichal might as well rest.

Marichal's catcher, Jack Hiatt, had one complaint. "He throws too many strikes," Hiatt said. ". . . With Marichal's control, he could drive the batters wild by flicking at a corner here, a corner there. But no, he rears back and pours the ball through the strike zone as though somebody might take the zone away before he gets the next pitch off." Marichal led the majors with thirty complete games—more than any National League *team* compiled in 1987—and came in at twenty-six and nine, 2.43.

The Yankees were in their period of decline, having finished last in 1966 and ninth in 1967. They climbed all the way to fifth place in

1968, and their star was not Mickey Mantle, who suffered through his final season with eighteen homers and a .237 batting average, but Mel Stottlemyre, a young pitcher who pitched six shutouts and won twenty-one games.

As a rookie, Stottlemyre helped pitch the Yankees to the 1964 pennant. He then suffered through the team's worst years. He won twenty games in 1965 and lost twenty in 1966. In 1988 Stottlemyre was working as pitching coach for the New York Mets and looked back on the pitching of 1968:

"They called 1968 the Year of the Pitcher. There just happened to be a lot of pitchers who were really at their peak. Don Drysdale and Bob Gibson were tremendous that year, and Denny McLain had the year of his life. Tiant was an outstanding pitcher for quite a few years. That just happened to be his peak season.

"In '68 I reacquired my breaking ball. When I broke into the league in 1964 and '65 I was basically a fastball pitcher. I threw a slider and an occasional changeup. In 1966 I tried to come up with a new pitch, and I lost my slider. I lost the feeling of my slider, and I had a poor year. I regained it in '67, and by 1968 I was able to use it a lot more. So I was probably on top of my game, too.

"They've always denied it, but I think they were messing with the baseball a little bit at that time. The hitters were screaming that the ball really would not carry. Some hits would really be juiced and they wouldn't go out of the ballpark. You can say, 'Well, if they did deaden the ball a little bit, it wouldn't make a lot of difference.' But it would make a great deal of difference if a lot of balls that were going out of the park were suddenly warning track balls. Outs. Everybody was trying to hit the three-run homer continuously. Maybe that was more the style.

"I see that in baseball today. If there's anybody to blame, it probably would be the fans. They have wanted to see home runs. They've made that known to the guys playing the game, and guys who were not necessarily home-run hitters tried to become home-run hitters, and averages went down a little bit. I don't see as many guys making adjustments with two strikes as I once did. The coaches talk to them continuously about it. But we have a few on our ballclub who take the same swing with two strikes that they do with no strikes. They accept a number of strikeouts and think they're going to get a few more home runs by continuously taking the bigger swing. They think it's worth it. They think they get rewarded more for hitting homers, maybe, than for batting average.

"After '68, I think because of the great year the pitchers had, they made a change in the baseball. The texture of the baseball was changed. The ball became very slick, and I had a lot of difficulty throwing a sinking fastball for a period of time."

In 1968 the hitting drought was epidemic. The White Sox limped through thirty-nine innings without a run, then scored one in a 5–1 loss to the Yankees. Their crosstown rivals, the Cubs, did them one worse. Phil Niekro and Jim Britton of the Braves beat the Cubs 1–0 in eleven innings, wasting ten shutout innings by Chicago ace Ferguson Jenkins. The Cubs traveled to St. Louis, where Nelson Briles beat them 1–0, Steve Carlton gave them one hit in a 4–0 win, and Bob Gibson outdueled Jenkins 1–0. On to Cincinnati, where George Culver blanked the Cubs for the first two innings. That ran the Cubs' scoreless streak to forty-eight innings, setting a new National League record and matching a record for hitting futility set by the Philadelphia Athletics in 1906.

For the season, Jenkins won twenty games and lost fifteen. He was shut out nine times, losing five of them by 1–0 scores. In the off-season, Jenkins played basketball for the Harlem Globetrotters; his job was to pitch the basketball to Meadowlark Lemon, who slammed it with his fists for a home run. "Meadowlark hit a home run off me every night," Jenkins said.

Fred Talbot of the Yankees lost his first eight decisions; his team scored only four runs. "The poor guy must be going nuts," said Ralph Houk, the Yankee manager. For the season, the major leagues rang up 339 shutouts, and in 82 of them the winning team scored only one run. The average number of runs scored per game was 6.84, second-lowest in history. The overall major league batting average was .237, two points lower than the previous low, set in 1908. Both *leagues* had earned run averages under 3.00. A few sluggers excelled—Frank Howard of Washington hit 44 homers, and Willie Horton of Detroit and Willie McCovey of San Francisco hit 36. But not many players were connecting. In total, home runs were down by 300 from 1967, by 700 from 1966, and by 1,000 from 1962, the year Roger Maris hit 61.

Attendance declined. Jim Lonborg, the injured Red Sox pitching ace, expressed the view of many fans. "I can't stand to watch a baseball game," Lonborg said. "There is just no action. It's dull. I do enjoy playing baseball, but I'd rather watch basketball or hockey."

Football had become a favorite of television viewers, and analysts said America was becoming too urban and fast-paced for baseball, which was described as bucolic and pastoral. The Lou Harris polling organization asked respondents to name their favorite sport, and though baseball came out on top with 39 percent, football's share climbed to 32 percent from 25 percent three years before. More foreboding were the responses of fans under thirty-five years old (football 46 percent, baseball 24) and high-income fans (football 52, baseball 22).

Baseball officials were anxious to revive fan interest. Everyone agreed that the way to do it was to increase scoring. In June 1968, Giles, the National League president, asked the league's general managers, managers, and coaches to suggest ways scoring could be increased without drastic changes in the rules. Joe Cronin, the American League's MVP in 1930 and the AL's president in 1968, viewed the controversy from a historical perspective.

"It's the 9 to 2 and 10 to 3 games that really can't be called exciting," Cronin said. "It's a funny thing, at that. When I was playing and we had big-score games, the cry was 'Give us back the good old days of good pitching, stolen bases, bunting, and the hit and run.' Well, now that type of game is back and everybody is complaining . . . I don't think anything radical should be done. I might be in favor of lowering the mound to ten or twelve inches. But that's about all."

Others preferred more drastic changes. Paul Richards, general manager of the Houston Astros, urged that the pitching rubber be moved back about five feet—the flip side of John McGraw's suggestion of 1930 that it be moved forward. Charlie Finley, the eccentric owner of the Oakland Athletics, suggested that the batter walk on three balls, rather than four. Others talked about narrowing home plate, letting a pinch hitter bat more than once, using an eight-man lineup with the pitcher never batting, and making the pitcher finish any inning he started.

Jim Fregosi of the Angels suggested that instead of pitching down from a mound, pitchers should have to pitch up from a hole. Tony Kubek said, "I believe pitching could be curbed and hitting stimulated by one simple move—limit each pitching staff to only eight men . . . The starter would have to stay in there longer."

It was too late to counteract one important change that benefited pitchers. Baseball teams had been building new ballparks at a record pace, and Ralph Kiner, the great slugger turned baseball broadcaster, said it was too bad. "These big ballparks we're getting now just make it that much tougher to score runs," Kiner told sportswriter Edgar Munzel. "The pitchers already have the upper hand and it's just giving them that much more of an edge. To my mind, there's no question that it takes a lot of romance out of the game. If a ballclub that had a home in one of these lopsided parks would have a bad trip, the fans could always say, 'Wait until they get home. They'll murder these other bums.' A team could be tailored to the ballpark dimensions and it would be almost invincible at home . . . I remember when they built those Greenberg Gardens in Pittsburgh. It was money in the bank for the owners of the Pirates. With Hank Greenberg and me as righthanded pull hitters and the fence 365 down the line in left and 406 in left-center, a bullpen area was built across left field to shorten the distance to 335 feet. The fans would love to see Hank and me pump homers in there. We drew 1.2 million fans that year, even though we were not pennant contenders."

Lee McPhail, general manager of the Yankees and later president of the American League, gave an educated view of what had happened and what might be done. "The fans like to see a lot of hitting, a lot of baserunners, and a lot of excitement," McPhail said. "There are many reasons for this change, one of which is the number of new parks. Every time a new park is built, its dimensions are much larger than the park it replaces. In the case of new teams, their parks are modern in size and are generally a pitcher's park with deep foul lines and distant fences.

"I also feel that the better equipment is responsible to a degree. The bigger gloves create better fielding, while something else has come into the game more or less unnoticed. There are more scientific defenses now, which could be the result of more scouting. It used to be that pitchers and hitters ran in cycles, but I don't know if the pendulum is ever going to swing the other way again.

". . . I think the first step should be the elimination of the pitcher as a hitter. Have a regular hitter in the lineup any place you want him, for the pitcher. . . . If you have a defensive shortstop hitting eighth and the pitcher ninth, there isn't much for the fans to anticipate during the inning they come up."

Little League and other organized boys' leagues came in for more than their share of criticism. "I think the pitching coaches are better than the hitting coaches," said Brooks Robinson of the Orioles. Hank Bauer, the Oriole manager until he was fired at midseason, said, "The hitters, the big husky guys, just aren't playing baseball. A lot of them are going into football." Bill Rigney, the Angels' veteran manager, said major league batters were "simply not concentrating."

Phil Rizzuto, the Yankee shortstop turned broadcaster, said too many hitters were swinging for the fences. "Today's hitters help the pitchers because so few of them know how to use the bat," Rizzuto said. "They all swing from the end, which makes life easier for the pitcher." Al Dark, the Giant shortstop turned Cleveland manager, agreed with him. So did Satchel Paige, whom the Braves hired as a player-coach so he could work enough days to qualify for a big league pension. "They all swing for those homers," Paige said. "They don't bunt anymore." Paige was listed at sixty-two years old but said he wasn't sure. "They couldn't find my record in Mobile because the jail had moved and the judge had died," he said. "They did a lot of checking on my family and found I had some relatives two hundred years old."

Life was anything but easy for the hitters. Rusty Staub of the Astros credited superior relief pitching and the change from small to large ballparks. "In these large parks, you just have to hit a line shot to get a hit unless it's right in the alleys," Staub said. "These guys playing the outfield now will just catch up to anything you hit out there."

Walt Alston, the Dodger manager, and Frank Robinson, the Oriole slugger, gave credit to the young pitchers. Robinson said, "Pitchers nowadays come up to the majors and they can get four pitches over the plate—fastball, curve, slider, and whatever else they're throwing.

It used to be they could get only two pitches over, fastball and curve, if that. You used to like to see new guys coming into the league because the fastball was the only thing most of them could get over consistently. After a while, they'd start getting their curve over, but it took some time. And in the meantime you could look for the fastball in a tough situation. Now it's really changed. The count's two and oh or three and one, and you don't get a fastball. You get a curve or something else because he can get that over just as well as a fastball.

"I know one thing," Robinson continued. "It's getting pretty tough to find a .300 hitter, never mind a guy who's going to hit .340 or .350."

Robinson was right. With the season winding down, Carl Yastrzemski of Boston, Danny Cater of Oakland, and Tony Oliva of Minnesota were competing for the American League batting championship, and none was hitting above .290. Yastrzemski went on a late-season tear and won the title at .301, the lowest in history for either league. The composite AL batting average was .230—another record low—so Yaz finished 31 percent higher than the league norm. Astounding as it may appear, that was almost as good a showing, in relative terms, as Bill Terry's .401 average in 1930. The National League had a composite batting average of .303 that year. Terry beat it by 32 percent.

The pitching dominance of 1968 was startling, but it was not the first time baseball had faced the need to change in order to revive hitting. In 1892 the National League expanded from eight to twelve teams. Pitching was dominant, attendance was low, and a pioneering sports editor, W. R. Lester of the Philadelphia *Record,* proposed radical changes. There was no pitching rubber back then; since 1880 pitchers had worked from a box five feet six inches long by four feet wide. The front of the box was fifty feet from home plate—a big advantage for pitchers. On the other hand, foul balls didn't count as strikes, and hitters were allowed to use bats with one side flat—a boon for bunts, or, as they were called back then, "baby hits."

Lester proposed that baselines be lengthened from ninety feet to ninety-three, that the pitcher's box be abolished in favor of a position sixty-five feet nine inches from home plate, that the flat bat be outlawed, and that foul balls count as strikes. He built that kind of diamond in a Philadelphia suburb, and amateur teams played on it, using Lester's rules, with apparent success.

As always, however, traditionalists were outraged. Cap Anson, playing manager of the Chicago Cubs and the most dominant baseball figure of his day, said, "There is enough batting now and the public is tired of the continuous tampering with the rules." (It was Anson who also purged blacks from organized baseball.)

National League owners met at the New Yorker Hotel on March 7, 1893, and argued into the night. A vote on the Lester plan resulted in a tie. The owners finally compromised, retaining the ninety-foot baselines, establishing a pitcher's rubber five feet from the back of the old box—in other words, sixty feet six inches from home plate—and outlawing the flat bat. They decided against counting foul balls as strikes, but finally took that step in 1901, with the new American League following in 1903. Although hammered out in compromise, all these rules are still in effect.

The 1892 changes worked, as the number of .300 hitters increased from twelve in 1892 to sixty-five in 1893. For all his complaints, Anson's own batting average climbed from a career low of .274 in 1892 to .322 in 1893. Fans responded enthusiastically to the hitting—they always do—and attendance increased.

In 1968 contact hitters gave the National League a respectable batting race. Pete Rose, proudly wearing a crew cut in defiance of '60s fashion, hit .335 to edge Matty Alou of the Pirates, at .332, and Matty's brother, Felipe, with the Braves, at .317. The National League hit .242, so Rose beat the norm by 38 percent. It was the first of three batting championships for Rose, whose all-around play impressed everyone. "Check the box scores," said Luman Harris, the Braves' manager. "Every time the Reds win, that hustling son of a gun plays a key role. Somehow he keeps figuring a way to beat you—with his bat, his speed, or his glove."

But baseball was not content to wait for other hitters to catch up. Following the 1968 season, the rules committee adopted two modest changes proposed in an editorial by C. C. Johnson Spink of *The Sporting News:*

"1. Go back to the old, narrower definition of the strike zone.

"2. Lower the pitcher's mound from the present 15-inch height to 10 inches."

Both leagues expanded in 1969, the American League moving into Seattle and putting a new franchise in Kansas City, which the Athletics had deserted a year before in favor of Oakland. The National League added franchises in San Diego and Montreal.

Hitting picked up. Bowie Kuhn, the new commissioner, thought more might be done. In spring training of 1970 a new ball, called the X-5, was thrown into play for a few exhibition games. It was supposed to be 5 percent more lively than the standard ball, but it seemed much quicker than that. "If they use that ball on AstroTurf or Tartan-Turf," said Leo Durocher, "somebody will get killed." The X-5 went back to the drawing board. So did a wider diamond, which was tried in a minor league exhibition game. It had the first and third base lines flared out by three degrees to give hitters more fair territory.

The designated hitter, suggested in 1968 by McPhail and others, was adopted by the American League in 1973. Charley Lau, whose undistinguished playing career ended in 1967, became a batting coach and an apostle of punching line drives and hard grounders through the gaps—an approach that appeared new, although it might have looked right at home eighty years before. Gradually, the delicate balance between hitting and pitching swung back toward center.

19

"Gibson . . . was at his peak. I almost got a sore arm that year from throwing the ball around the infield after he'd strike people out."

Philosophical sportswriters often wax poetic about the smooth fit of summer and baseball, a sport slow enough for the season yet intense enough to occupy a fan's attention every day. Many fans ride baseball as their vehicle to an annual summertime escape from the anxieties of life.

But the summer of 1968 was too turbulent for escape. Events accelerated, and emotions ran out of control. On June 5 Senator Robert F. Kennedy was shot to death in the kitchen corridor of a Los Angeles hotel, minutes after claiming victory in California's Democratic primary election for president. Sirhan Bishara Sirhan, twenty-four, a Jordanian, was arrested and charged with murdering Kennedy. Three days later, James Earl Ray was arrested in London and charged with the assassination of Martin Luther King.

On June 25 more than fifty thousand people, followers of King and his civil rights movement, marched through Washington in a "Poor People's Walk." They demanded deliverance from poverty and discrimination, set up camp on the Mall, near the Lincoln Memorial, and called their tent community "Resurrection City."

On campus after campus, college students took over administrative offices, closed classrooms, and demanded more racial justice and less cooperation with the Defense Department and other U.S. government agencies. In France, students occupied the Sorbonne and joined with workers in a general strike.

Eastern Europeans took hope from reforms instituted by Alexander Dubček, head of Czechoslovakia's Communist party, who said his goal was "socialism with a human face." Czechs were allowed to express independent political views and newspapers published accounts of atrocities by the secret police. On August 20 Soviet tanks led several hundred thousand soldiers into Prague, crushing the independent movement.

North Vietnam's Tet offensive, launched January 30, intensified opposition to continued U.S. involvement in the war. Thousands of young Americans—and plenty of older Americans, too—pronounced themselves "radicalized" by the war. On August 8 the Republican National Convention, meeting in Miami Beach, nominated Richard M. Nixon for president. He chose Spiro T. Agnew, little-known governor of Maryland, as his running mate, and promised to bring "an honorable end to the war in Vietnam."

Democrats convened in Chicago two weeks later, and thousands of protestors gathered to support the antiwar candidate, Senator Eugene McCarthy of Minnesota, and to oppose the nomination of Vice-President Hubert Humphrey. Chicago police clashed violently with the protestors, injuring many, in what came to be called the "days of rage." On the convention floor, Senator Abraham Ribicoff of Connecticut accused Chicago Mayor Richard J. Daley of "gestapo tactics" against the protestors. Television cameras caught Daley, in the convention audience, mouthing an angry insult at Ribicoff. Humphrey was nominated, but many Democratic liberals who used to view him as a hero said they would not support him because he would not come out against the war.

Baseball had always put on the right patriotic face in wartime, but the game stumbled in trying to keep pace with the tumult of 1968. A few sports figures were involved in the political campaign: Stan Musial, senior vice-president of the Cardinals, headed a national committee of sports figures in support of Robert Kennedy. Slugger Hank Aaron of the Braves was a member, as were basketball star Bill Russell and football celebrities Gale Sayers, Herb Adderley, and Paul Hornung.

But by and large baseball operated in a vacuum. The Houston Astros came into Chicago during the Democratic National Convention, and the players watched in wonder as their bus driver navigated through battle lines of demonstrators and police. Outside their hotel, demonstrators were throwing stink bombs at police, who responded with tear gas.

Commissioner William Eckert tried to pay tribute to Robert

Kennedy without impairing the economic interests of the club owners who paid his salary, but his compromise didn't quite work. Funerals for Kennedy were held June 8 in both New York and Washington. Eckert postponed games scheduled for those cities and told other clubs not to start their games until the funerals were over. The funeral in Washington ran late, and games in Boston, Baltimore, Detroit, and Cincinnati began before the funeral cortege arrived at Arlington National Cemetery. "It was as though someone was standing by the side of the bier with a stopwatch and a starter's gun," wrote Dick Young of the New York *Daily News.*

The Giants were expecting a bat day crowd of thirty thousand or more and postponed their game until 4:00 P.M., Pacific time, to allow time for the funeral. But the visiting team, the New York Mets, refused to play. Ed Kranepool, the Mets' player representative, explained, "We're from New York. It's a matter of respect for us not to play." Gil Hodges, the New York manager, said he probably would go to church and advised his players not to be seen in pleasure spots.

The Giants lapsed into poor taste with this statement: "The Giants sincerely regret the disappointment of thousands of young fans who had intended to attend the bat day game tomorrow and now are compelled to rearrange their plans."

President Johnson had declared June 9 a national day of mourning for Senator Kennedy. Eckert told each team to decide for itself whether to play. The Red Sox and Orioles postponed home games, but other teams played.

Some players were upset. The Reds voted thirteen to twelve to play, against the recommendation of Milt Pappas, their player representative. He angrily resigned the post—and the Reds quickly traded him to Atlanta. Houston players voted unanimously not to play, but Spec Richardson, the team's general manager, threatened to fine anyone who refused to take the field. Only Rusty Staub and Bob Aspromonte of the Astros and Maury Wills of the visiting Montreal Expos sat out. Wills said, "I was out of uniform when Dr. King died and if I didn't respect Senator Kennedy's memory, too, I felt I would be hypocritical."

Roberto Clemente of the Pirates wanted to sit out, but Manager Larry Shepard persuaded him to play. "I preferred not to play," Clemente said. "The disturbing thing to me was the indifferent attitudes of some of our players. Some didn't take a stand either way—just said they didn't care whether they played or not."

A year later, a nationwide protest against the war called Vietnam Moratorium Day coincided with a World Series game at New York's Shea Stadium. A few weeks before, Tom Seaver had responded positively to someone's suggestion for an advertisement saying, "If the Mets can win the pennant, why can't we end the war?" When Seaver arrived at Shea on Moratorium Day, he was handed a radical newspaper with his picture on the front page. Inside, he was quoted as saying, "I think it's perfectly ridiculous what we're doing about the Vietnam situation. It's absurd. When this Series is over, I'm going to have a talk with Ted Kennedy, convey some of my ideas to him, and then take an ad in the paper. I feel very strongly about this."

Seaver was upset by the use of his name. "The people are being misled by that and I resent it," he said. "I'm a ballplayer, not a politician. I did not give them permission to use me."

About a hundred college students picketed Shea Stadium on Moratorium Day, but most fans ignored them, and the ballpark was packed for the Series contest. John Lindsay, the mayor of New York, had ordered the flag flown at half-mast on public buildings in honor of the Vietnam dead. Shea is a city building, but 250 wounded Vietnam veterans attending the game said they disliked the half-mast gesture. Lindsay conferred with Bowie Kuhn, the baseball commissioner, and they agreed to raise the flag to the top.

As a business—but a *public* business—baseball had a thin tightrope to walk. But its business side is always secondary to the game itself, and in 1968 baseball provided two heroes, welcome diversions from the protestors and politicians who often seemed too angry or petty or defensive to earn widespread public acclaim. An athlete can become a hero entirely by virtue of his performance, and both Bob Gibson and Denny McLain filled the role. As they excelled, so did their teams; Gibson and McLain seemed to inspire their teammates, giving baseball two truly outstanding clubs.

When Gibson shut out the Houston Astros on June 6, the Cardinals had already pulled out of their slump and back into first place. Steve Carlton started the comeback by shutting out the Giants on Memorial Day. Larry Jaster, another lefthander, shut out the Mets the following night. Gibson beat the Mets 6–3. The Cards swept four from the Mets in New York, and then four from the Astros in Houston.

In consecutive starts, Gibson beat the Astros 4–0, the Braves 6–0, the Reds 2–0, the Cubs 1–0, and the Pirates 3–0. He went up against Drysdale July 1 in Los Angeles. With two out in the Dodger first, Len Gabrielson singled and went to third on a bad-hop single by Tom Haller. A fastball got away from Gibson—wild pitch—and Gabrielson scored, jumping twice on the plate to emphasize the end of Gibson's shutout streak, which was endangering Drysdale's brand-new record.

Gibson didn't allow another run, and the Cardinals won, 5–1. In the cheerful Cardinal clubhouse, Gibson put the needle to his friend Tim McCarver. "It was the catcher's fault," Gibson shouted, making it clear that he was only kidding. "He loused it up." More seriously, he said, "It was a shame that I had to miss the doggone thing the way I did with a wild pitch, but I don't care. We won. Pressure? Call it aggravation. There was more pressure on me when I was growing up as a kid."

Mike Shannon remembered playing third base behind Gibson in 1968:

"Gibson was maturing. He was at his peak. I almost got a sore arm that year from throwing the ball around the infield after he'd strike people out. Not only did he still have his great ability, but he also was a tremendous *pitcher.*

"See, everybody thought that Gibson was simply a fastball pitcher, that he'd just rear back and throw it past everyone. Bob Gibson's best pitch was a slider. Not his fastball, his slider. He used his fastball to get double plays. He'd strike everybody out with his slider. But if he had a guy on first base, less than two out, he'd take the fastball, turn it over a little bit to a righthanded batter. Boom! He'd hit a one-hop shot to me. Bing-bang! A double play."

The Cardinals' slump had aggravated the whole team, which scored only twenty-one runs while losing eleven of thirteen games. "I must have left three hundred men on third base with less than two out," said Shannon. "So one day I decided to forget everything. Judy and I took the kids to a school picnic on Memorial Day. We stayed at the amusement park all day and when we got home, I rushed to the ballpark. I didn't even bother to take batting practice, and on my first swing I hit a homer."

Shannon, McCarver, Cepeda, Flood, Brock, Javier, and Maxvill started to hit, and the Cardinal pitching was almost beyond belief. Carlton threw three shutouts out of five starts. His teammates used to call him "Ichabod Crane" because he was so thin, but he was gaining strength through a strict conditioning and body-building regimen.

Carlton stopped the Cubs on one hit June 19, and Leo Durocher said, "You know, for a while I thought they had sneaked in Sandy Koufax when I wasn't looking." As good as he was, Carlton was only twenty-three and hadn't yet developed his famous slider, relying instead on a fastball, curve, and change. "He can think about adding pitches when he gets older," said the Cardinal pitching coach, Billy Muffett.

Nelson Briles and Ray Washburn also were pitching well, and Joe Hoerner, the relief ace, was working toward a season record of eight wins—all in extra innings—seventeen saves, and an ERA of 1.47. The Cardinals unveiled a statue of Stan Musial, and the old Cardinal hero put on the uniform with his teammates from 1941 before an adoring crowd of 47,455. But even Musial was more impressed with the Cardinals of 1968.

"This present Cardinal team will mold the greatest dynasty in the club's history," Musial said. ". . . This is a strong, solid club, one that will continue to win for the next five or six years." In fact, the Cards lost to the Mets—the "Miracle Mets"—in 1969, and management impatiently broke up the team, trading McCarver, Hoerner, and Flood to the Phillies for slugger Dick Allen and infielder Cookie Rojas.

Flood refused to report and filed suit against the contractual reserve clause that bound a player to his team until traded. He sat out the 1970 season and fought his case all the way to the U.S. Supreme Court. But he lost, and his playing career was virtually finished. Flood's lawsuit is often credited with eventually winning free agency for players in 1975, but in fact free agency came from an arbitration case involving pitchers Dave McNally and Andy Messersmith. McNally and Messersmith won on an issue involving interpretation of the language in a baseball contract—an issue that was not even raised in Flood's case.

Ironically, the 1968 Cardinals were criticized as fat cats. Their payroll, tabulated by Curt Matthews of the St. Louis *Post-Dispatch,* came to an alarming $950,000. Spread among the team's twenty-five players, that was $38,000 a man—or $134,500 when translated into 1989 dollars. Gibson drew the team's highest salary at about $85,000 ($301,000 in 1989 dollars). "Some highly placed baseball people believe that by paying so well the Cardinals are undermining the very structure of baseball," reported *Sports Illustrated.* By 1989 the average big leaguer was making $513,730, and top stars were making more than $2 million.

Flood batted second, behind Lou Brock, who was off and running toward the third of eight stolen base championships and a record career total of 938. "That Brock's worth one run a game," said Bill White of the Phillies. Maury Wills used to take a big lead off base, but Brock, a college math major, figured he would get to second base faster with a running start off a short lead. He also perfected the quick pop slide, and made base-stealing more of a science than ever before.

"There are ways to tell when a pitcher is going to throw to the plate and when he's going to throw to first base," Brock said. ". . . Most of them throw on a certain count, which you can study from the bench even before you get on base. You can count, 'one, two, three, four' or whatever the sequence of timing happens to be with the individual pitcher."

Gibson sometimes faltered in hot weather, but not in 1968. After yielding a run to the Dodgers, he shut out Marichal and the Giants 3–0, beat Houston 8–1, pitched four scoreless innings in a game that was rained out, beat Houston 8–1, shut out the Mets 2–0, and blanked the Phillies and Chris Short 5–0. Next time out he beat the Mets 7–1, then edged the Braves and Phil Niekro 1–0. He gave up a run to the Cubs, winning 3–1, and then blanked the Phils 3–0. That made fifteen straight wins, ten of them shutouts. All fifteen were complete games. Gibson yielded 7 runs and 77 hits in 135 innings. He struck out 114 and walked only 21.

On August 24 Gibson set a personal high with fifteen strikeouts. But Willie Stargell reached him for a three-run homer and hurt Gibson again with a double in the ninth inning. Dal Maxvill threw wildly on a ground ball and Stargell scored the winning run in a 6–4 Pittsburgh win. The loss sent Gibson's ERA soaring from 0.99 to 1.07.

The Cardinals had long since run away from the rest of the league. In June and July they won forty-six games and lost fifteen, sweeping seven straight from the Dodgers and Giants on the West Coast just before the All-Star break. They led the Reds and Braves by ten games, but faced a backbreaking schedule of fifty-nine games in fifty-six days. "We looked at that," recalled Mike Shannon, "and we thought, 'What are they trying to do to us?' What happened, we went out and we kicked everybody's butt."

The Cards won thirty-six of those games. Their lead grew to as much as fifteen games. The clubhouse rang with full-volume recordings of the team's favorite songs, "Here Comes the Judge" and "Fistful of Dollars," and the Cardinals put together a makeshift band of their own. Dick Hughes, a country music man, played the guitar and yodeled. Nelson Briles played electric guitar and sang. Ed Spiezio, a reserve infielder, played the accordion, and Cepeda banged the bongo drums.

Gibson and Flood strummed the ukelele, and the Cardinals, like old folks on a bus tour, sang along to while away long airplane rides. Delayed at the Philadelphia airport, Cardinal players behaved like boys. McCarver manned an airport information desk and sent passengers in various directions. Maris took a wheelchair, and Maxvill and Hoerner pushed him into a soaking collision with a janitor's water bucket. Upon arrival in St. Louis at 3:00 A.M., Hoerner emerged with the luggage on the suitcase conveyor chute. Gibson read off names on the bags: "Frankie Frisch . . . Pepper Martin . . . Dizzy Dean . . ."

Gibson complained frequently of aches, pains, hay fever and other allergies, and in the middle of one shutout he lay down on the clubhouse floor between innings, complaining that the St. Louis heat was wearing him out. But he kept winning, and no one ever knocked him out. He beat the Reds 1–0 in ten innings for his twentieth win of the year. "Maybe you'll pass Juan Marichal," said a teammate. "Not if you guys keep getting only one run a game," Gibson cracked.

Although Drysdale had the record for consecutive shutouts, Gibson set two marks of his own, giving up only two runs in 92 innings, three in 101. "I'd say control has been a big thing," Gibson said. "I haven't walked many. And I haven't been making as many mistakes as I used to."

For the season, he wound up 22 and 9, with an ERA of 1.12, the lowest of the century. He led the league in strikeouts with 268 and walked only 62. "I never pace myself," he said. "I just go out there and give all I've got as long as I can." Yet Gibson never looked to the bullpen. He started 34 games, finished 28, and was taken out for a pinch hitter in the other 6. In fact, from September 12, 1967, until July 4, 1969, Gibson pitched 53 straight games without *once* getting knocked out. In addition, he pitched six straight complete games in two World Series.

Even in the Year of the Pitcher, Gibson's 1968 performance stands out as one of the greatest seasons any pitcher has ever registered. Looking back, McCarver said, "The amazing thing about that year is how he ever lost nine games." Dizzy Dean was proud to identify with Gibson. "Great pitchers like Gibson and me never fool around with the hitters," Dean said. "We both like to throw the ball with something on it."

Gibson pitched thirteen shutouts. The Cardinal staff pitched 30 shutouts, 31 one-run games, and 21 two-run games—a total of 82 games in which the opposition scored two or fewer runs. The team ERA was 2.49; in 1930 and again in 1987 no *pitcher* had an ERA that low. The Cardinals led the league all but thirteen days of the season, and clinched the pennant September 15 as Maris hit the 275th and last home run of his career. By then baseball was looking past the season to a World Series matchup between Gibson and McLain, whose pitching achievements—and personality—were getting his name in headlines even more than Bob Gibson.

20

"I'd like to see Dennis curb his cockiness just a bit. . . . It could hurt his career."

McLain seemed impervious to doubt and misfortune. Six times he stopped Detroit losing streaks at two or three games. His mouth was big, but his achievements were bigger. He said he preferred to pitch away from Tiger Stadium, and he won his first sixteen decisions on the road.

He was pitching every four days, and he wasn't resting much between starts. "It was like I was on a high-speed treadmill," McLain wrote in his autobiography. ". . . The momentum I built up with my activities between starts seemed to carry over to the games I pitched."

McLain was not exactly playing around. He was working, or thought he was. In fact, he was exercising his ego, jumping into associations and businesses that carried him to ruin—or at least to bankruptcy and suspension from baseball, before he got into even deeper trouble and wound up in prison.

But in the summer of 1968 McLain was pure pitcher, and he knew it. When he won his tenth game on June 13, a sportswriter reminded him that he had had ten wins on the same date two years before and asked him whether he was now a better pitcher. "Sure I am," McLain replied. "I know the hitters better and know more about all phases of pitching."

The Tigers played inspired baseball. By the standards of 1968, when a run was a precious commodity, they were an old-fashioned wrecking crew. A pitch by Lew Krausse of the Athletics broke Al Kaline's right arm on May 25, and when Kaline returned five weeks later Manager Mayo Smith didn't know where to play him. In early July, Jim Northrup, playing in Kaline's old right field spot, hit three grand-slam homers in a week. Mickey Stanley, always a superb center fielder, became a strong hitter as well. Willie Horton, the left fielder, was the team's best slugger and most consistent hitter.

That left first base, held down since 1960 by Norm Cash, a dependable slugger. Cash batted lefthanded and Kaline righthanded, so Smith tried platooning them. Kaline's first day back was July 1, and he drove in the winning run with a single. Cash then got his turn and hit three homers in his next six times up.

Kaline and Cash, both thirty-three, were Detroit's veterans. Kaline had been a Tiger regular since 1954, when he was nineteen years old. He hit .340 in 1955 to become the youngest batting champion in history, and though he never again approached that mark he was a steady all-around star, year after year. Kaline's father made brooms in a Baltimore factory, and young Kaline's success was a storybook example of poor parents sacrificing to help a talented and ambitious son.

"We lived right behind a power factory," Kaline told an interviewer in 1968. "Every time I take my kids to Baltimore, I take them around to Cedley Street and show them where I lived. I show them that power factory and those three smoke stacks. I just want them to know that life was never always this easy.

"My dad was always there to play catch with me. He'd be on his feet all day long at the factory and he'd come home dead tired, but we'd go down to the corner and start playing catch. He'd hit me some fly balls. Pretty soon some of the other kids would come around and then he'd slip off and go home. It wasn't until later—a lot of years later—that I realized what my parents had done for me. They never asked me to get a job. They never asked me to work. God knows we could have used the money. Once they saw I had a chance to be a ball player, they let me alone. They let me play."

In 1961, the year Roger Maris hit 61 homers, Norm Cash had a spectacular season for the Tigers. He led the league in hitting at .361, hit 41 homers and drove in 132 runs. He never again hit .300—his lifetime average over seventeen seasons was .271—and after his retirement he acknowledged use of a corked bat in his big year. But he continued to play well, hitting more than his share of homers—377 lifetime—and driving in runs from the middle of the Tiger lineup.

*　*　*

Like every other team in baseball, the Tigers couldn't hit for average in 1968—they wound up with a team BA of .235—but they led the American League in runs and hit 185 home runs to lead the majors. Horton hit 36 homers, Cash and Bill Freehan 25 each, Northrup 21, and second baseman Dick McAuliffe 16. The Detroit sluggers delivered at the right time. Forty times the Tigers won after trailing through six innings. On May 17 Joe Sparma, the Tigers' weakest starter, took a one-hitter into the ninth inning, only to have Washington's Frank Howard homer for a 3 to 2 Washington lead. In the Detroit ninth, Northrup hit a grand slam to give Sparma his win. Northrup hit five grand-slam homers that season and led the team in RBI with 90. Twenty years later, he fondly recalled the attitude of the 1968 Tigers:

"We were confident. We felt that if we were close going into the seventh, eighth, or ninth inning, if we were within two or three runs, we were going to come back and win it. We got it rolling. By the halfway point, we didn't have any doubt whatsoever that we were going to do it. It just kept growing and growing and growing, because we were doing it.

"And it wasn't just one guy. It was everybody on the team. Tom Matchick hit a home run off Moe Drabowsky, the only homer hit off Moe all year, and beat him in a ballgame. Ray Oyler hit one home run, and it won a game. . . . Dick Tracewski hit a three-run home run in the tenth inning off Sam McDowell to win a game over in Cleveland.

"Those kind of things happened. It was momentum and attitude. We believed we could do it, and we did it."

Horton's slugging won seven late-inning games, and Gates Brown went eighteen for thirty-nine as a pinch hitter, winning six games with dramatic hitting. On August 11 Brown hit a pinch-hit homer to beat the Red Sox 5 to 4 in the fourteenth inning. That was the opening game of a doubleheader; in the nightcap he singled home the winning run as the Tigers scored four in the ninth inning to win, 6 to 5.

Horton was the big threat, and opposing pitchers frequently decked him. "I haven't been knocked down so often in my life," he said. "I remember only a couple of games I haven't been on the ground. I thank God for giving me the reflexes to get out of the way." Horton homered against the Angels, and next time up pitcher Jim McGlothlin decked him. Horton got up, dusted off, and turned to catcher Tom Satriano. "If the next one is close, I'm going to punch you in the nose," Horton said. He wasn't brushed back again that night.

Tiger batters were hit by pitches thirty-four times in the season's first half, and Horton was beaten out for first place by Freehan, who got hit twelve times. Freehan was such a good catcher, and such a dependable hitter, that he got more votes to the All-Star team than anyone else, including Carl Yastrzemski, the defending Triple Crown champ. Freehan's votes didn't come from sentimental fans, but from a panel of experts; back then players and managers elected their league's All-Star starters.

At the season's halfway mark, McLain won his sixteenth game in the opener of a doubleheader, beating Oakland 5 to 4 on a three-run homer by Horton. Kaline hit a three-run homer in the nightcap for a 7 to 6 win, a sweep, and a lead of nine and one-half games.

Baltimore was in second place, and at the All-Star break the Orioles fired their manager, Hank Bauer, and replaced him with Earl Weaver, an obscure coach who had managed for years in the minor leagues. "Weaver . . . stepped into the job as if he had been waiting for it for half a century," reported *The Sporting News*. Frank Lane, an Oriole scout, said of Weaver, "In the International League they hated the little guy's guts. Of course, that may have been because he was usually one or two innings ahead of the other managers." The Orioles won eleven of their first fifteen games under Weaver, taking three of four from the Tigers, who were in a slump, losing eight of twelve games. The Indians got hot, too, and the Detroit lead shrank to five and one-half games over Baltimore and Cleveland.

The Tigers came to Baltimore for three games, and in the opener Earl Wilson pitched the Tigers to a 4–1 win. The next day McLain won his twentieth game, stopping the Orioles 9–0 with the help of two homers by Horton and one each by Dick McAuliffe, Don Wert, and Al Kaline. It was July 27. Only twice before had a pitcher won his twentieth earlier in the season. Rube Marquard of the Giants did it on July 19, 1912, and Lefty Grove on July 25, 1931.

George Vecsey covered McLain's twentieth win for the *New York Times* and gave Denny this personal salute:

"The success of the 24-year-old pitcher is a boost for every fun-loving young man in the land. McLain has pursued his version of the good life since joining the Tigers in 1964."

Baltimore's Dave McNally beat Detroit's Mickey Lolich 5–1 in the series finale, and the Tigers lost to the Yankees the next day, but Wilson and McLain then pitched back-to-back shutouts.

McLain was on a roll. In successive starts he beat the Twins and Jim Kaat 2–1, the Indians 13–1, the Indians again 6–3, and the Red Sox, 4–0. His record was twenty-five and three, and it was only August 16. Writers were speculating that he might win thirty games, and McLain did nothing to discourage the speculation. As he talked to writers one day, Joe Sparma, whose locker was nearby, cracked, "Don't be humble, Denny. Just be yourself."

McLain had a telephone installed in his car—quite a status symbol in 1968—and talked of buying a $700,000 Lear jet. Glen Campbell, the singer, and Ed Sullivan, the talk-show host, visited McLain in the Tiger clubhouse. When the Tigers went West to play the Angels, McLain visited comedian Tommy Smothers. "Tommy's got a house worth $350,000 to $400,000," McLain said. "I want one of those."

His father-in-law, Lou Boudreau, said, "He's a great kid, and I'm really proud of him. I'd like to see Dennis curb his cockiness just a bit. Being confident and cocky is one thing, but being too cocky is something else again. It could hurt his career, just as it has hurt other young athletes."

During an airplane trip, sportswriter Joe Falls kidded with McLain about "Denny McLain for President" signs that were sprouting up in Detroit.

"Are you going to run?" Falls asked.

"I'm thinking about it," McLain replied.

"Who'll be your running mate?"

"Joe Sparma. I've got to get the Italian vote."

"And your secretary of defense?"

"Gates Brown. I've got to get the colored vote, too."

"Why not run? Then you'll be sure to get your hundred grand."

"I'll ask the Tigers for it. I'm having a better year than the president." Shades of Ruth!

The Tigers slumped, and the Orioles made one more pull at the chinning bar. On August 23 in New York, Stan Bahnsen of the Yankees outdueled Wilson 2–1. After a nineteen-inning game that wound up in a 3–3 tie and wore down both pitching staffs, Mel Stottlemyre, the Yankee ace, beat McLain 2–1. The two teams played a doubleheader the next day, and the Tigers led the opener 5–0 in the fourth inning and had two men on base.

Ralph Houk, the Yankee manager, waved in Rocky Colavito from the bullpen. Colavito was an outfielder, a former slugging star for the Tigers, and in 1968 he was playing his final season at age thirty-five. Still, he had a strong arm. He retired Kaline and Horton to end the Tiger threat, and went on to pitch two and two-thirds scoreless innings, earning the win as the Yankees came back and won, 6–5. "Don't forget I was signed as a pitcher-outfielder," Colavito said after the game. ". . . I used mostly fastballs with a few curves and sliders."

The Yankees completed the four-game sweep on August 25 by defeating Detroit's Mickey Lolich in the nightcap. The Orioles were hot, pulled within four games, and eagerly took on the Washington Senators, whom they had beaten twelve straight times. This time, the Senators won two, while the Tigers were winning two from the Angels behind McLain and Lolich.

On August 30 the Orioles came to Detroit for a final shot. Earl Wilson, who could hit as well as pitch, stopped them in the first game with a four-hitter, coupled with a three-run homer of his own; Detroit, 9–1. Next day Dave McNally won his tenth straight for Baltimore, 5–1, as Paul Blair homered and tripled.

McLain pitched the finale, and he was shaky. The Tigers led 4–2 in the third inning, but the first two Oriole batters reached base, and Boog Powell, who hit McLain better than anyone else in the league, rifled a line drive at the box. McLain somehow caught it—it could have caught *him*—and started a triple play. The Tigers won, 7–3, for McLain's twenty-seventh, and the pennant race, if there had been one, was over.

On September 17 the Tigers' magic number was down to one. A home crowd of 46,512 was cheering for the clincher, and the Tigers led 1–0 after eight innings. As the Yankees came to bat, Tom Yawkey, owner of the Red Sox, telephoned Jim Campbell in his private box and told the Tiger GM that the Red Sox had beaten the Orioles, clinching the pennant for Detroit.

Campbell kept that news off the Tiger Stadium scoreboard and off the Tiger radio broadcast, fearing that otherwise the fans would take over the field and force a Tiger forfeit. The Yankees tied the game in their half of the ninth. With two out in the Tiger ninth, Kaline walked, Freehan singled, Brown walked, and third baseman Don Wert singled home the winning run. Detroit fans, never decorous, tore down the left field screen in their rush to the field.

The clincher was fun, but the big game had come against Oakland three days before, with McLain pitching for his thirtieth win. No pitcher had won thirty since Dizzy Dean did it for the Cardinals in 1934, and Dean was in Detroit September 14 to share broadcasting duties with Sandy Koufax, who won only twenty-seven games in his biggest year. Talking to writers before the game, McLain said, "Yes, I'm going to ask for one hundred thousand dollars, and that's a low figure."

The game was on nationwide television, and McLain was in his element. So was young Reggie Jackson of the A's. He homered in the fourth with a man on for a 2–0 lead. Norm Cash answered with a three-run homer for Detroit, but the A's quickly tied the game. Jackson came up in the sixth inning and hit a changeup into the upper deck for a 4–3 lead.

Kaline batted for McLain in the last of the ninth. He walked. Mickey Stanley singled him to third. Northrup topped a ball down the first base line, and Danny Cater of Oakland threw wildly to home, Kaline scoring. With one out and Horton up, the A's played in to cut off the run from third. Horton drove the ball over left fielder Jim Gosger, and Stanley scored the winning run.

Detroit, 5–4; winning pitcher, McLain, thirty and five. He jumped for joy in the Tiger dugout, bumped his head against the ceiling, and almost knocked himself silly. Al Kaline grabbed him and helped him step proudly out onto the field. McLain hugged his teammates, and they hugged him. He went into the clubhouse, but the crowd kept chanting "We want Denny," so he came out and waved.

He went to the clubhouse interview room. "I made a few bad pitches, especially the one Jackson hit for the second homer," he said. "It was a changeup, a high one. But this team is fantastic. They've been winning like that for me all year."

The season still had two weeks to go, and McLain started three more games. Anything after number thirty would be anticlimactic for most pitchers, but McLain gave his thirty-first win a memorable touch. The Yankees were in town, and it was Mickey Mantle's last visit to Tiger Stadium; he retired following the 1968 season. At the time he had 534 homers, tying him with Jimmie Foxx for third place on the all-time list.

The Tigers took a 6–1 lead, and when Mantle came up late in the game McLain had an idea. He related the incident this way in his autobiography:

"When Mantle came to the plate with one out, I called Bill Freehan out to the mound.

" 'Tell Mickey it's coming right down the pipe,' I said.

"Freehan looked at me like I was nuts and said, 'What do you mean?'

" 'Just what I said. Tell him he's going to get one right where he wants it.'

"Freehan seemed a bit confused and went back behind the plate. I saw him say something to Mantle, who spun his head around to look at Freehan and then looked back at me. He must have been confused, too. Mickey got ready for my pitch, which was right down the middle with nothing on it. He couldn't call room service and order a better pitch than that. But he never moved his bat. The umpire called strike one and I called Freehan back out to the mound.

" 'What the hell is wrong?' I asked. 'Why didn't he swing?'

" 'I don't think he believes you,' Freehan answered.

" 'Well, tell him again. I'm going to give him another one.'

"Freehan still looked bewildered, but he delivered my message again. I lobbed in another pitch that must have looked as big as a grapefruit, but Mickey took a rather tentative swing and fouled it off. Then he looked at me and grinned. At last. The message had gotten through. He finally believed me.

"When I started my windup a third time, Mantle was ready. He swung so hard, he nearly popped his shoelaces. This time he made solid contact. The ball sailed far over the right field fence, just inside the foul screen. With the crowd again on its feet cheering, Mickey began his home-run trot. He rounded third and headed for home plate, where he looked right at me and tipped his cap.

"I got the message—'Thanks, Denny'—and so did most everyone else in Tiger Stadium. But I didn't give a damn. I thought it was hilarious.

". . . The next batter was Joe Pepitone, who placed his hand over the plate and suggested that I lay one in there for him, too. My first pitch was a fastball behind his head, and all you could see was Joe's butt wiping the batter's box as he hit the dirt."

McLain won that game 6–2, then lost to the Orioles 2–1 and had a no-decision. He finished at thirty-one and six; no one had won thirty-one games since Lefty Grove, in 1931. The Tigers scored an average of five runs a game for McLain, but he didn't need that much support; he allowed only 1.96 earned runs a game. Even in 1968 that was a phenomenally low ERA, considering that McLain pitched in a hitter's ballpark and worked a league-leading 336 innings. He also led the league in winning percentage (.838), games started (41), and complete games (28). He struck out 280 and walked only 63.

He was unanimously chosen the winner of the American League's Cy Young and Most Valuable Player awards. Bob Gibson won the same awards in the National League—the only time in history that pitchers won the MVP in both leagues. The World Series promised the greatest pitching matchup in history.

21

"Bob Gibson just overmatched us completely. There wasn't any human being alive who could have hit him."

The World Series opened in St. Louis, and the first game was scoreless for three innings. By then, however, the batters had things figured. Gibson was unhittable. McLain was weak.

Gibson struck out Dick McAuliffe and Al Kaline in the first inning. He fanned Norm Cash, Willie Horton, and Jim Northrup in the second, and Bill Freehan and McLain in the third. He didn't walk anyone. Mickey Stanley hit a harmless single in the first inning and Don Wert hit one in the third.

The Cardinals wasted a triple by Tim McCarver in the second and stranded Lou Brock on third base in the third. They broke through in the fourth. McLain walked Roger Maris and McCarver. Mike Shannon singled Maris home and took second when Willie Horton fumbled the ball. Julian Javier singled, scoring McCarver and Shannon.

The Cardinals showed off their speed, too. Brock stole a base and took another on Bill Freehan's bad throw. Javier stole second after his RBI single. The stolen bases didn't contribute to the scoring, and didn't matter anyway. With three St. Louis runs on the board, the game belonged to Gibson.

McLain was removed for a pinch hitter in the sixth, and the Tigers threatened. With one out, McAuliffe singled. Gibson struck out Stanley, but Kaline doubled into the left field corner, McAuliffe stopping at third. That brought up Norm Cash, a strong lefthanded hitter. Gibson struck him out.

Gibson got stronger. He struck out Horton, Northrup, and Freehan in the seventh. In the eighth he fanned veteran Eddie Mathews, who was pinch hitting. That gave him fourteen. The record for a

World Series game was fifteen, set by Sandy Koufax against the Yankees in 1963.

Gibson was a fast worker. He wanted the game over. His catcher, McCarver, swears that Gibson was unaware of the record, and Gibson says so, too. Mickey Stanley singled to lead off the Tiger ninth. Gibson struck out Kaline for the third time, the Tiger right fielder flailing at a fastball. The St. Louis crowd was cheering, and the cheers crescendoed, because the scoreboard flashed a message saying that Gibson was one strikeout away from sixteen, a new Series record. McCarver pointed at the message, trying to get Gibson to pay attention to it, but Gibson impatiently demanded the ball. "Come on, come on, let's *go!*" he said.

Gibson tipped his cap, though he didn't want to. He was never one to indulge fans—except, as he put it himself, with his performance. McCarver threw him the ball, crouched, gave the sign, and Gibson went to work on Cash. He struck him out on a slider. Horton took the count to two and two, fouled off a couple of pitches, and moved back from an inside pitch—which broke sharply over the inside corner. Strike three. The score was 4–0, St. Louis, and Gibson had seventeen strikeouts, a World Series record.

In the old tradition, the New York *Daily News* hired Gibson to write a daily story about the World Series games. "I didn't even know about the record," he wrote. "I couldn't imagine what all the shouting was about. Then I happened to turn around and look at the scoreboard. I saw something about sixteen strikeouts and a World Series record and I knew what all the shouting was about. When I got Willie Horton for my seventeenth strikeout I was happy because the game was over."

The Tigers knew what the shouting was about. "Nobody could have done anything against him," said Mayo Smith, the Detroit manager, after the game.

In interviews twenty years later, Jim Northrup, Mike Shannon, and Tim McCarver recalled that game.

Northrup, the Detroit center fielder, had this to say:

"We couldn't hardly touch him. I'd never faced Gibson before, and when he comes at you with that stuff it's amazing. He was throwing

B-Bs, and he had some of the nastiest breaking stuff I've faced. I faced Nolan Ryan in no-hitters, but I don't think I've ever faced anybody on one given day who could so completely overmatch an entire team of fastball hitters. That's what we were, and Bob Gibson just overmatched us completely. There wasn't any human being alive who could have hit him.

"He really came at you hard and strong. It was you against him. He liked to pitch fast. He didn't like it if you stepped out on him and held him up. He wanted to get the ball and throw it. McLain was like that, too. He and McLain would pitch, and if you let them they'd probably pitch a one-hour game between them, every time out."

Shannon had a good vantage point from his third base position:

"It was like he was pitching against Little Leaguers. And you know, they were a hell of a hitting team, probably one of the best in ten or twenty years. They had Norm Cash, Al Kaline, Bill Freehan, Horton. Years later, talking to those guys, I asked them the same thing. I said, 'Have you ever been overmatched more than on that particular day? Have you ever seen anything like that?' To the man, they say they never, ever, witnessed anything like that.

"McLain? I wasn't impressed by him. He was all tuckered out. I think that was the beginning of the end for him."

McCarver, the Cardinal catcher, agreed that McLain had lost it:

"McLain's stuff? Terrible! When you crank it up that many times over a seven-month period, you wear down. There's no question that he was hurting during the Series."

Gibson and McLain met again in the fourth game of the Series, played in Detroit, and the results were even more lopsided. Gibson gave up five hits, struck out ten, and walked one. Lou Brock, the first batter to face McLain, hit a homer, and the Cardinals pounded McLain in the third inning—a single by Flood, a triple by McCarver, a double by Shannon. The weather was lousy, and with two out in the Cardinal third the game was delayed an hour and fourteen minutes by rain. When play resumed, McLain was gone. The Cardinals won, 10–1.

Twenty years later, McLain looked back on that World Series:

"I was absolutely through for the season. I hurt very badly going into the month of September. *Very* badly. As far as that first game, hey, the guy strikes out seventeen. Gibson had one of those days. Every pitcher has one or two of those games in his career, and Gibson chose his on the day of the first game of the World Series. I don't care what kind of stuff I had that day. What did we get beat, four to nothing? How bad is that?

"The next ballgame we pitched should have never been played. It was played in a downpour. I know that affects both sides. But it's a World Series game. It should be given more consideration. How about the fans at the ballpark? They deserved better. For forty- or fifty-dollar tickets you deserve better than that. It was Eckert, the commissioner. Eckert, I don't think ever called a shot on his own. It was abysmal. It was one of the worst decisions I've ever seen. I've never been a mudder anyway. I hate it when it's wet. I couldn't believe we played.

"My arm was killing me. Then they shot me up for the sixth game and I was able to go out and pitch. I had everything in the sixth game."

It is tempting to attribute Gibson's glory and McLain's downfall to the contrast in their characters—Gibson, the severe and uncompromising perfectionist, a fierce symbol of black achievement, defeats McLain, the selfish, bubble-headed playboy. That was the result, but the cause had nothing to do with virtue or its absence. The decisive factor was as basic as a game of catch. Gibson had a resilient arm. McLain's arm was sore. He had tendonitis, and that—not his foolish transgressions—impaired his World Series performance and cut short his baseball career.

Few things are as fragile as a pitcher's arm, and McLain's started going bad in 1965, when he was twenty-one years old. That was his first big year; he was sixteen and six for the Tigers, with an ERA of 2.61. It was also the year he started getting cortisone shots for the painful tendonitis in his right shoulder.

Lots of pitchers get shots, and some of them pitch successfully for years. But by 1968 McLain needed more and more cortisone. "Late

1965 was the first time I had a cortisone shot and then it just multiplied from there," McLain recalled. "In 1968 I probably got a dozen."

Mayo Smith, the Tiger manager, told author Donald Honig that the doctors told him the cortisone shots "would help him for only so long and then it was going to be rough on Denny." So McLain, winning thirty-one games at age twenty-four, was playing out a short string, while Gibson, eight years older, had a lot more pitching to look forward to.

Anyway, a World Series is not scripted, and this one did not come down to Gibson, the hero, and McLain, the foil. The hero turned out to be a guy whom Mayo Smith once called "my sway-backed left-hander," Mickey Lolich.

Lolich was the number two man on the Detroit staff, and he had a habit of pitching his best toward the end of the season. He won his last five decisions in 1968, and in the second game of the World Series he cut down the Cardinals on six hits, striking out nine in an 8–1 romp. Horton and Cash homered, and so did Lolich—the first and only home run of his career.

That evened the Series, reviving the appetite of many baseball purists who viewed the 1968 World Series as the best for many years, and as the last uncorrupted test of major league baseball as it had been and should remain. It was the best, they said, because pitching would dominate hitting, as in the olden days, and it was the last pure test because divisional play would begin in 1969, requiring playoffs—or League Championship Series, as they are grandly called—to determine the pennant winners.

The Cardinals won the third game, 7–3, behind Ray Washburn and Joe Hoerner, and when Gibson beat McLain in the rainy fourth game the Cards were on top three games to one. No National League team had won back-to-back World Series since John McGraw's New York Giants of 1921 and 1922. The Cardinals seemed on the verge.

Lolich started the fifth game and was quickly rocked. Lou Brock, who was setting World Series records with his hitting and baserunning, led off the first inning with a double. Curt Flood singled him home, and Orlando Cepeda homered. The Tigers reached Nelson Briles for two runs in the fourth when Stanley tripled, Norm Cash hit a sacrifice fly, Horton tripled, and Northrup singled.

Willie Horton came up with the key play in the fifth inning, and it was not a home run. Brock—again Brock—doubled and sped home on Javier's single. Freehan blocked the plate, and Brock elected to score standing up, fearing that if he slid Freehan would block him from the plate. Horton made the throw of his life. The play was as close as a play can be; umpire Doug Harvey called Brock out.

That run would have put the Cardinals two up and would have forced Smith to pinch hit for Lolich. Instead, he let Lolich bat with one out in the seventh. He blooped a single. Joe Hoerner relieved Briles, and the Tigers mauled him. Dick McAuliffe singled, Mickey Stanley walked, and Al Kaline singled two runs home. Cash singled home a third run, and Lolich stopped the Cardinals in the eighth and ninth—stopped them cold, in fact, after their three-run rally in the first inning. The final score was Detroit 5, St. Louis 3.

Kaline's key hit, and his all-around play in the Series, made Mayo Smith look good on a move that could have made him look terrible. Going into the Series, Smith faced the same pleasant problem he encountered at midseason—where to play Al Kaline, who was in his sixteenth season and was looking forward to his first World Series. Cash had been hitting well—he always hit well toward the end of the season—so Smith wanted him at first base. He decided to move his center fielder, Mickey Stanley, to shortstop, bench Ray Oyler, his good-field-no-hit shortstop, move Jim Northrup to center field, and play Kaline in right.

Shortstop is not a fill-in position, but Stanley, a good all-around athlete, often took grounders there in practice. Smith had him drill with Dick McAuliffe, the second baseman. "Mayo, you've got to be kidding," McAuliffe said after a few workouts. But they kept at it. Stanley made two errors in the World Series, both on difficult plays in the hole. In general he fielded well. He got six hits and scored four runs—almost surely more than Oyler would have contributed. Cash hit .385 with a homer and five RBI. Kaline glittered, batting .379, hitting two homers, and leading both clubs in RBI with eight.

With McLain's arm sore, Smith did not know whom he would start in the sixth game. McLain got a cortisone shot, but Smith wasn't sure his arm would come around. The teams had an off-day between the fifth and sixth games, and Smith was talking to reporters during a

Tiger workout. McLain, who had been throwing, walked by and winked at his manager.

Smith had his pitcher. McLain scattered nine hits and struck out seven. In the third inning, Jim Northrup hit a grand-slam homer as the Tigers scored ten runs to tie a record set by the Athletics in 1929—that fateful inning that overcame an 8–0 Cub lead and was blamed on Hack Wilson, who lost two fly balls in the sun. This time—October 9, 1968—the result was a lopsided 13–1 win for the Tigers.

The seventh game matched Gibson, on three days' rest, and Lolich, on two. Gibson already had won seven straight World Series games, a record. He had won the seventh game of the 1964 and 1967 Series. No pitcher in history was a better bet for that Series finale, and it seemed fit that this premier pitcher would close out the Year of the Pitcher with a final masterpiece.

Lolich had an opportunity to steal McLain's thunder, and he must have relished it. Although it was not publicized at the time, Lolich and McLain did not get along. Their feud became public knowledge at the All-Star break in 1969. Both pitchers made the American League All-Star team. McLain had bought himself an airplane and planned to fly to the game, in Washington, D.C., with his wife. Lolich asked if he and his wife could go along, and McLain agreed. According to McLain, he told Lolich that the lefthander and his wife would have to fly back on their own, because the McLains had to fly to Lakeland, Florida, for a business meeting. According to Lolich, McLain rudely stranded him and his wife in Washington. Petty stuff, of just the kind that boils up between two prickly rivals.

Lolich had a little pot belly and was not a particularly athletic-looking man. But his skill did not surprise the Cardinals. Red Schoendienst, the Cardinal manager in 1968, recalled Lolich's role in an interview twenty years later:

"Joe Monahan, our head scout, scouted the Detroit ballclub, and we had him in a meeting before the World Series started. We went over the Detroit ballclub, and he said, 'The pitcher who's going to give you the most trouble is Lolich. He's going to give our ballclub more trouble than Denny McLain.'

"He was right. Lolich had good control and he had the good hard sinker and he had the good hard slider. He was a tough pitcher, a great competitor, hard to beat. He [went] out there and [kept] you in the ballgame all the time."

According to Mike Shannon, a teammate warned the Cardinal players about Lolich. "Maris told us that in July," Shannon recalled. "He said, 'Don't worry about McLain. The guy we have to worry about is Lolich.' "

The Tigers were still worrying about Gibson, who struck out five in the first three innings to break his own record of thirty-one strike-outs in a World Series. Neither team threatened until two were out in the top of the seventh. Then Cash singled to right, Horton singled to left, and Northrup hit a line drive to deep center field. Curt Flood made a false start in, slipped on the wet ground as he switched directions, and failed to reach the ball. It fell for a triple. Freehan doubled Northrup home, and the score was 3–0.

Schoendienst did not pinch hit for Gibson in the eighth—who would pull Bob Gibson at such a time? The Tigers scored one run in the ninth and so did the Cardinals, on a solo homer by Mike Shannon. The Tigers won, 4–1, and won the World Series, four games to three. The heroes were pitchers, as they should have been in 1968—Mickey Lolich, with three wins, and Bob Gibson, who won two, lost one, and struck out thirty-five. Both Lolich and Gibson posted Series ERAs of 1.67.

Lolich had spent a long time in baseball. As a kid he was a batboy for Portland of the Pacific Coast League, and 1968 was his sixth season in the big leagues. As a newly minted World Series star, he said, "All my life somebody has been a big star and Lolich has been number two. I figured my day would come, and this was it. Everybody thought it would be a big showdown between McLain and Gibson. I'm glad it turned out to be me."

McLain was not glad. "Anyone but him," he wrote in his autobiography. In later years, Lolich said his World Series performance improved his confidence and helped his pitching. He went on to win nineteen games in 1969, twenty-five in 1971, and twenty-two in 1972. He rounded out his major league career in 1979, at the age of thirty-nine.

Jim Northrup recalled the friction between McLain and Lolich:

"Here we had two guys who could flat *pitch.* Two of the top pitchers in the game. But McLain had excelled over everybody with his thirty-one and six, and then twenty-four and nine. Lolich was having good years, but he was sitting in front of his locker all alone, and there were twelve guys over talking to McLain.

"Denny got along with his teammates very, very well. It's hard not to like Denny McLain. But a lot of times Denny wouldn't do his work. He wasn't there always, and he was flying here and flying there.

"Little nitpicking things. Like the pitcher who's supposed to pitch the next night is supposed to shag the fly balls from the outfield and put them on the stand for the guy throwing batting practice. That's no big deal, except Denny didn't do it. That made the guys mad who had to do it. They had to be there. They couldn't leave and do the things Denny was doing with his airplane. They had to do their running, and Denny didn't run. He didn't like to run. They weren't big rules, but he broke enough rules to cause dissension on the pitching staff. That was the only problem."

Bob Gibson continued to star for the Cardinals, continued to strike fear in his opponents, and continued to earn the affection and respect of his teammates. He complained about the lower pitcher's mound that came into use in 1969. He said he couldn't pitch shutouts anymore; after pitching thirteen shutouts in 1968, he never again rang up more than five in a season, although five was enough to lead the National League in 1971.

Gibson won twenty games in 1969 and twenty-three in 1970, earning his second Cy Young Award. He pitched a no-hitter against the Pirates in 1971. He was forty years old when he finally retired in 1975, and to the end he was a fastball pitcher. He returned to Omaha, his hometown, where he bought a restaurant and became an officer of a bank. During the summer, he hosted a sports talk show in St. Louis. His old teammates still talk of him in reverent tones, and his old opponents still talk of him with awe.

McLain won twenty-four games in 1969 and shared the Cy Young Award with Mike Cuellar of Baltimore. He struck out ninety-nine fewer batters than he had in 1968 and attributed much of the decline to the lower pitching mound—a change that reduced the effectiveness of virtually all power pitchers, particularly those with an overhand delivery.

After the 1968 World Series, McLain went to work in earnest, playing the organ, making speeches, endorsing products: earning several times his baseball salary. The pitching celebrity played the organ for two weeks at a hotel in Las Vegas, where he enjoyed the gambling tables. He expanded his business interests. McLain didn't get the hundred thousand dollars he wanted for 1969, but the Tigers more than doubled his salary, to sixty-five thousand dollars.

McLain and a handful of other players made a USO tour of Vietnam after the 1969 season, and while he was there his wife, Sharyn, back in Detroit, came up against a sudden and unexpected shortage of cash. The lawyer McLain had hired to handle their finances had, according to McLain, taken their money. In June 1970 McLain declared bankruptcy.

His troubles were piling up. *Sports Illustrated* hit the stands in February 1970 with a cover story alleging that McLain was a bookie, with ties to the mob. McLain admits making book but says it was small-time stuff, that he never gambled on baseball, and that he knew no organized crime figures. In his autobiography, he says he could have won a big libel judgment against *Sports Illustrated,* but was talked out of suing by a lawyer.

A grand jury questioned McLain. So did baseball commissioner Bowie Kuhn, who suspended him until July 1 because of his gambling connections. McLain considered Kuhn's action unfair, believing he had earned leniency by talking candidly to the commissioner.

A crowd of more than fifty-three thousand came to watch McLain's return on July 1, 1970. But the Yankees bombed him, and as the season wore on, so did everyone else. In late August he dumped a bucket of water on Jim Hawkins, a young Detroit sportswriter. McLain thought that was fun, so he dumped a bucket on Watson Spoelstra, an older writer. Spoelstra complained to Tiger management, and the team suspended McLain for a week. Before the week was up, Kuhn suspended McLain again, this time for carrying a gun on road trips. McLain denied it, saying he carried a gun only under the seat of his car and only while driving in dangerous sections of Detroit.

That suspension lasted through the remainder of the 1970 season. The Tigers then traded McLain to the Washington Senators in a package deal that brought the Tigers two excellent infielders, shortstop Ed Brinkman and third baseman Aurelio Rodriguez. Ted Williams was the Washington manager. Some of the men who played for Williams speak of him fondly, but not McLain. "Williams was a loudmouthed, egotistical, selfish sonofabitch," McLain wrote of the old slugger.

As a pitcher, McLain was washed up. He lost twenty-two games for the Senators in 1971, and in 1972 he flunked trials with the Oakland Athletics and Atlanta Braves. He even tried to come back in the minor leagues, but failed. The tendonitis that had pained him even during his superb 1968 season had ruined his pitching arm for good.

McLain hopped from business to business, from city to city. He owned taverns in Atlanta, but gave them up when his wife threatened to divorce him. He was a talk-show host in Detroit, but quit because it tired him. He ran a mall in Detroit and he ran a minor league baseball team in Memphis, Tennessee. Nothing worked out, and in 1977 he again filed for bankruptcy.

He tried making and selling giant-screen television sets, mortgage brokering, operating walk-in clinics, and various other ventures, most of which seemed to put him in touch with shady characters. McLain says he took pains to avoid participation in their criminal activities. He was a scratch golfer and made a good living hustling golf, but he wanted more. He bought an airplane, tried other businesses, met other shady characters. He put some businesses and debts in Sharyn's name, and when they failed she filed for bankruptcy, and for divorce. It was not the first time their marriage almost collapsed, but Sharyn was a forgiving wife, and they reconciled.

On March 19, 1984, a federal grand jury indicted McLain on charges of racketeering, conspiracy to commit racketeering (including loan-sharking), extortion, and possession of cocaine with intent to distribute; his golf bag had somehow gotten packed full of cocaine. He was convicted a year later after a long and tumultuous trial.

McLain contends he did nothing but make book, a crime with which he was not even charged. He says his colleagues framed him on the other charges, testifying against him in exchange for government leniency in their own cases.

He was sentenced to twenty-three years in prison. He suffered—mostly, he says, because of the pain he caused his family. Serving time in the federal penitentiary at Atlanta, Georgia, he bet three thousand dollars on a baseball game between his team and another prison team. Luckily for McLain, the other bettors dropped out. McLain pitched several innings, leaving with a sore arm and the score tied, 4 to 4. His team lost, 25 to 5, and McLain was so sore he had to spend five days in bed. His weight, which had ballooned to 300 pounds, was down to 275; his playing weight with the Tigers had been 185.

An appeals court overturned his conviction, ruling that the judge had not conducted the trial properly. McLain was released on September 4, 1987. He was reunited with his family. They moved to Fort Wayne, Indiana, where McLain found employment as promotional manager for a minor league hockey team. He lost that job, but signed with a publisher to write his autobiography, with the help of a sportswriter. It was published in September 1988. A month later McLain and his lawyers negotiated a plea bargaining agreement with the government, and McLain pleaded guilty to charges of racketeering and possession of cocaine with intent to distribute. On December 15, 1988, Judge Elizabeth Kovachevich of the U.S. District Court in Tampa sentenced McLain to the time he had already served in prison, plus five years on probation. The effect of the ruling was to let the former pitching star remain free.

"I screwed up," McLain told the judge. "I'm sorry. Whatever I did, I did. I've said I'm sorry and agreed to the plea agreement. I don't know what else to say."

Sharyn Boudreau McLain told Judge Kovachevich that her husband was not the same man who went off to prison in 1984. "If he had not changed, if he was the same man he was when he went to prison, I wouldn't be standing here today," Mrs. McLain said. "You may have done us a big favor by taking him from us at the time you did."

* * *

Maybe Denny McLain's life wasn't much, but in 1968, the greatest pitching year in baseball history, he won more games than anyone else among the brilliant group of pitchers who excelled that season. If you could pick a man at his prime to pitch a game for you, you wouldn't go wrong with the Denny McLain of 1968, though some might prefer Bob Gibson. Looking further back, you might consider Lefty Grove and wonder what he might have accomplished had he pitched in 1968, when pitching was king, rather than 1930, when hitters ruled the game. As the old-timers say, those things go in cycles, but baseball is always baseball, the best game of them all.

Statistical Summary
Seasons of Extremes—A Statistical Sampling

Batting: League Leaders

NATIONAL LEAGUE

1930		1968	
*Bill Terry, New York	.401	Pete Rose, Cincinnati	.335
Babe Herman, Brooklyn	.393	Matty Alou, Pittsburgh	.332
*Chuck Klein, Philadelphia	.386	Felipe Alou, Atlanta	.317
Lefty O'Doul, Philadelphia	.383	Alex Johnson, Cincinnati	.312
*Fred Lindstrom, New York	.379	Curt Flood, St. Louis	.301
		Glenn Beckert, Chicago	.294
George Watkins, St. Louis	.373	*Willie McCovey, San Fran.	.293
*Paul Waner, Pittsburgh	.368	*Roberto Clemente, Pitt.	.291
Riggs Stephenson, Chicago	.367	Rusty Staub, Houston	.291
		Lee May, Cincinnati	.290
*Pie Traynor, Pittsburgh	.366		
*Lloyd Waner, Pittsburgh	.362		
*Hack Wilson, Chicago	.356		
*Kiki Cuyler, Chicago	.355		
*Mel Ott, New York	.349		
*Frank Frisch, St. Louis	.346		
Pinky Whitney, Philadelphia	.342		
Shanty Hogan, New York	.339		
*Gabby Hartnett, Chicago	.339		
*Travis Jackson, New York	.339		
*Chick Hafey, St. Louis	.336		
Del Bissonette, Brooklyn	.336		

*Member, Baseball Hall of Fame

*Al Simmons, Philadelphia	.381	*Carl Yastrzemski, Boston	.301
*Lou Gehrig, New York	.379	Danny Cater, Oakland	.290
*Heinie Manush, Washington	.362	Tony Oliva, Minnesota	.289
		Willie Horton, Detroit	.285
*Babe Ruth, New York	.359	Ted Uhlaender, Minnesota	.283
Carl Reynolds, Chicago	.359	Don Buford, Baltimore	.282
*Mickey Cochrane, Philadelphia	.357	Bert Campaneris, Oakland	.276
		Ken Harrelson, Boston	.275
Johnny Hodapp, Cleveland	.354	Rick Monday, Oakland	.274
Dick Porter, Cleveland	.350	Rod Carew, Minnesota	.273
*Sam Rice, Washington	.349		
Eddie Morgan, Cleveland	.349		
*Joe Cronin, Washington	.346		
*Earle Combs, New York	.344		
*Bill Dickey, New York	.339		
*Earl Averill, Cleveland	.339		
*Jimmie Foxx, Philadelphia	.335		
*Charlie Gehringer, Detroit	.330		

Home Runs

NATIONAL LEAGUE

1930		1968	
*Hack Wilson, Chicago	56	*Willie McCovey, San Fran.	36
*Chuck Klein, Philadelphia	40	Dick Allen, Philadelphia	33
Wally Berger, Boston	38	*Ernie Banks, Chicago	32
*Gabby Hartnett, Chicago	37	*Billy Williams, Chicago	30
Babe Herman, Brooklyn	35	*Hank Aaron, Atlanta	29

AMERICAN LEAGUE

*Babe Ruth, New York	49	Frank Howard, Washington	44
*Lou Gehrig, New York	41	Willie Horton, Detroit	36
*Goose Goslin, St. Louis	37	Ken Harrelson, Boston	35
*Jimmie Foxx, Philadelphia	37	Reggie Jackson, Oakland	29
*Al Simmons, Philadelphia	36	Bill Freehan, Detroit	25
		Norm Cash, Detroit	25

Runs Batted In

1930		1968	
*Hack Wilson, Chicago	190	*Willie McCovey, San Fran.	105
*Chuck Klein, Philadelphia	170	*Billy Williams, Chicago	98
*Kiki Cuyler, Chicago	134	Ron Santo, Chicago	98
Babe Herman, Brooklyn	130	Tony Perez, Cincinnati	92
*Bill Terry, New York	129	Dick Allen, Philadelphia	90

AMERICAN LEAGUE

*Lou Gehrig, New York	174	Ken Harrelson, Boston	109
*Al Simmons, Philadelphia	165	Frank Howard, Washington	106
*Jimmie Foxx, Philadelphia	156	Jim Northrup, Detroit	90
*Babe Ruth, New York	153	Boog Powell, Baltimore	85
*Goose Goslin, St. Louis	138	Willie Horton, Detroit	85

Pitching: Earned Run Average

NATIONAL LEAGUE

1930: League Leaders

	W	L	ERA
*Dazzy Vance, Brooklyn	17	15	2.61
*Carl Hubbell, New York	17	12	3.76
Bill Walker, New York	17	15	3.93
Pat Malone, Chicago	20	9	3.94
*Burleigh Grimes, St. Louis	13	6	4.07

1968: ERAs under 2.60

	W	L	ERA
*Bob Gibson, St. Louis	22	9	1.12
Ron Kline, Pittsburgh	12	5	1.68
Bob Bolin, San Francisco	10	5	1.99
Bob Veale, Pittsburgh	13	14	2.05
Jerry Koosman, New York	19	12	2.08
Steve Blass, Pittsburgh	18	6	2.12
*Don Drysdale, Los Angeles	14	12	2.15
Phil Regan, Chicago	10	5	2.20
*Tom Seaver, New York	16	12	2.20
Ray Washburn, St. Louis	14	8	2.26

Clay Carroll, Cincinnati	7	7	2.29
Milt Pappas, Atlanta	10	8	2.37
Gary Nolan, Cincinnati	9	4	2.40
*Juan Marichal, San Fran.	26	9	2.43
Gaylord Perry, San Fran.	16	15	2.45
Ted Abernathy, Cincinnati	10	7	2.46
Cecil Upshaw, Atlanta	8	7	2.47
Dock Ellis, Pittsburgh	6	5	2.50
Phil Niekro, Atlanta	14	12	2.59
Don Sutton, Los Angeles	11	15	2.60
Pat Jarvis, Atlanta	16	12	2.60

AMERICAN LEAGUE

1930: League Leaders

*Lefty Grove, Philadelphia	28	5	2.54
Wes Ferrell, Cleveland	25	13	3.31
Lefty Stewart, St. Louis	20	12	3.45
George Uhle, Detroit	12	12	3.65
Bump Hadley, Washington	15	11	3.73

1968: ERAs under 2.60

Luis Tiant, Cleveland	21	9	1.60
Sam McDowell, Cleveland	15	14	1.81
Wilbur Wood, Chicago	13	12	1.87
Dave McNally, Baltimore	22	10	1.95
Denny McLain, Detroit	31	6	1.96
Tommy John, Chicago	10	5	1.98
Stan Bahnsen, New York	17	12	2.05
Jose Santiago, Boston	9	4	2.25
Jim Perry, Minnesota	8	6	2.27
Jim Nash, Oakland	13	13	2.28
John Hiller, Detroit	9	6	2.30
Joe Horlen, Chicago	12	14	2.37
Mel Stottlemyre, New York	21	12	2.45
Blue Moon Odom, Oakland	16	10	2.45
Stan Williams, Cleveland	13	11	2.50
Jim Hardin, Baltimore	18	13	2.51
Dean Chance, Minnesota	16	16	2.53

Acknowledgments

I am particularly grateful to the players, managers, coaches, and sportswriters who shared their recollections with me. I talked to a number of players a decade ago, when I first became fascinated with the 1930 season. Some of these men have died: Bill DeWitt, Charlie Grimm, Bill Hallahan, Babe Herman, and Charley (Red) Ruffing. All the other interviews were conducted in 1988.

Most other sources are identified in the text. I got lots of help from Dave Kelly and Pablo Calvan at the Library of Congress in Washington, D.C., and from Tom Heitz, Bill Deane, Pat Kelly, and John Blomquist at the National Baseball Library in Cooperstown, New York. Ted Patterson, a Baltimore sportscaster and a broadcasting historian, helped me on the early days of baseball broadcasting.

Much of my information came from old issues of *The Sporting News, Baseball Digest, Baseball Research Journal, Sports Illustrated, Baseball Magazine,* and a number of daily newspapers.

For background on Hack Wilson, I am deeply grateful to Robert S. Boone and Gerald Grunska, authors of *HACK: The Meteoric Life of One of Baseball's First Superstars: Hack Wilson* (Highland Press, Highland Park, Illinois, 1978).

The autobiographies of Denny McLain and Bob Gibson were equally helpful. McLain gave me permission to quote his autobiographical account of the home-run pitch he fed to Mickey Mantle. It's from *Strikeout: The Story of Denny McLain,* by Denny McLain with Mike Nahrstedt (The Sporting News Publishing Company, St. Louis, 1988). Gibson's book is *From Ghetto To Glory: The Story of Bob Gibson,* by Bob Gibson with Phil Pepe (Prentice-Hall, Englewood Cliffs, New Jersey, 1968).

This is not the kind of formal book that calls for a bibliography, so I am not going to list the two or three dozen books that helped me in writing this book. Because I used them so much, I'll single out *The Baseball Encyclopedia,* seventh edition, edited by Joseph L. Reichler and published by Macmillan Publishing Company, New York; *The Sports Encyclopedia: Baseball,* seventh edition, by David S. Neft and Richard M. Cohen, published by St. Martin's Press, New York; *Baseball: A Comprehensive Bibliography,* compiled by Myron J. Smith, Jr., published by McFarland & Company, Jefferson, North Carolina; *The Sport Americana Baseball Address List,* by R. J. Jack Smalling and Dennis W. Eckes, published by Edgewater Book Company, Cleveland; and *Green Cathedrals,* by Philip J. Lowry, published by the Society for American Baseball Research, Garrett Park, Maryland.

—William B. Mead

Index